CHAMPAGNE

To
Henri Lauga,
who always believed in the idea
Nicolas Ducrot
who made the believing come true

CHAMPAGNE

Text and Photographs
by
William I. Kaufman
chevalier et officier
de
l'Ordre des Coteaux
assisted by Lazare S. Kaufman

A Studio Book
The Viking Press
New York

Acknowledgments

There are so many who helped me in my work that I only hope that I have not omitted anyone. If I have, forgive me. I am only mentioning names, and for a very specific reason: my purpose is simply to say "Thank you," whether you be tycoon or worker. Kindness is a word that means the same to all, and this work would not have been possible without the kindness of many.

Michel André, Jean-Marie Arnoult, François d'Aulan, Edward H. Benenson, M. and Mme. Christian de Billy, Christian Bizot, Mme. Jacques Bollinger, Colonel François Bonal, the Brasserie du Boulingrin, Bernard Breuzon, Arnauld Bro de Comères, Michel Budin, Raoul Chandon-Moët, M. and Mme. Jean Couten, Tom Crimmins, Jean Dapremont, Joseph Dargent, M. and Mme. Jean Daunay, J. P. Davot, M. Dellinger, André Dévignes, Mme. Geneviève Dévignes, Henri Druart, Mlle. Marguerite Dubuisson, René Dumont, Pierre Ernst, Patrick Forbes, M. and Mme. Charles Gaillard, Mlle. Marie France Gardot-Renevey, Odil Girardin, M. and Mme. Bernard de la Giraudière, Mme. Annie de Sainte Goresille, Mme. Claude Gosset, Edward Gottlieb, Pierre Gouttier, Mme. André Guy, Alain Harmel, M. and Mme. Jean-Marc Heidsieck, William Kaduson, Jean Lallier, François Lanson, Roger Laslier, Mlle. Irène Lassare, Comtesse Guillaume Lecointre, Leleu and Son, R. Levresse; Pierre, Roland, and Jean-Jacques Lorin; Pierre Maquin, Jean Marcandier, Arnaud de Mareuil, Charles Marq, Abbé Albert Mathieu, Roger Mazerot, Mme. F. Merand, Emile Moreau, Bernard de Nonancourt, Xavier Oury, Mme. Geneviève d'Adhemar de Panat, Roland d'Adhemar de Panat, Bernard Pieds, M. and Mme. Poirette, François Pomarède, Alphonse Pottevin, Marcel Poussin, Georges Prade, Miss Anne Price, M. and Mme. César Prieto, Jean Pierre Ravaux, Jean Rodez, Mme. Pol Roger, Henry LeRoux, M. Sainte Marie, M. and Mme. Max Schosseler, Mlle. Anne-Marie Seconde, M. and Mme. Jacques Simone, Henry Supper, Claude Taittinger, Philippe du Verdier, M. and Mme. Alain Vesselle, Ghislain de Vogue, Mme. René Welche.

CONTENTS

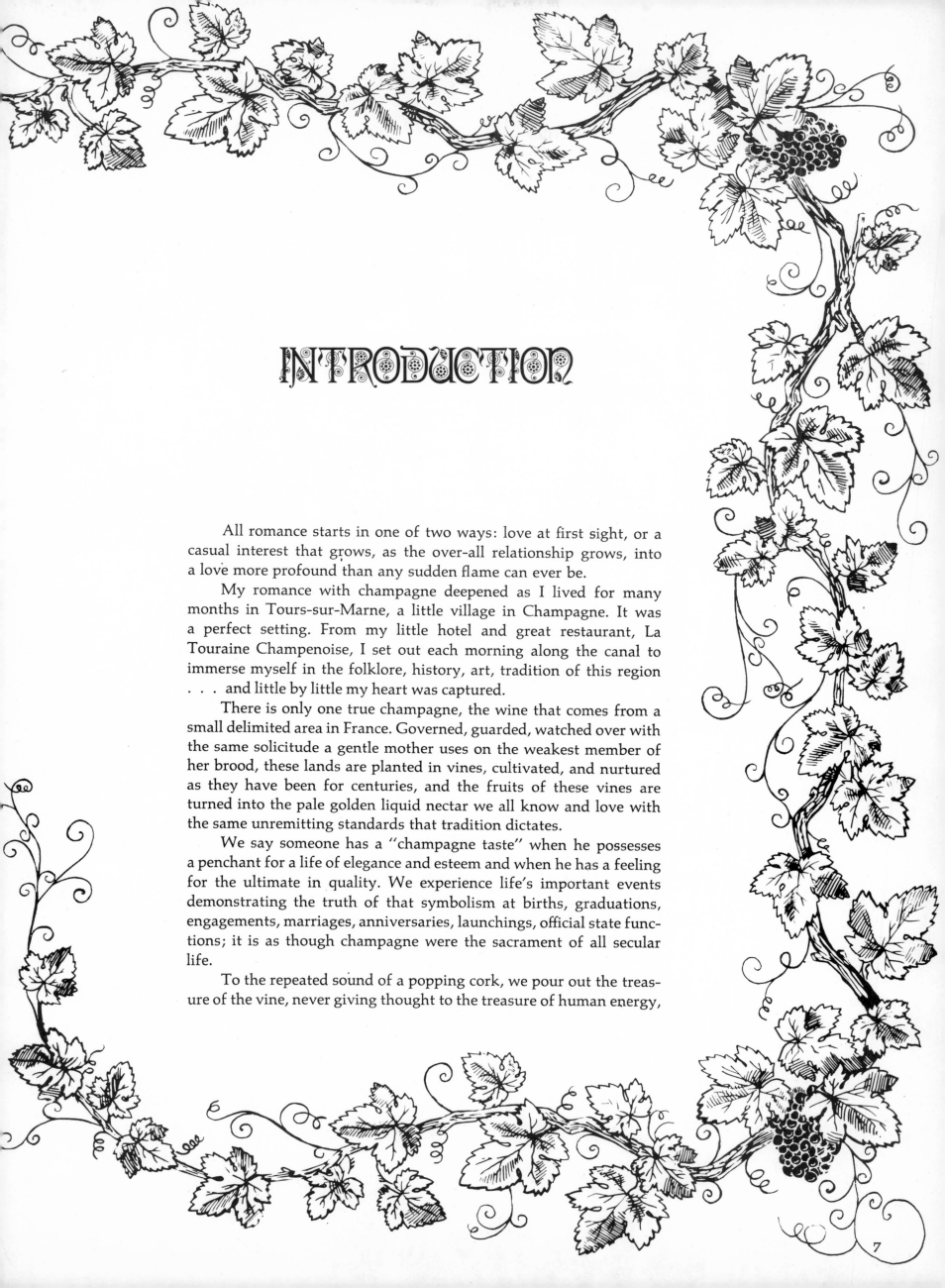

INTRODUCTION

All romance starts in one of two ways: love at first sight, or a casual interest that grows, as the over-all relationship grows, into a love more profound than any sudden flame can ever be.

My romance with champagne deepened as I lived for many months in Tours-sur-Marne, a little village in Champagne. It was a perfect setting. From my little hotel and great restaurant, La Touraine Champenoise, I set out each morning along the canal to immerse myself in the folklore, history, art, tradition of this region . . . and little by little my heart was captured.

There is only one true champagne, the wine that comes from a small delimited area in France. Governed, guarded, watched over with the same solicitude a gentle mother uses on the weakest member of her brood, these lands are planted in vines, cultivated, and nurtured as they have been for centuries, and the fruits of these vines are turned into the pale golden liquid nectar we all know and love with the same unremitting standards that tradition dictates.

We say someone has a "champagne taste" when he possesses a penchant for a life of elegance and esteem and when he has a feeling for the ultimate in quality. We experience life's important events demonstrating the truth of that symbolism at births, graduations, engagements, marriages, anniversaries, launchings, official state functions; it is as though champagne were the sacrament of all secular life.

To the repeated sound of a popping cork, we pour out the treasure of the vine, never giving thought to the treasure of human energy,

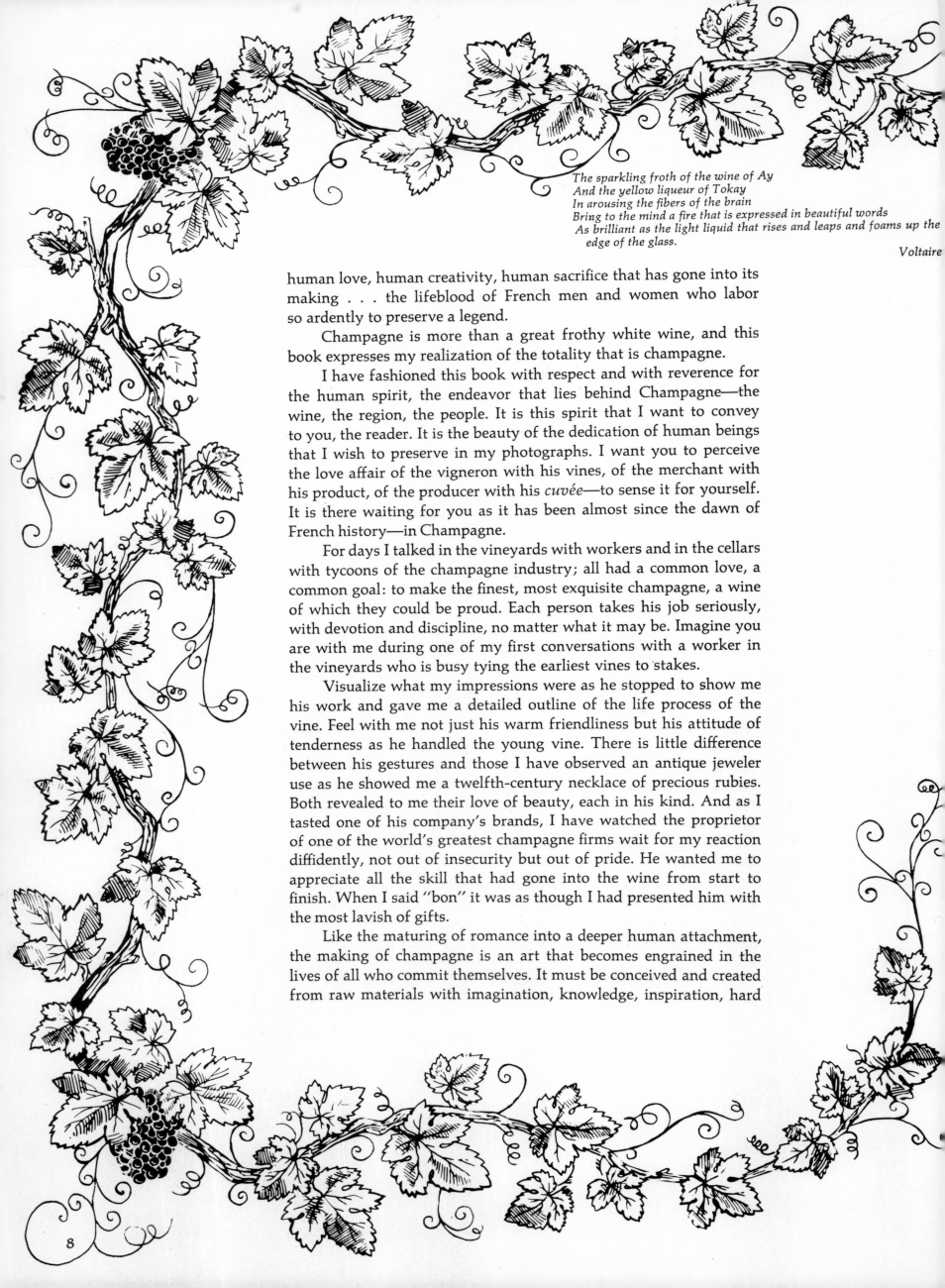

The sparkling froth of the wine of Ay
And the yellow liqueur of Tokay
In arousing the fibers of the brain
Bring to the mind a fire that is expressed in beautiful words
As brilliant as the light liquid that rises and leaps and foams up the
edge of the glass.

Voltaire

human love, human creativity, human sacrifice that has gone into its making . . . the lifeblood of French men and women who labor so ardently to preserve a legend.

Champagne is more than a great frothy white wine, and this book expresses my realization of the totality that is champagne.

I have fashioned this book with respect and with reverence for the human spirit, the endeavor that lies behind Champagne—the wine, the region, the people. It is this spirit that I want to convey to you, the reader. It is the beauty of the dedication of human beings that I wish to preserve in my photographs. I want you to perceive the love affair of the vigneron with his vines, of the merchant with his product, of the producer with his *cuvée*—to sense it for yourself. It is there waiting for you as it has been almost since the dawn of French history—in Champagne.

For days I talked in the vineyards with workers and in the cellars with tycoons of the champagne industry; all had a common love, a common goal: to make the finest, most exquisite champagne, a wine of which they could be proud. Each person takes his job seriously, with devotion and discipline, no matter what it may be. Imagine you are with me during one of my first conversations with a worker in the vineyards who is busy tying the earliest vines to stakes.

Visualize what my impressions were as he stopped to show me his work and gave me a detailed outline of the life process of the vine. Feel with me not just his warm friendliness but his attitude of tenderness as he handled the young vine. There is little difference between his gestures and those I have observed an antique jeweler use as he showed me a twelfth-century necklace of precious rubies. Both revealed to me their love of beauty, each in his kind. And as I tasted one of his company's brands, I have watched the proprietor of one of the world's greatest champagne firms wait for my reaction diffidently, not out of insecurity but out of pride. He wanted me to appreciate all the skill that had gone into the wine from start to finish. When I said "bon" it was as though I had presented him with the most lavish of gifts.

Like the maturing of romance into a deeper human attachment, the making of champagne is an art that becomes engrained in the lives of all who commit themselves. It must be conceived and created from raw materials with imagination, knowledge, inspiration, hard

work, and persistence. It doesn't just happen. It is a lifetime work. It is a magnum opus.

If my book inspires the reader to visit Champagne, to taste champagne, to come in contact with the Champenois for a touch of the romance that has changed my horizons, I shall feel that I have become in some measure part of that strong *confrérie* or brotherhood of men and women dedicated to Champagne—the country, the people, and the wine of France.

A votre santé.

William I. Kaufman
Chevalier et Officier
de
l'Ordre des Coteaux de Champagne

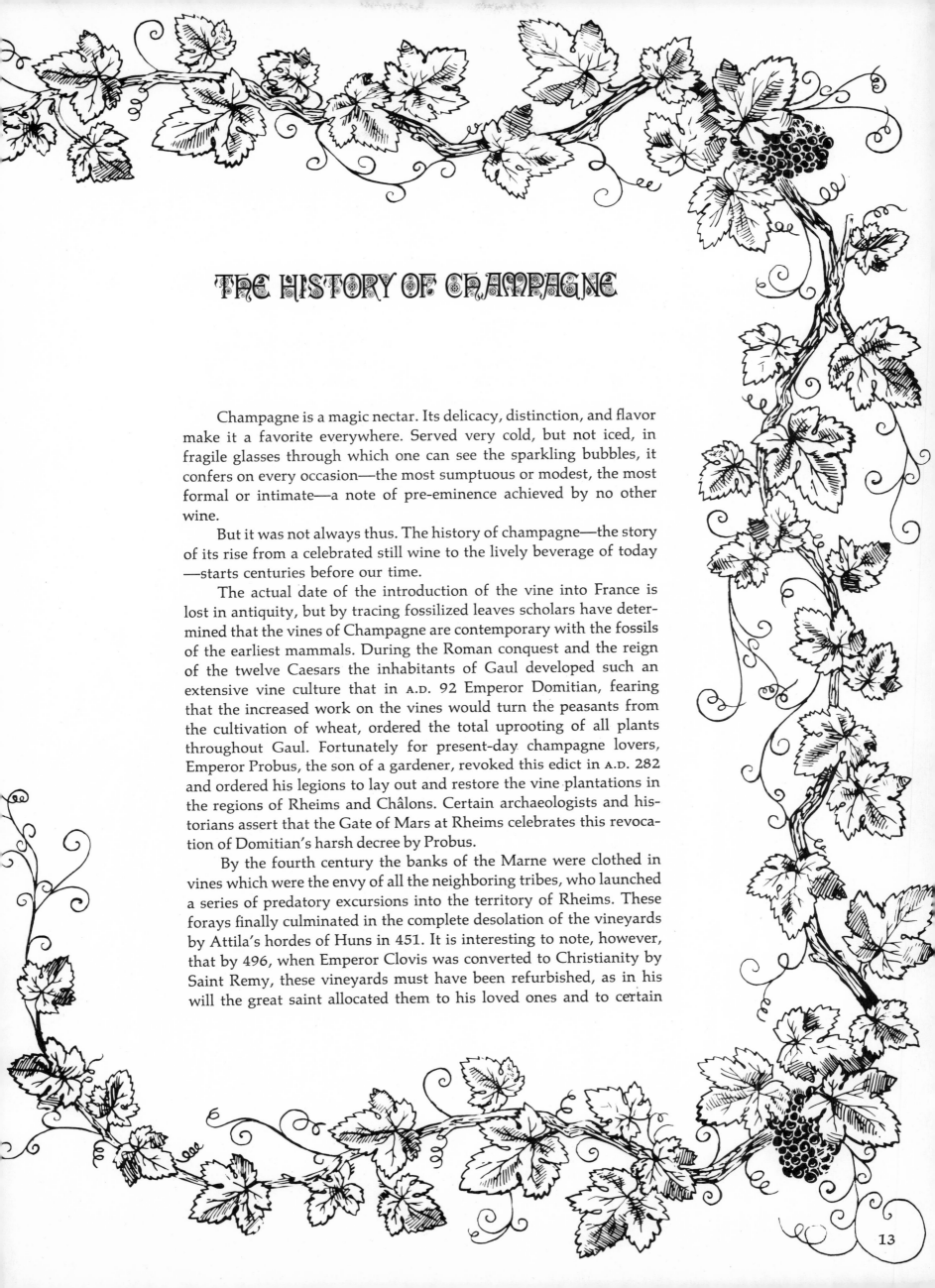

THE HISTORY OF CHAMPAGNE

Champagne is a magic nectar. Its delicacy, distinction, and flavor make it a favorite everywhere. Served very cold, but not iced, in fragile glasses through which one can see the sparkling bubbles, it confers on every occasion—the most sumptuous or modest, the most formal or intimate—a note of pre-eminence achieved by no other wine.

But it was not always thus. The history of champagne—the story of its rise from a celebrated still wine to the lively beverage of today —starts centuries before our time.

The actual date of the introduction of the vine into France is lost in antiquity, but by tracing fossilized leaves scholars have determined that the vines of Champagne are contemporary with the fossils of the earliest mammals. During the Roman conquest and the reign of the twelve Caesars the inhabitants of Gaul developed such an extensive vine culture that in A.D. 92 Emperor Domitian, fearing that the increased work on the vines would turn the peasants from the cultivation of wheat, ordered the total uprooting of all plants throughout Gaul. Fortunately for present-day champagne lovers, Emperor Probus, the son of a gardener, revoked this edict in A.D. 282 and ordered his legions to lay out and restore the vine plantations in the regions of Rheims and Châlons. Certain archaeologists and historians assert that the Gate of Mars at Rheims celebrates this revocation of Domitian's harsh decree by Probus.

By the fourth century the banks of the Marne were clothed in vines which were the envy of all the neighboring tribes, who launched a series of predatory excursions into the territory of Rheims. These forays finally culminated in the complete desolation of the vineyards by Attila's hordes of Huns in 451. It is interesting to note, however, that by 496, when Emperor Clovis was converted to Christianity by Saint Remy, these vineyards must have been refurbished, as in his will the great saint allocated them to his loved ones and to certain

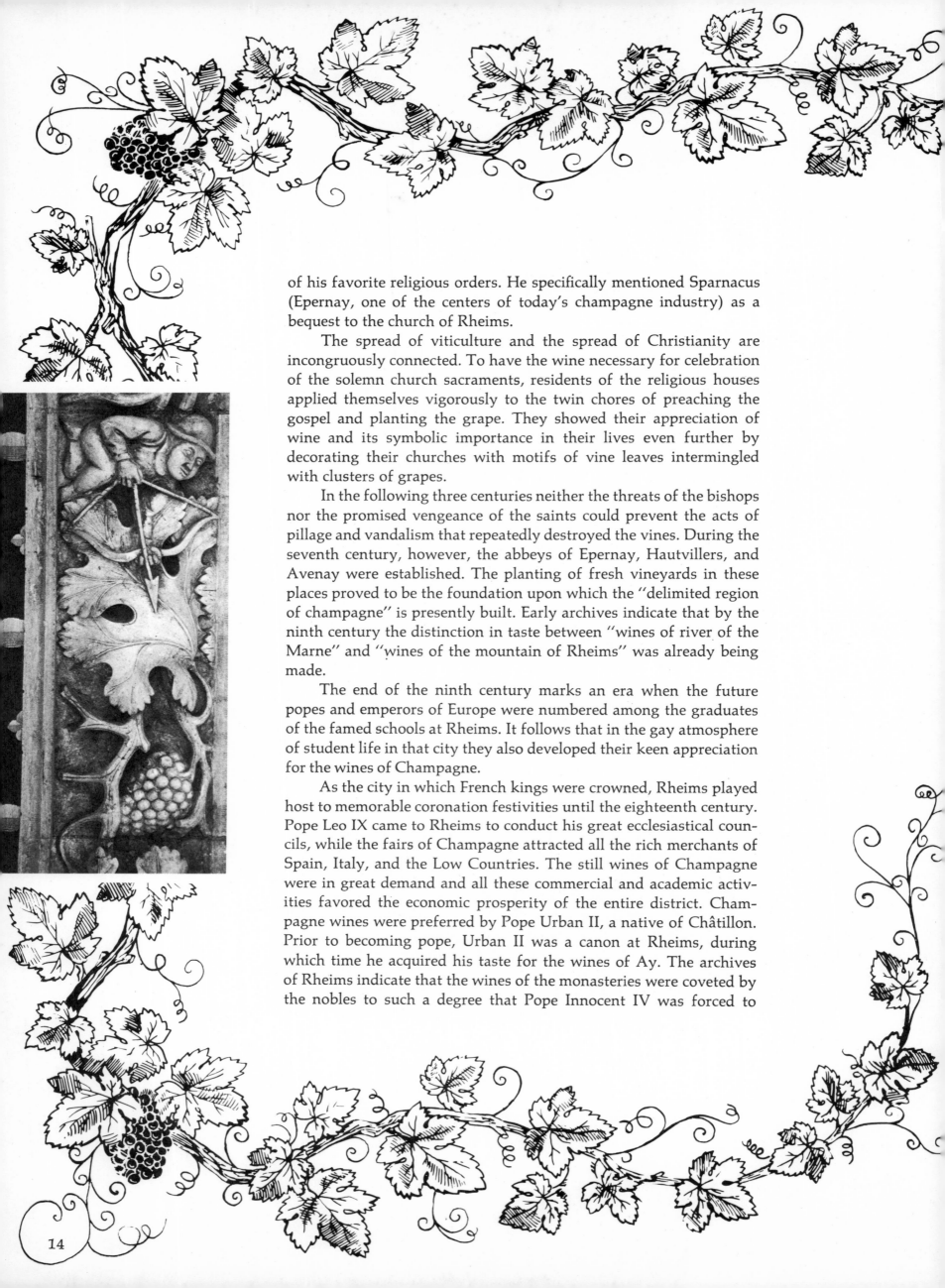

of his favorite religious orders. He specifically mentioned Sparnacus (Epernay, one of the centers of today's champagne industry) as a bequest to the church of Rheims.

The spread of viticulture and the spread of Christianity are incongruously connected. To have the wine necessary for celebration of the solemn church sacraments, residents of the religious houses applied themselves vigorously to the twin chores of preaching the gospel and planting the grape. They showed their appreciation of wine and its symbolic importance in their lives even further by decorating their churches with motifs of vine leaves intermingled with clusters of grapes.

In the following three centuries neither the threats of the bishops nor the promised vengeance of the saints could prevent the acts of pillage and vandalism that repeatedly destroyed the vines. During the seventh century, however, the abbeys of Epernay, Hautvillers, and Avenay were established. The planting of fresh vineyards in these places proved to be the foundation upon which the "delimited region of champagne" is presently built. Early archives indicate that by the ninth century the distinction in taste between "wines of river of the Marne" and "wines of the mountain of Rheims" was already being made.

The end of the ninth century marks an era when the future popes and emperors of Europe were numbered among the graduates of the famed schools at Rheims. It follows that in the gay atmosphere of student life in that city they also developed their keen appreciation for the wines of Champagne.

As the city in which French kings were crowned, Rheims played host to memorable coronation festivities until the eighteenth century. Pope Leo IX came to Rheims to conduct his great ecclesiastical councils, while the fairs of Champagne attracted all the rich merchants of Spain, Italy, and the Low Countries. The still wines of Champagne were in great demand and all these commercial and academic activities favored the economic prosperity of the entire district. Champagne wines were preferred by Pope Urban II, a native of Châtillon. Prior to becoming pope, Urban II was a canon at Rheims, during which time he acquired his taste for the wines of Ay. The archives of Rheims indicate that the wines of the monasteries were coveted by the nobles to such a degree that Pope Innocent IV was forced to reprove the barons in 1252 for interfering with the monastic vintage. Moreover he threatened them with excommunication should they repeat their offense.

At nearby Troyes the counts of Champagne, to whom Epernay was ceded as a fief, held court in the manner of sovereign princes. Seated at great banquet tables surrounded by their knights and barons, they gorged themselves on all manner of victuals, washing down their meats with native vintage while they feasted their eyes on the entertainment provided by minstrels, court fools, jugglers, and dancing girls.

At all the coronations of the French kings held in Rheims, champagne wines were an essential part of the festivities. At the crowning of Philip the Fair (1285) the wines flowed like water, and at the coronation of Charles IV (1322) so much wine was purchased in advance that Pierre Remi, the King's Minister of Finance, was able to initiate the illicit wine dealings which cost him his head some years later.

After 1328 and the coronation of King Philip VI the records of fourteenth-century Rheims show that wine brokers or *courtiers de vin* had come into being. They were in the habit of increasing their trade by offering a taste of as much as two to four gallons of wine from their cellars to all visiting merchants and to all persons of distinction who passed through the town. In 1361 the citizens of Rheims were so certain of their revenues from the sale of their famous vintages that they willingly imposed upon themselves an *octroi* or tax on all wines sold, in order to maintain the ramparts which protected their city.

With the coronation of Charles V (1364) the wines of Champagne began to gain a foothold on the international reputation that they still enjoy. At this event the King and Queen were accompanied by such foreign dignitaries as King Peter of Cyprus, King Wenceslas of Bohemia, the Dukes of Burgundy and of Anjou, and many other prelates and nobles who partook fully of the wines of Rheims and Epernay during the five days of royal feasting.

The greatest planting of vines in the champagne region plainly dates from this event, for these foreigners, having once savored these delicious wines, were determined to serve them in their own kingdoms. They were willing to import them no matter what the cost. A

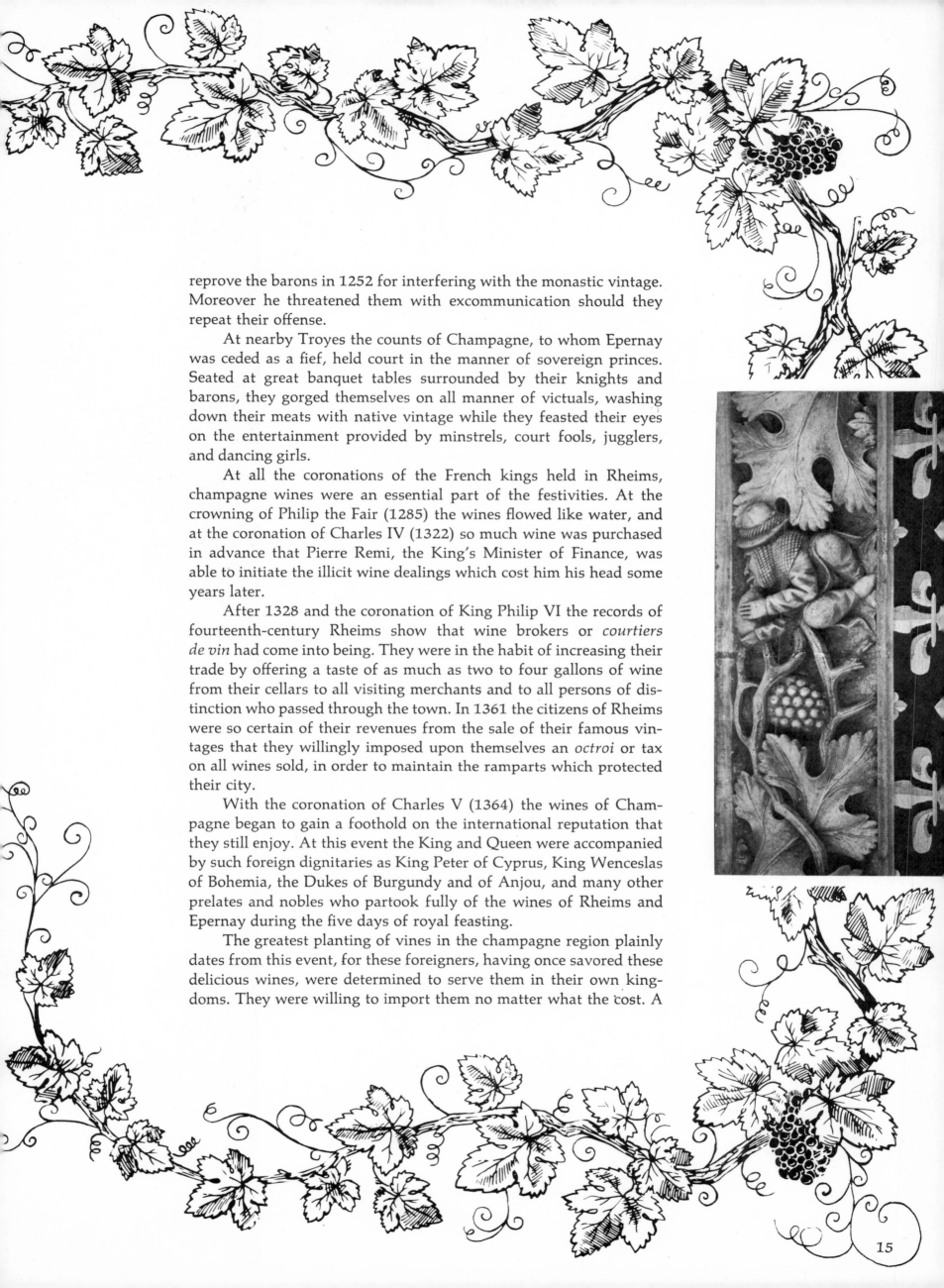

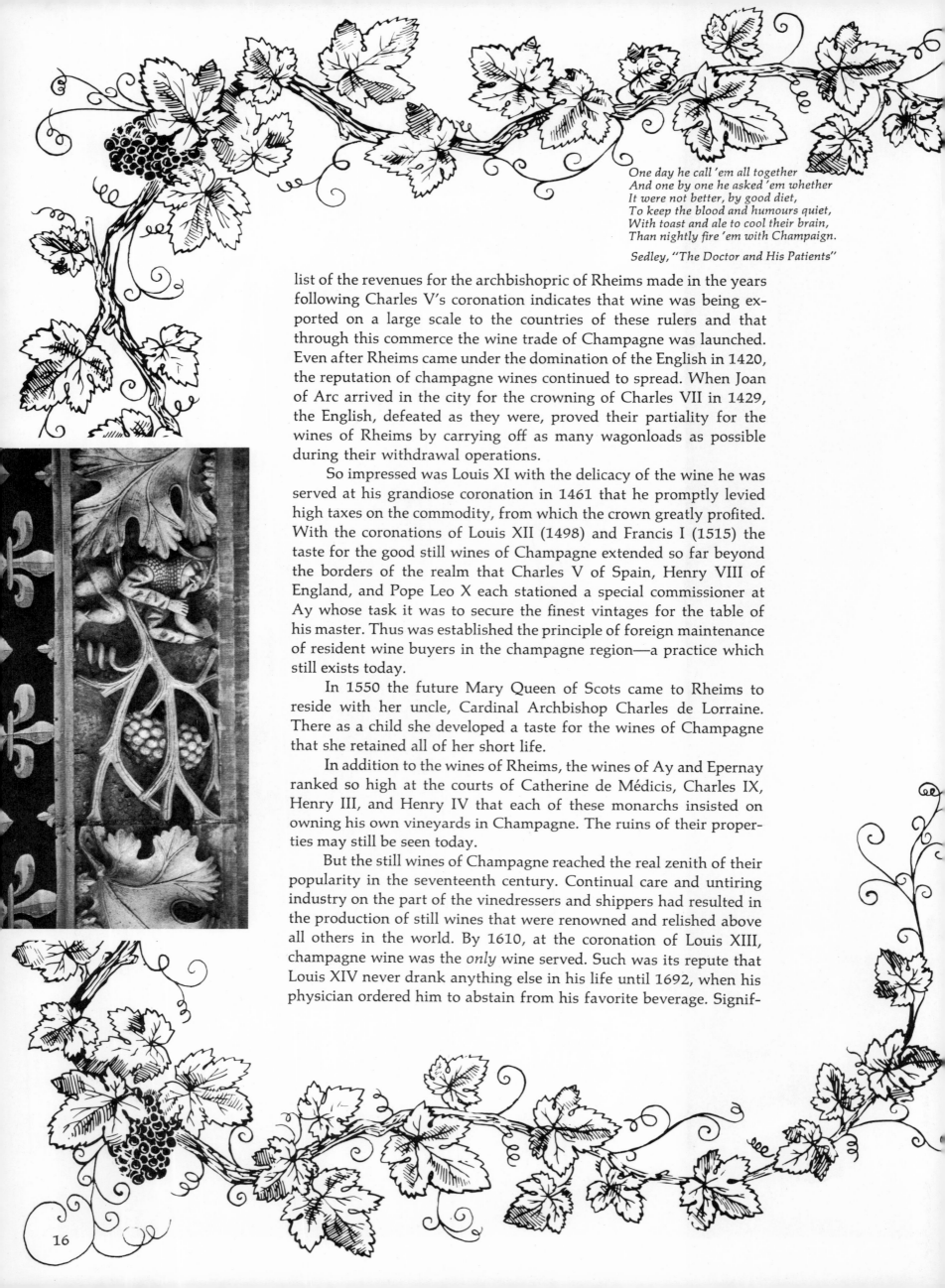

list of the revenues for the archbishopric of Rheims made in the years following Charles V's coronation indicates that wine was being exported on a large scale to the countries of these rulers and that through this commerce the wine trade of Champagne was launched. Even after Rheims came under the domination of the English in 1420, the reputation of champagne wines continued to spread. When Joan of Arc arrived in the city for the crowning of Charles VII in 1429, the English, defeated as they were, proved their partiality for the wines of Rheims by carrying off as many wagonloads as possible during their withdrawal operations.

So impressed was Louis XI with the delicacy of the wine he was served at his grandiose coronation in 1461 that he promptly levied high taxes on the commodity, from which the crown greatly profited. With the coronations of Louis XII (1498) and Francis I (1515) the taste for the good still wines of Champagne extended so far beyond the borders of the realm that Charles V of Spain, Henry VIII of England, and Pope Leo X each stationed a special commissioner at Ay whose task it was to secure the finest vintages for the table of his master. Thus was established the principle of foreign maintenance of resident wine buyers in the champagne region—a practice which still exists today.

In 1550 the future Mary Queen of Scots came to Rheims to reside with her uncle, Cardinal Archbishop Charles de Lorraine. There as a child she developed a taste for the wines of Champagne that she retained all of her short life.

In addition to the wines of Rheims, the wines of Ay and Epernay ranked so high at the courts of Catherine de Médicis, Charles IX, Henry III, and Henry IV that each of these monarchs insisted on owning his own vineyards in Champagne. The ruins of their properties may still be seen today.

But the still wines of Champagne reached the real zenith of their popularity in the seventeenth century. Continual care and untiring industry on the part of the vinedressers and shippers had resulted in the production of still wines that were renowned and relished above all others in the world. By 1610, at the coronation of Louis XIII, champagne wine was the *only* wine served. Such was its repute that Louis XIV never drank anything else in his life until 1692, when his physician ordered him to abstain from his favorite beverage. Signif-

QVO
NI
A ^{3}
QVI
DEM
MVL
TI
CONATI
SVNT

ORDINARENARRATIONEMQVEINNOBIS

DOMC · VIIII · POST OCT PE

LC STI EV · SCDM MATHEV

NEMO R · DIXIT IHC DI

cipulis suis; Nemo potest

duobus dominis seruire;

Et cetera; OMEL VENER BE

PBRI · DE EADE

Nemo

potest

duob

dom

serui

quia

ualet

simul ta

toria

na

&cetera

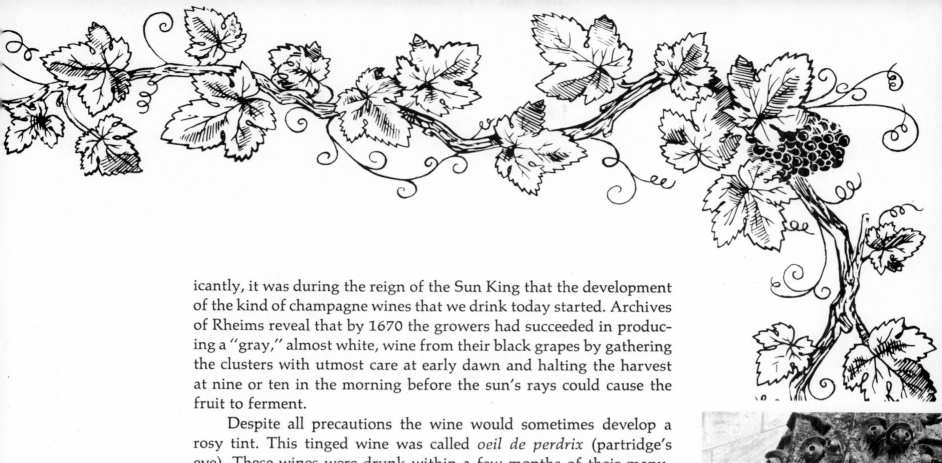

icantly, it was during the reign of the Sun King that the development of the kind of champagne wines that we drink today started. Archives of Rheims reveal that by 1670 the growers had succeeded in producing a "gray," almost white, wine from their black grapes by gathering the clusters with utmost care at early dawn and halting the harvest at nine or ten in the morning before the sun's rays could cause the fruit to ferment.

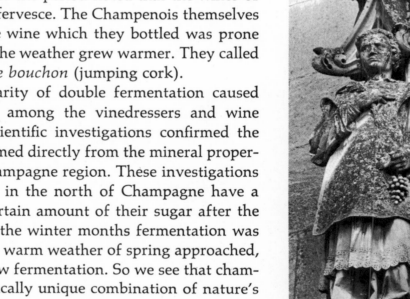

Despite all precautions the wine would sometimes develop a rosy tint. This tinged wine was called *oeil de perdrix* (partridge's eye). These wines were drunk within a few months of their manufacture inasmuch as gourmets of the period noted that the wines of this region had a tendency to effervesce. The Champenois themselves were aware that the new white wine which they bottled was prone to ferment a second time when the weather grew warmer. They called this twice-fermented wine *saute bouchon* (jumping cork).

Champagne is the only wine a woman can drink and still remain beautiful.

Madame Pompadour

The origin of this peculiarity of double fermentation caused many arguments and debates among the vinedressers and wine brokers until finally certain scientific investigations confirmed the fact that the phenomenon stemmed directly from the mineral properties of the chalky soil of the champagne region. These investigations showed also that wines grown in the north of Champagne have a natural tendency to retain a certain amount of their sugar after the first fermentation; that during the winter months fermentation was arrested, but that as soon as the warm weather of spring approached, this sugar retention caused a new fermentation. So we see that champagne is the result of a romantically unique combination of nature's gifts found only in the small corner of the world called "Champagne."

It is a coincidence of great consequence that in this same year of 1670 a monk named Dom Pierre Pérignon became cellar master of the abbey of Hautvillers. Founded ten centuries earlier by the Benedictines, the abbey was at the peak of its glory when he took up his work. It had produced no less than nine archbishops and twenty-two abbots who distinguished themselves in both civil and religious affairs. Its territorial possessions were vast, its revenue ample. The wine of its fertile vineyards was highly esteemed at home and abroad.

Dom Pierre was a charitable, pleasant, sensitive monk. A contemporary of Louis XIV, he was known to be intelligent and knowledgeable. The exactitude with which he fulfilled his monastic duties

made him eminently well suited to his appointed post: director of finances for the abbey and administrator of the cellars. As cellar master of this rich monastery he was led by his exceptional instinct and unceasing curiosity to penetrate into the smallest details in the creation of sparkling champagne. He was a true pioneer. His experiments firmly established the principles that are still followed in champagne production. Since his time nothing of fundamental importance has been invented in this field and the scientific research of modern times has merely rationalized his basic work on sparkling champagne.

Dom Pierre first studied the phenomenon of double fermentation. Having observed that fermentation occurred once after harvest and a second time in the spring, he succeeded through arduous tests in controlling and accelerating this fermentation at will, thus producing wines which were lighter and more delicate. His examination of the sugar content of the wine enabled him to create and control the force of the bubbles which made the wine so unique. But his greatest contribution lay not in capturing the principles which lay behind the sparkle but in his discovery that by "marrying" the juices of grapes grown in different fields and by blending them in certain proportions, he could produce the same distinctive champagne tastes year after year. He was able to repeat his formulae over and over again, each time proving that he would get exactly the same results. Striving always for better champagne, he developed the secret of mixing the new wines with old reserved wines to produce a higher quality of taste and refinement. These methods marked the origin of the *cuvée* or blending of champagne wines. *This discovery of the technique for marrying the wines is the single most important contribution to the entire history of champagne and champagne production that has ever been made.* The pre-eminence of champagne is based on the consistency of its high quality: a high quality that is ensured by adherence to the principles first realized by this great and creative Benedictine monk.

Over the years, following the rules established by Dom Pierre, each champagne producer has developed a cuvée prized and preserved as its own secret formula. By this means each company offers its clientele a particularly consistent champagne taste positively identified with its brand name.

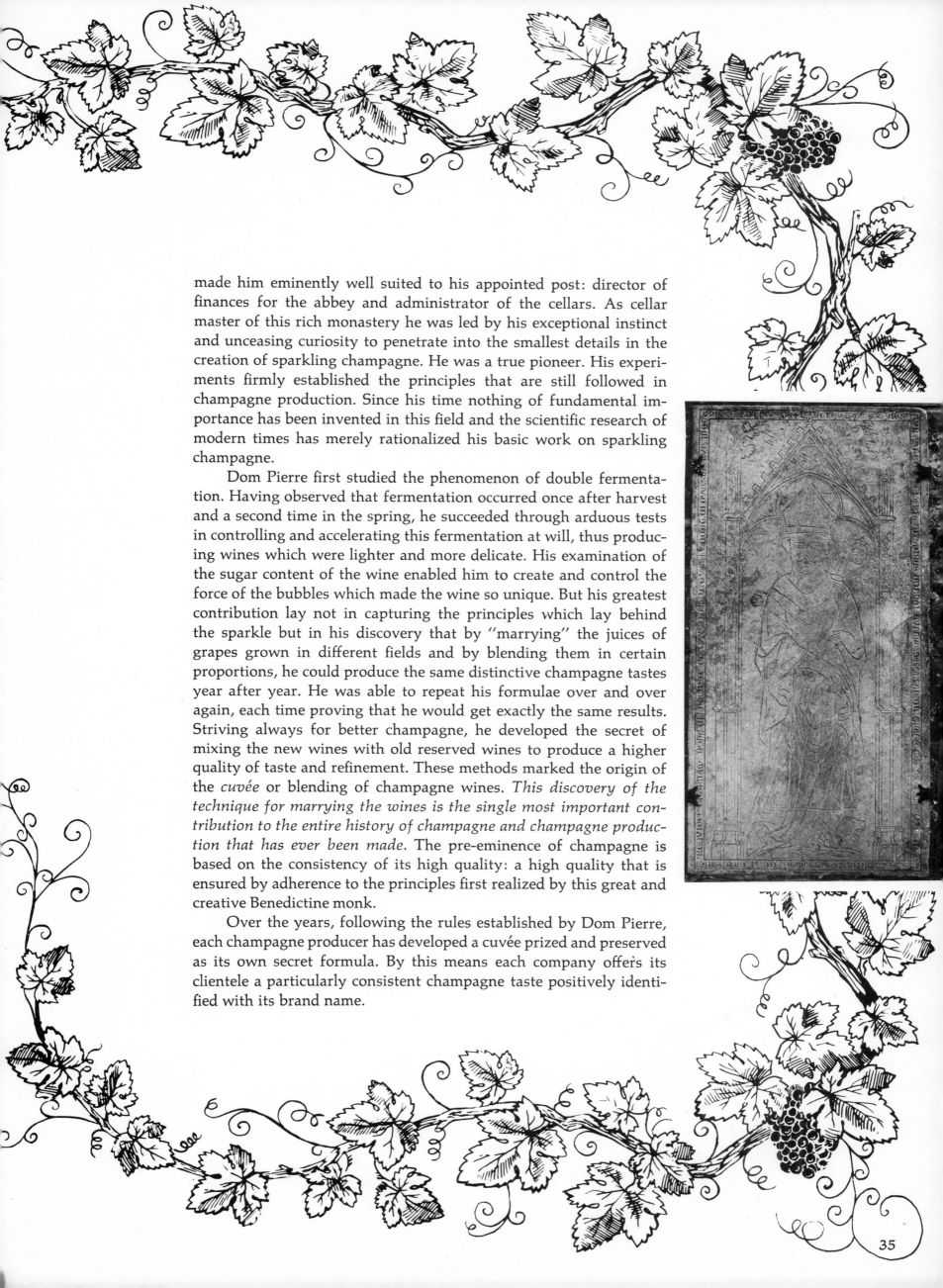

Dom Pierre introduced the use of the cork into the champagne region, although it had been previously utilized in England. He realized that he would be able to control the speed of fermentation and the sparkle in the champagne more precisely if he replaced the old wooden staples wrapped in hemp and soaked in oil with the living cork, which would expand in the bottle and seal it more thoroughly. He was also the first to recognize the natural advantages of the chalky soil as a storage place in which to mature wines. He observed that the low constant temperatures of the old Roman stone quarries were ideal for the repose and aging of the wines he had "married" so carefully. In the course of his experimentation he was the first to use these enormous caverns. Among his other experiments, we know that he discovered a way of clearing the wine without being obliged to decant it into fresh bottles. Unfortunately his secret was never revealed beyond the confines of his own monastery, and shortly after his death the process of *dépotage* (decanting) fell into disuse and was replaced by *dégorgeage:* removal of the sediment from the neck of the bottle without removing the wine from its original container.

The abbey in which Dom Pierre did his work is still standing just north of Epernay. In the courtyard of the abbey is a larger-than-life-size statue of the famous monk who must be credited with the development of the formula for the champagne that bears his name. The abbey and the cellars in which he did his work are open to the public by appointment and by permission.

The fame of the new sparkling wine, known variously as "vin de Pérignon," "vin du diable," "flacon pétillant," "flacon mousseux," "vin sautant," "vin mousseux," "saute bouchon," etc., quickly spread. The discovery of the "sparkle" came just in time: the glory of France was on the wane; the once brilliant King Louis XIV had become a bigoted, almost isolated invalid; the French economy was toppling. It was at this moment that the wines of Champagne were preserved for posterity by Saint-Evremond, a remarkable Frenchman, brave soldier, learned philosopher, and witty courtier who introduced the beverage into England. Seeking refuge from the displeasure of Louis XIV, he settled down in his new-found homeland to become the arbiter of good taste in royal and fashionable society. While a young man in France Saint-Evremond had been one of the three

One day Henry IV dropped in to see his minister Sully. After drinking several glasses of wine he exclaimed: "By Saint Gris!—here is a good wine. It holds its own with mine from Ay and from other good vineyards. I want to know where it comes from."

"My friend Tassy sent it to me," replied the great Minister of the Treasury.

"That's a man I'd like to know myself," responded the king— and so he did.

CHAMPAGNE IN ENGLAND.

Jones : 'I say, Brown, things are deuced bad in the City.'
Brown : 'Then I'm deuced glad I'm at Epsom.'

(From a drawing by John Leech in 'Punch.')

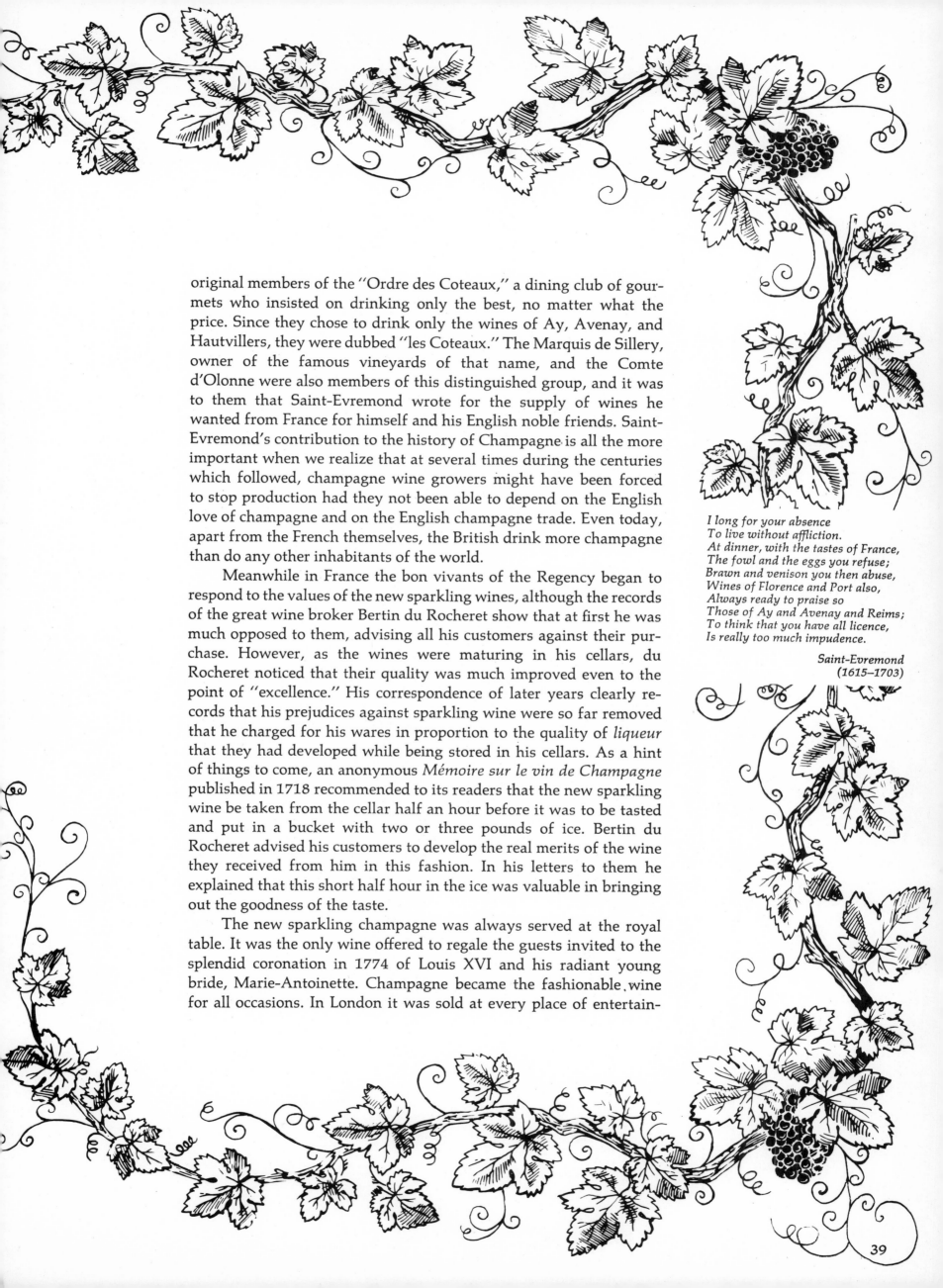

original members of the "Ordre des Coteaux," a dining club of gourmets who insisted on drinking only the best, no matter what the price. Since they chose to drink only the wines of Ay, Avenay, and Hautvillers, they were dubbed "les Coteaux." The Marquis de Sillery, owner of the famous vineyards of that name, and the Comte d'Olonne were also members of this distinguished group, and it was to them that Saint-Evremond wrote for the supply of wines he wanted from France for himself and his English noble friends. Saint-Evremond's contribution to the history of Champagne is all the more important when we realize that at several times during the centuries which followed, champagne wine growers might have been forced to stop production had they not been able to depend on the English love of champagne and on the English champagne trade. Even today, apart from the French themselves, the British drink more champagne than do any other inhabitants of the world.

Meanwhile in France the bon vivants of the Regency began to respond to the values of the new sparkling wines, although the records of the great wine broker Bertin du Rocheret show that at first he was much opposed to them, advising all his customers against their purchase. However, as the wines were maturing in his cellars, du Rocheret noticed that their quality was much improved even to the point of "excellence." His correspondence of later years clearly records that his prejudices against sparkling wine were so far removed that he charged for his wares in proportion to the quality of *liqueur* that they had developed while being stored in his cellars. As a hint of things to come, an anonymous *Mémoire sur le vin de Champagne* published in 1718 recommended to its readers that the new sparkling wine be taken from the cellar half an hour before it was to be tasted and put in a bucket with two or three pounds of ice. Bertin du Rocheret advised his customers to develop the real merits of the wine they received from him in this fashion. In his letters to them he explained that this short half hour in the ice was valuable in bringing out the goodness of the taste.

The new sparkling champagne was always served at the royal table. It was the only wine offered to regale the guests invited to the splendid coronation in 1774 of Louis XVI and his radiant young bride, Marie-Antoinette. Champagne became the fashionable wine for all occasions. In London it was sold at every place of entertain-

I long for your absence
To live without affliction.
At dinner, with the tastes of France,
The fowl and the eggs you refuse;
Brawn and venison you then abuse,
Wines of Florence and Port also,
Always ready to praise so
Those of Ay and Avenay and Reims;
To think that you have all licence,
Is really too much impudence.

Saint-Evremond
(1615–1703)

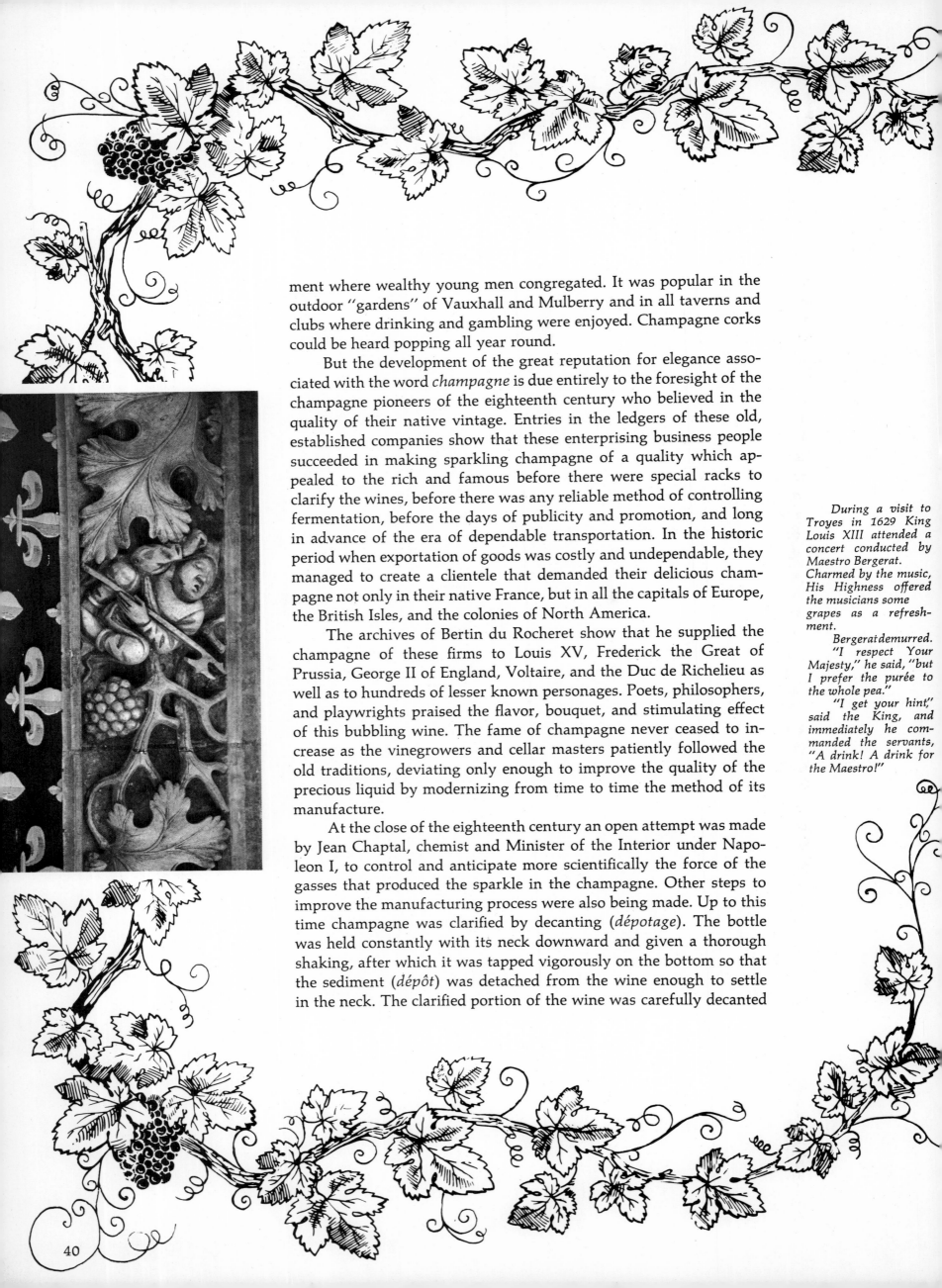

ment where wealthy young men congregated. It was popular in the outdoor "gardens" of Vauxhall and Mulberry and in all taverns and clubs where drinking and gambling were enjoyed. Champagne corks could be heard popping all year round.

But the development of the great reputation for elegance associated with the word *champagne* is due entirely to the foresight of the champagne pioneers of the eighteenth century who believed in the quality of their native vintage. Entries in the ledgers of these old, established companies show that these enterprising business people succeeded in making sparkling champagne of a quality which appealed to the rich and famous before there were special racks to clarify the wines, before there was any reliable method of controlling fermentation, before the days of publicity and promotion, and long in advance of the era of dependable transportation. In the historic period when exportation of goods was costly and undependable, they managed to create a clientele that demanded their delicious champagne not only in their native France, but in all the capitals of Europe, the British Isles, and the colonies of North America.

The archives of Bertin du Rocheret show that he supplied the champagne of these firms to Louis XV, Frederick the Great of Prussia, George II of England, Voltaire, and the Duc de Richelieu as well as to hundreds of lesser known personages. Poets, philosophers, and playwrights praised the flavor, bouquet, and stimulating effect of this bubbling wine. The fame of champagne never ceased to increase as the vinegrowers and cellar masters patiently followed the old traditions, deviating only enough to improve the quality of the precious liquid by modernizing from time to time the method of its manufacture.

At the close of the eighteenth century an open attempt was made by Jean Chaptal, chemist and Minister of the Interior under Napoleon I, to control and anticipate more scientifically the force of the gasses that produced the sparkle in the champagne. Other steps to improve the manufacturing process were also being made. Up to this time champagne was clarified by decanting (*dépotage*). The bottle was held constantly with its neck downward and given a thorough shaking, after which it was tapped vigorously on the bottom so that the sediment (*dépôt*) was detached from the wine enough to settle in the neck. The clarified portion of the wine was carefully decanted

During a visit to Troyes in 1629 King Louis XIII attended a concert conducted by Maestro Bergerat. Charmed by the music, His Highness offered the musicians some grapes as a refreshment.

Bergerat demurred. "I respect Your Majesty," he said, "but I prefer the purée to the whole pea."

"I get your hint," said the King, and immediately he commanded the servants, "A drink! A drink for the Maestro!"

into fresh bottles after the solid particles had been removed, and later the remaining sediment was removed by the *dégorgement* process. Now a new method evolved for clarifying the wine. The bottles were no longer shaken, turned upside down, or rapped smartly on the bottom. Instead they were placed in sloping racks. Each day the bottles were rotated by hand and the slope of the racks was modified until all the sediment settled on the cork.

As a result of all this special care and expert handling, champagne prices rose. But the more delicious the wine became because of its added delicacy, the more the demand for it grew. While the rich and royal enjoyed their champagne, and the wine merchants of Rheims who sold it at great profit lived in high style, the heavy duties and taxes levied against it crushed the poor vignerons who grew the grapes. Nevertheless, even though they were overwhelmed by poverty, the vinedressers, out of deep love for their small plots of land and out of devotion to their traditional calling, must have continued their production of fine champagne through the trying period of the Wars of the Revolution and the Allied invasion of 1814–1815. We read in the archives of the champagne region that Napoleon I visited the cellars at Epernay to choose his wines. After him Charles X, Louis Philippe, and Napoleon III successively visited Epernay for the purpose of sampling and purchasing champagnes. Meanwhile the breakage of the bottles (*la casse*) was seldom less than 10 per cent and sometimes as high as 80 per cent. This damage caused the loss of many fine wines and the cost of champagne soared. Already highly speculative, the champagne trade became still more so.

These mounting difficulties stimulated François, a druggist from Châlons, to try some tentative experiments to control this bursting of bottles. Using the work of Chaptal as his point of departure, François was finally able to develop a process called *réduction François*. For the first time it was possible to determine accurately how much sugar was in the wine when it was bottled, and the exact volume of carbonic acid gas created by this natural sugar to produce the sparkling bubbles in the champagne. François discovered that he could also control the vinosity of the champagne and in so doing was able to produce wines of varying flavor: brut, sec, demi-sec, and sweet. But his most important contribution lies in the fact that, as a result of the réduction François, the breakage of champagne bottles was reduced from 80 to

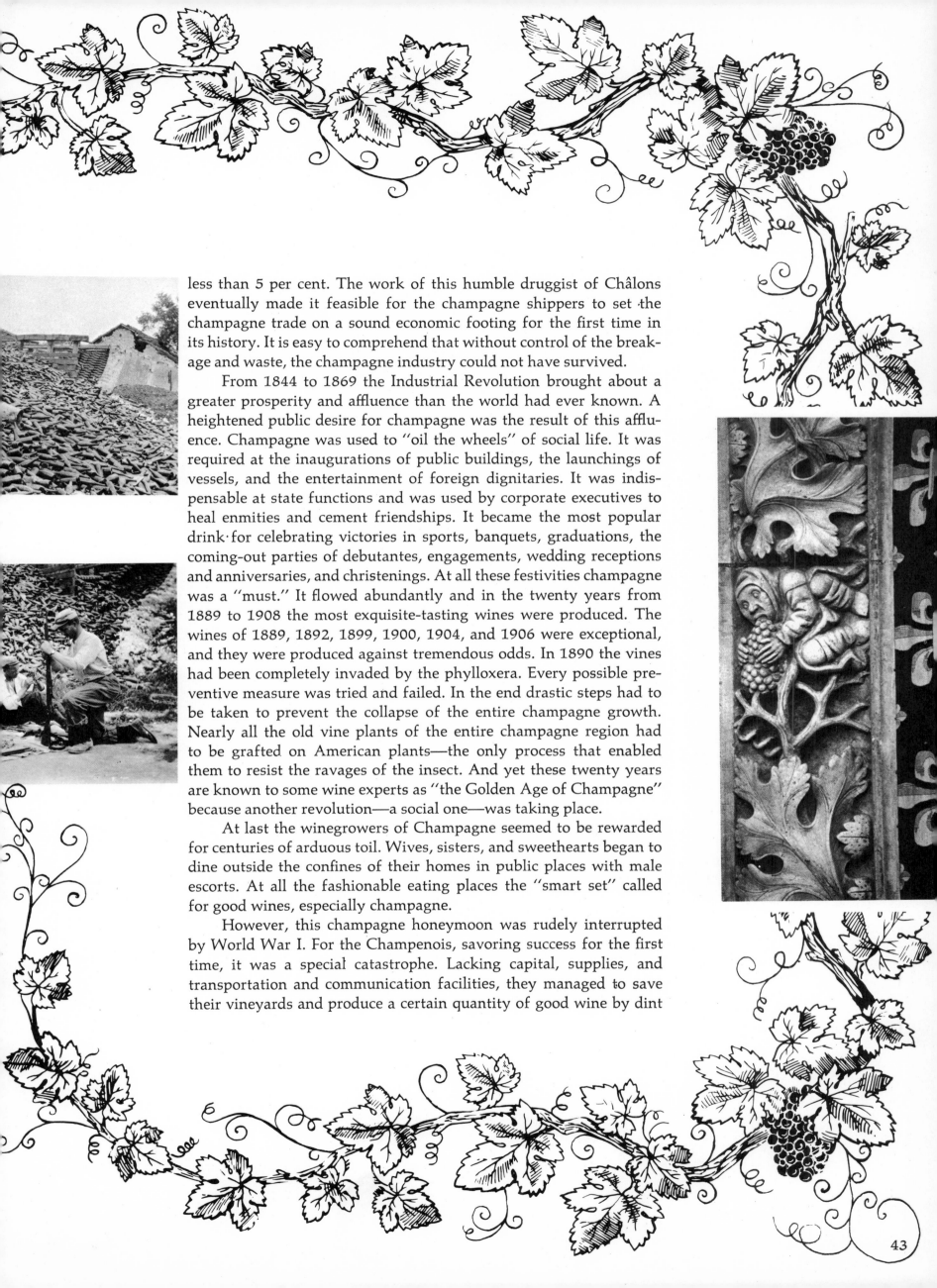

less than 5 per cent. The work of this humble druggist of Châlons eventually made it feasible for the champagne shippers to set the champagne trade on a sound economic footing for the first time in its history. It is easy to comprehend that without control of the breakage and waste, the champagne industry could not have survived.

From 1844 to 1869 the Industrial Revolution brought about a greater prosperity and affluence than the world had ever known. A heightened public desire for champagne was the result of this affluence. Champagne was used to "oil the wheels" of social life. It was required at the inaugurations of public buildings, the launchings of vessels, and the entertainment of foreign dignitaries. It was indispensable at state functions and was used by corporate executives to heal enmities and cement friendships. It became the most popular drink·for celebrating victories in sports, banquets, graduations, the coming-out parties of debutantes, engagements, wedding receptions and anniversaries, and christenings. At all these festivities champagne was a "must." It flowed abundantly and in the twenty years from 1889 to 1908 the most exquisite-tasting wines were produced. The wines of 1889, 1892, 1899, 1900, 1904, and 1906 were exceptional, and they were produced against tremendous odds. In 1890 the vines had been completely invaded by the phylloxera. Every possible preventive measure was tried and failed. In the end drastic steps had to be taken to prevent the collapse of the entire champagne growth. Nearly all the old vine plants of the entire champagne region had to be grafted on American plants—the only process that enabled them to resist the ravages of the insect. And yet these twenty years are known to some wine experts as "the Golden Age of Champagne" because another revolution—a social one—was taking place.

At last the winegrowers of Champagne seemed to be rewarded for centuries of arduous toil. Wives, sisters, and sweethearts began to dine outside the confines of their homes in public places with male escorts. At all the fashionable eating places the "smart set" called for good wines, especially champagne.

However, this champagne honeymoon was rudely interrupted by World War I. For the Champenois, savoring success for the first time, it was a special catastrophe. Lacking capital, supplies, and transportation and communication facilities, they managed to save their vineyards and produce a certain quantity of good wine by dint

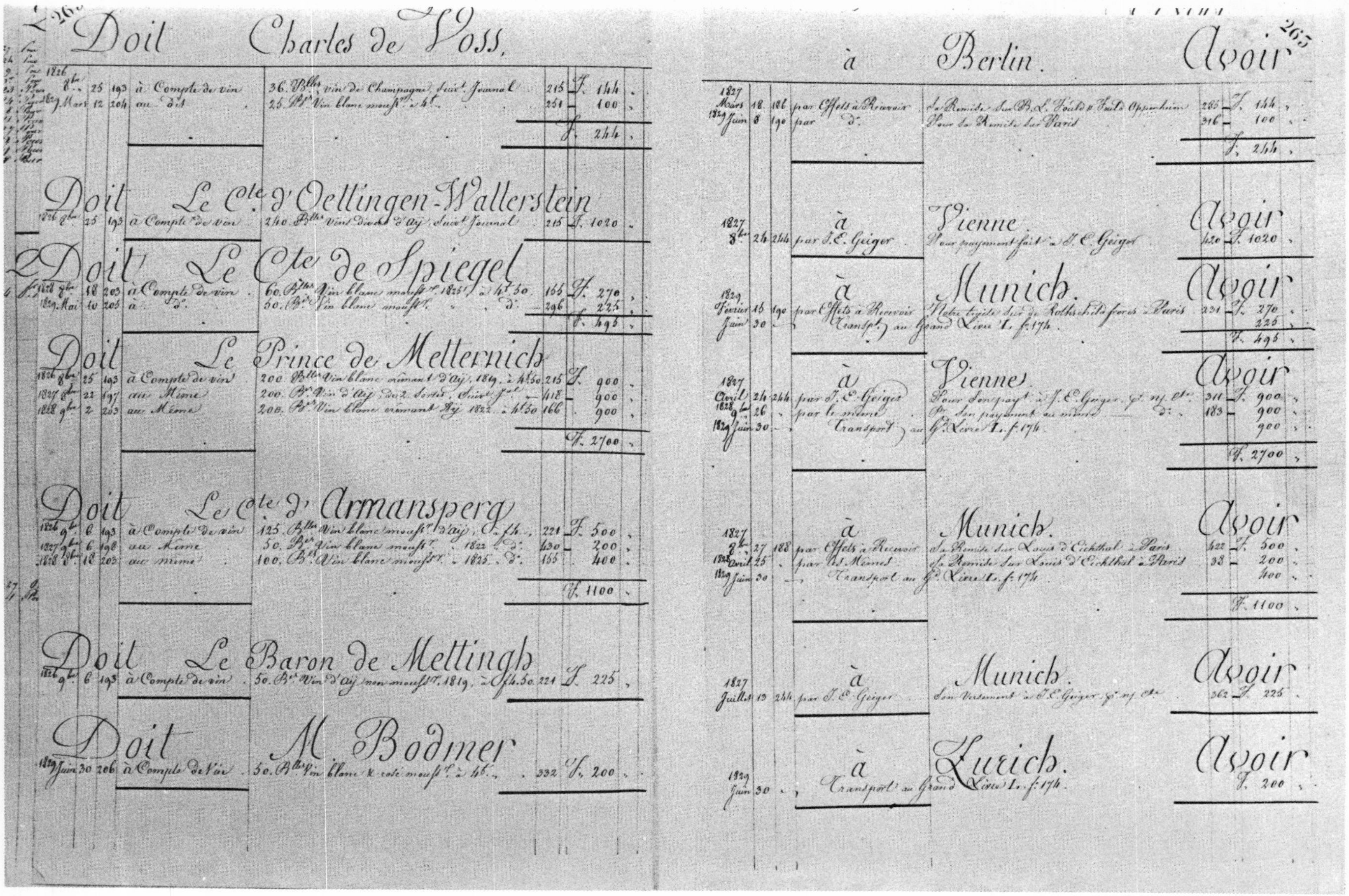

Doit Charles de Voss, à Berlin. Avoir

1826 8bre 25 193 à Compte de vin 36. Bllles vin de Champagne, suivt Journal 215 F. 144 .
1829 Mars 12 204 au dit 25. Bles Vin blanc mousst à 4f. 251 — 100 .
F. 244 .

1827 Mars 18 186 par Effets à Recevoir sa Remise sur B. L. Fould & Fould Oppenheim 285 F. 144 .
1829 Juin 8 190 par d° Pour sa Remise sur Paris 316 — 100 .
F. 244 .

Doit Le Cte d'Oettingen-Wallerstein à Vienne Avoir

1826 8bre 25 193 à Compte de vin 240. Blles Vins divers d'Aÿ, suivt Journal 215 F. 1020 .

1827 8bre 24 244 par J. E. Geiger Pour payement fait à J. E. Geiger 420 F. 1020 .

Doit Le Cte de Spiegel à Munich. Avoir

1828 8bre 18 203 à Compte de vin 60. Blles Vin blanc mousst 1825, à 4f.50 166 F. 270 .
1829 Mai 10 205 à d° 50. Bles Vin blanc mousst d° 296 225 .
F. 495 .

1829 Février 15 190 par Effets à Recevoir Notre traite sur de Rothschild frères à Paris 231 F. 270 .
Juin 30 Transpt au Grand Livre L. f. 174. 225 .
F. 495 .

Doit Le Prince de Metternich à Vienne Avoir

1826 8bre 25 193 à Compte de vin 200. Blles Vin blanc crémant d'Aÿ, 1819, à 4f.50 215 F. 900 .
1827 8bre 22 197 au Même 200. Bles Vin d'Aÿ, de 2 sortes, suivt Jal 418 — 900 .
1828 9bre 2 203 au Même 200. Bles Vin blanc crémant Aÿ 1822 à 4f.50 166 900 .
F. 2700 .

1827 Avril 24 244 par J. E. Geiger Pour son payt à J. E. Geiger p. n/ Cte 311 F. 900 .
1828 9bre 26 par le même Pr son payement au même d° 183 — 900 .
1829 Juin 30 Transport au Gd Livre L. f. 174. 900 .
F. 2700 .

Doit Le Cte d'Armansperg à Munich. Avoir

1826 9bre 6 193 à Compte de vin 125. Blles Vin blanc mousst d'Aÿ, à f4. 221 F. 500 .
1827 9bre 6 198 au Même 50. Bles Vin blanc mousst 1822 d° 430 — 200 .
1828 8bre 18 203 au même 100. Bles Vin blanc mousst 1825 d° 165 400 .
F. 1100 .

1827 8bre 27 188 par Effets à Recevoir sa Remise sur Louis d'Eichthal à Paris 422 F. 500 .
1828 Avril 25 par les Mêmes sa Remise sur Louis d'Eichthal à Paris 38 — 200 .
1829 Juin 30 Transport au Gd Livre L. f. 174. 400 .
F. 1100 .

Doit Le Baron de Mettingh à Munich. Avoir

1826 9bre 6 193 à Compte de vin 50. Bles Vin d'Aÿ non mousst 1819, à f4.50 221 F. 225 .

1827 Juillet 13 244 par J. E. Geiger Son Versement à J. E. Geiger p. n/ Cte 362 F. 225 .

Doit M. Bodmer à Zurich. Avoir

1829 Juin 30 206 à Compte de Vin 50. Blles Vin blanc & rosé mousst à 4f. 332 F. 200 .

1829 Juin 30 Transport au Grand Livre L. f. 174. F. 200 .

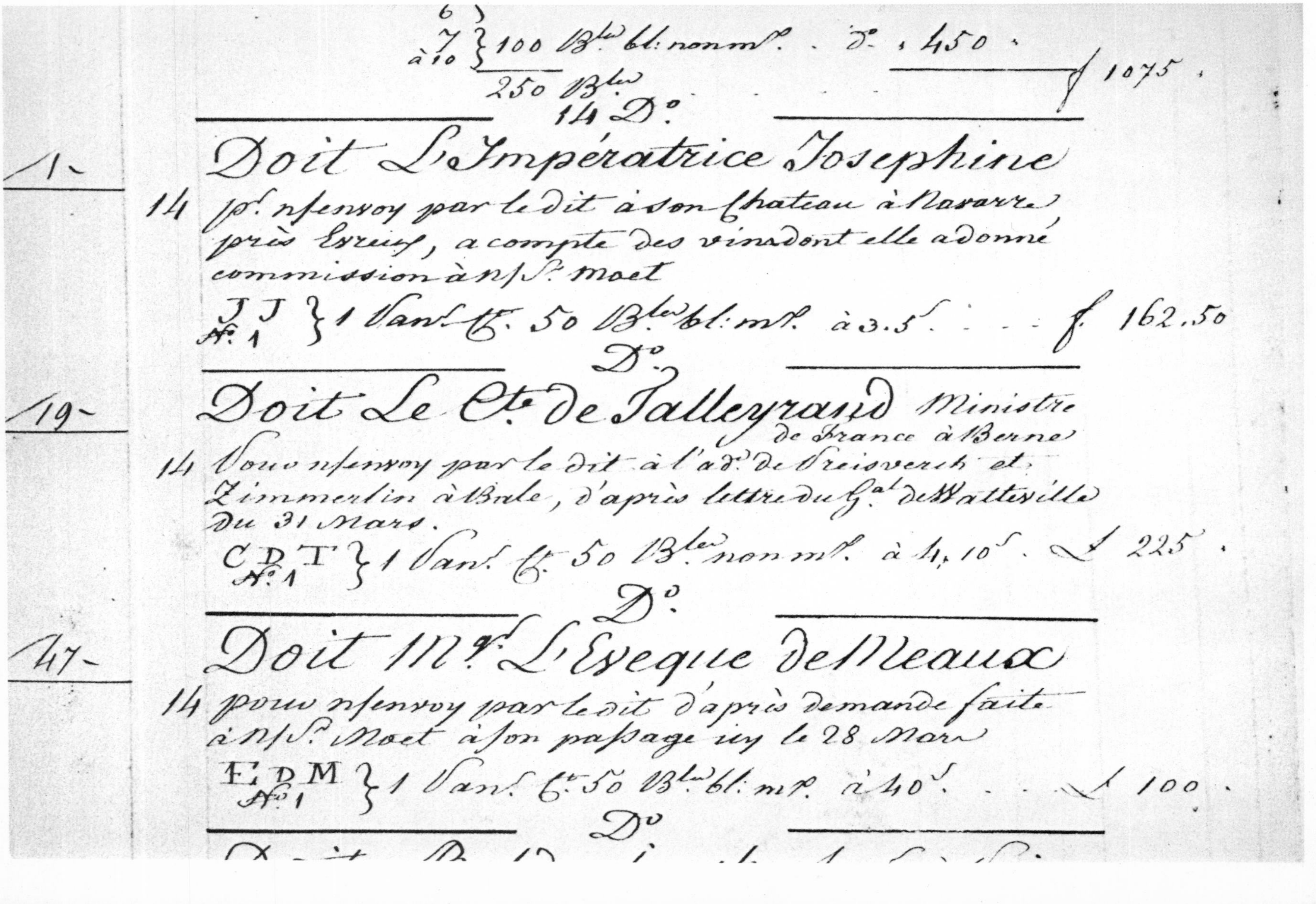

6
à 7 } 100 Bles bl: non mt . d° . 450 .
10
250 Bles | 1075 .

14 D°.

1 — Doit L'Impératrice Josephine

14 pr n/envoy par ledit à son chateau à Navarre près Evreux, a compte des vins dont elle a donné commission à n/ Sr Moet

JJ
N° 1 } 1 Van. Cr 50 Bles bl: mt. à 3.5 . . . f 162.50

D°.

19 — Doit Le Cte de Talleyrand Ministre de France à Berne

14 Vous n/envoy par le dit à l'adr. de Preiswerk et Zimmerlin à Bale, d'après lettre du Gal de Watteville du 31 Mars.

CDT
N° 1 } 1 Van. Cr 50 Bles non mt. à 4,10s . £ 225 .

D°.

47 — Doit Mgr L'Eveque de Meaux

14 pour n/envoy par ledit d'après demande faite à n/ Sr Moet à son passage icy le 28 Mar

EDM
N° 1 } 1 Van. Cr 50 Bles bl: mt. à 40s . . . £ 100 .

D°

Doit   **Christie**, Chargé des Caves du Prince

fr 2	P.r notre Envoi de 200 Bles vin mousseux	à 6 —	244	f.
fb 14	S.r 792 Bles vin de champt. divers		345	
Mars 26	72 Dites D. Tisanne à f. 3.50.r		1	
l 6	288 Dites D. Divers à f. 6.		7	
ai 17	75 Dites D. à f. 7.		23	
et 16	n.e Traite de $108.4.11 fa 30. 8bre qui a été payée par Martell		54	
e 24	204. à Compte de vin 72 b.es vin de Sillery à f. 7.55.r 2505.		112	
re 7	256. au Dit 90 bout.s vin de Sillery		269	
r 14	257. au Dit 504 Dites vins Divers		255	
	Porté au f. 99		f.	

Doit S.M. Le Roi de Naples

Mars	6	S.r n.e envoy de 600 Bles bl. mt. à 4 dont 100 b.es p.r le Mont Cenis 366	d	

Doit   **Bonaparte**   Prem

		322	1100
		27	500
27	Pour s.r envoy de 300 Bles vin de champagne à 3.10. à 4	125	1320
24	Pour s.r envoi de 200 Bles à 30. à 3.10.	133	350
9	Pour u.e envoi de 350 Bles à 3. 10.r 5.r 6.r	349	574
25	Pour id de 100 Bles non mousseux à 3.10.	365	1455 6
23	Pour id à 150 D.r dont 100 bl. Tysanne & 50 blanc Rose 349	370	155
14	Pour id de 200 D.r blanc m.t à 5	686	750
11	Pour frais d. Deux caisses adressées à Strasbourg	424	1950
27	Pour Id envoy de 150 b.es blanc m.t	431	585 14
23	Pour Go. à Munic de 400 Bles divers à Munic	509	300
29	Pour frais sur 4 caisses b.es blanc m.t 400 Bles envoyées à Munic à 5	2534	133
18	Pour envoy de 100 Bles blanc m.t à 5 D.r Mayence		
	Go. de 50 D.r Tysanne à 50.r		

Doit L'Impératrice Joseph

			385 f.	162.50
avril	14	S.r n.e envoy à Navare de 50 Bles bl. mt. à 3.5.r		

of almost superhuman labor—but to no practical purpose, as the champagne remained in the cellars. The entire future of champagne was now in the balance. Two thirds of the export markets were lost. There were no more royal dukes, no more gay life in the glittering capitals of Europe. Prohibition affected the markets of the United States and Scandinavia, where those who had the financial means were shut off by law from the possibility of its purchase. Outside of France and England, everyone who knew and loved champagne could no longer afford it. Once more it seemed like the end.

A welcome change occurred, however, when American Prohibition came to an end in 1933. Exports to the United States rose quickly. Then just at harvest time in 1939 World War II broke out, bringing with it the miseries and indignities of occupation, the inevitable shortages, and again the total loss of all export markets save Germany. So dire were the general results that a committee was formed by the vignerons (wine growers) and the wine shippers to bring a measure of discipline and concerted action into the production and distribution of their wine. The committee was so successful in its work that it was perpetuated after the cessation of hostilities. During a period of trial and error many changes were effected, until finally it became stabilized into a truly representative organization called the Comité Interprofessionnel du Vin de Champagne (C.I.V.C.) or Interprofessional Committee for Champagne Wine, which has a definitive working program. This committee has constantly and impartially done its utmost for the common good. Its efforts have helped solve some of champagne's severest problems in marketing and merchandising. In the areas of education and publicity the committee has succeeded in making the champagne-loving public realize why champagne is so unique. Champagne is expensive because the grapes from which it is made are costly and because it takes long hours and many highly paid skilled experts to bring the wine to perfection. Furthermore, champagne must be given time to age in the bottle, and it is obvious that interest rates on capital which is bottled and stored in cellars for six or more years must be exceedingly high. Champagne costs more but it is worth more. Its supremacy as the best of all sparkling wines is unquestioned. At present, when the buying public has so many fine commodities to choose from, there are people whose tastes are highly educated, people who are well-

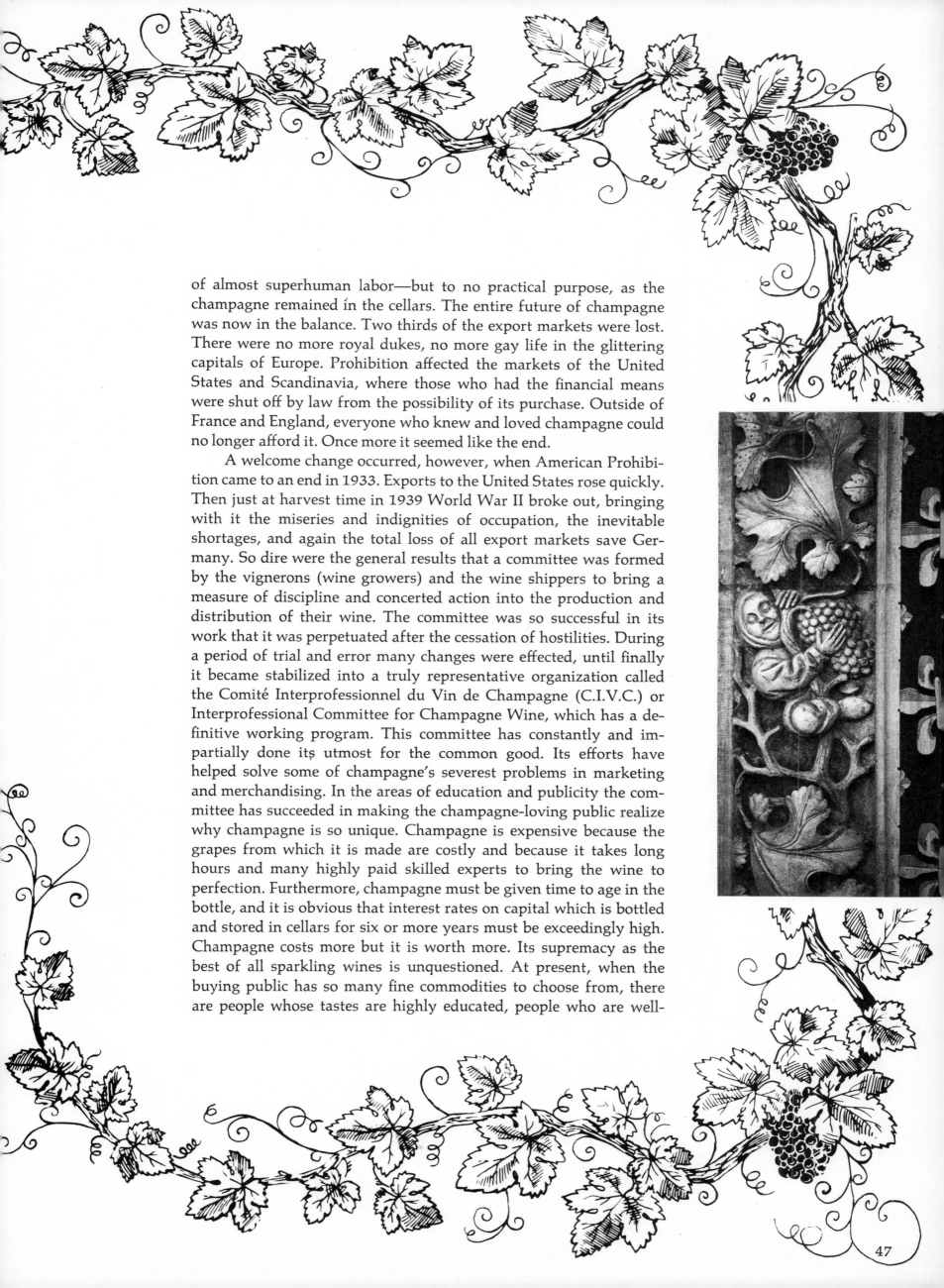

traveled, cultivated, and in possession of refined judgment, who know the differences among these products. They choose to serve champagne, the peerless beverage of sophisticated elegance and incomparable perfection. And they are right!

Today champagne is fulfilling the destiny marked out for it by the Romans who long ago discovered the delights of the vineyards of northern Gaul. They hailed champagne as the King of Wines. Thanks to their early perception, we are able to raise our delicate glasses filled with the laughing, sparkling bubbles of this noblest of all wines, and to keep the long thread of champagne history going as we toast the future: Long live the King of Wines, long live Champagne!!!

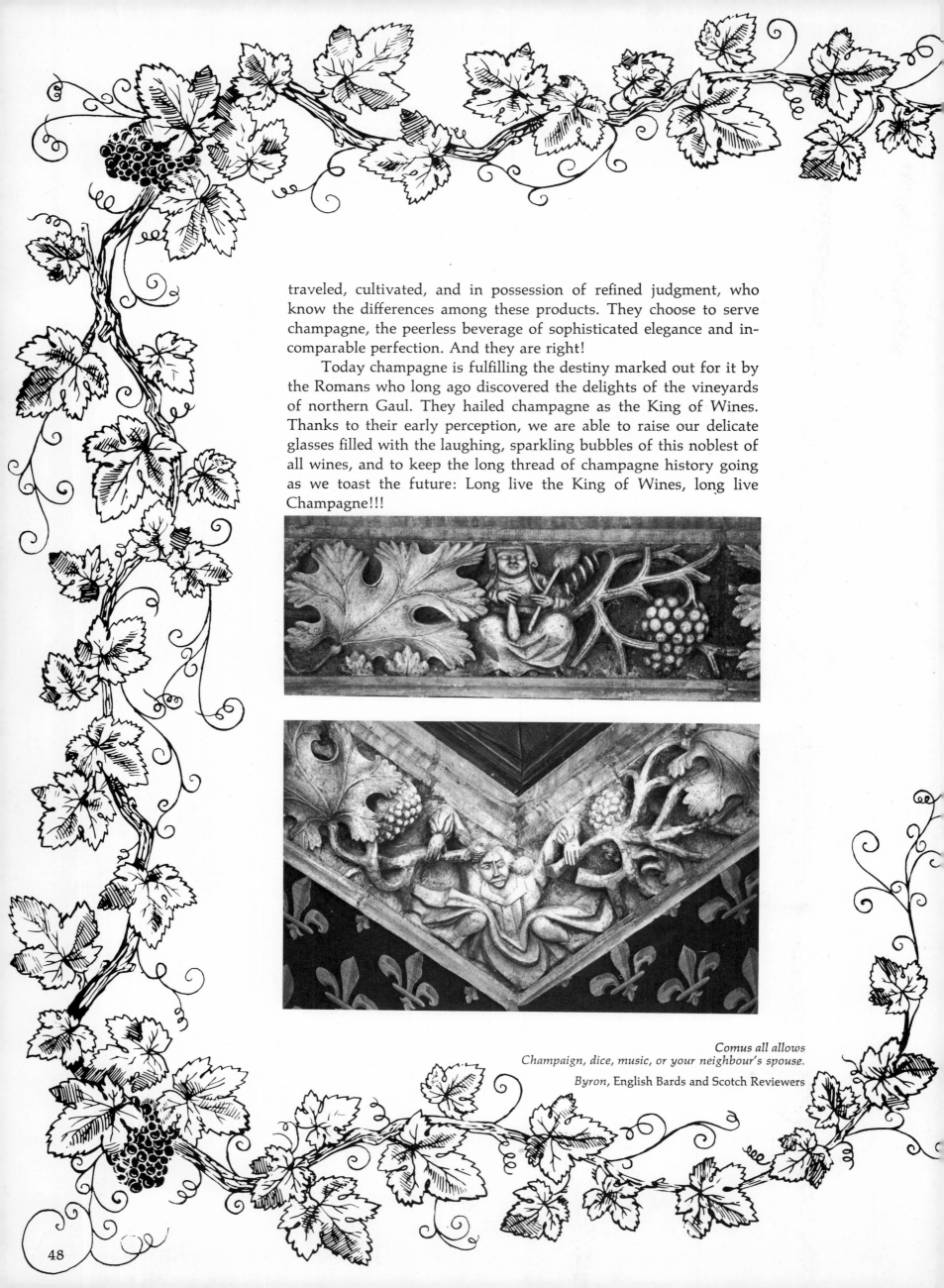

Comus all allows
Champaign, dice, music, or your neighbour's spouse.

Byron, English Bards and Scotch Reviewers

48

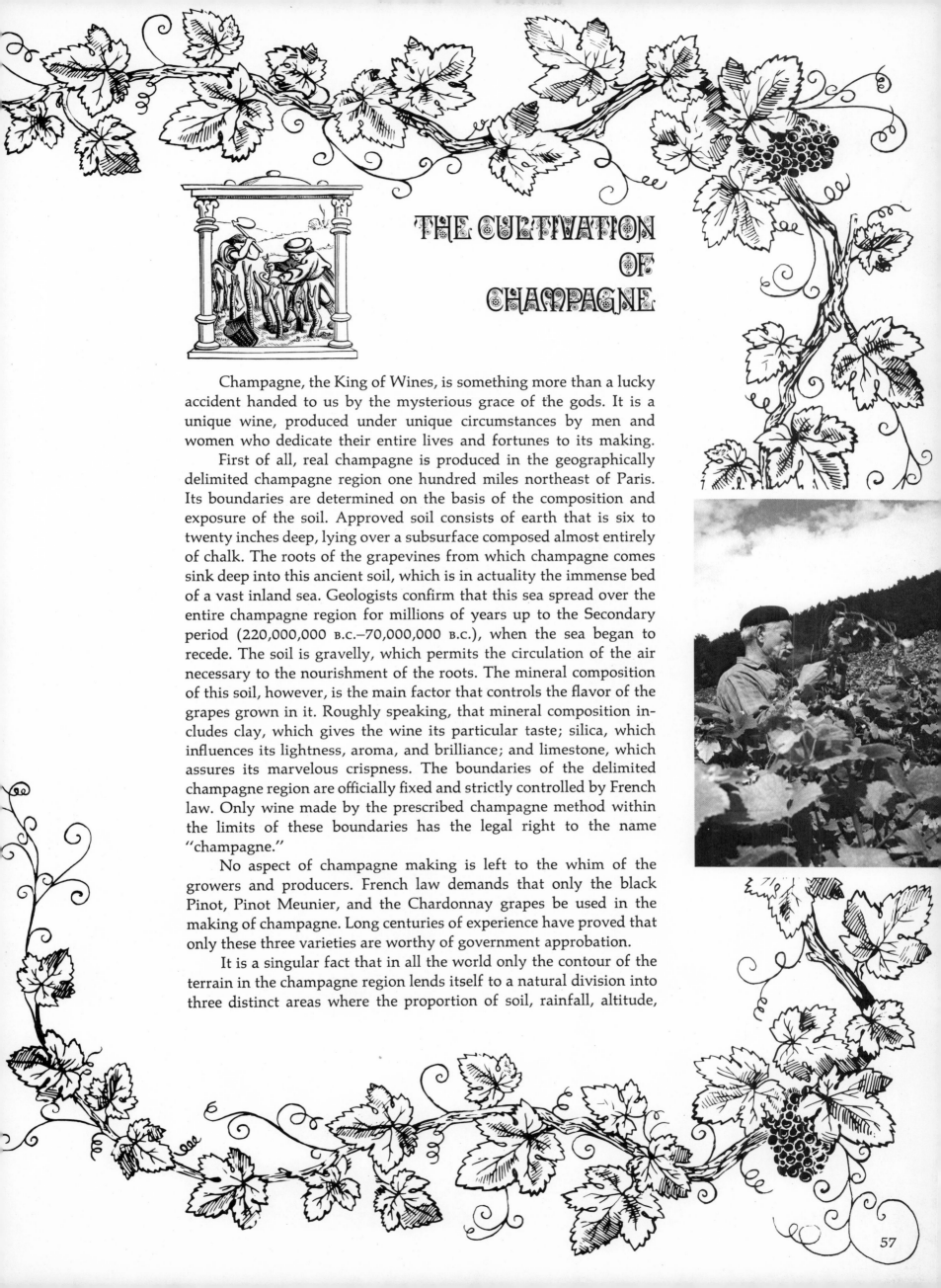

THE CULTIVATION OF CHAMPAGNE

Champagne, the King of Wines, is something more than a lucky accident handed to us by the mysterious grace of the gods. It is a unique wine, produced under unique circumstances by men and women who dedicate their entire lives and fortunes to its making.

First of all, real champagne is produced in the geographically delimited champagne region one hundred miles northeast of Paris. Its boundaries are determined on the basis of the composition and exposure of the soil. Approved soil consists of earth that is six to twenty inches deep, lying over a subsurface composed almost entirely of chalk. The roots of the grapevines from which champagne comes sink deep into this ancient soil, which is in actuality the immense bed of a vast inland sea. Geologists confirm that this sea spread over the entire champagne region for millions of years up to the Secondary period (220,000,000 B.C.–70,000,000 B.C.), when the sea began to recede. The soil is gravelly, which permits the circulation of the air necessary to the nourishment of the roots. The mineral composition of this soil, however, is the main factor that controls the flavor of the grapes grown in it. Roughly speaking, that mineral composition includes clay, which gives the wine its particular taste; silica, which influences its lightness, aroma, and brilliance; and limestone, which assures its marvelous crispness. The boundaries of the delimited champagne region are officially fixed and strictly controlled by French law. Only wine made by the prescribed champagne method within the limits of these boundaries has the legal right to the name "champagne."

No aspect of champagne making is left to the whim of the growers and producers. French law demands that only the black Pinot, Pinot Meunier, and the Chardonnay grapes be used in the making of champagne. Long centuries of experience have proved that only these three varieties are worthy of government approbation.

It is a singular fact that in all the world only the contour of the terrain in the champagne region lends itself to a natural division into three distinct areas where the proportion of soil, rainfall, altitude,

and sunlight are perfect enough for the growing of these three types of grapes. These three areas are the Montagne de Reims (Mountain of Rheims), nurturing the famous growths of Verzenay, Sillery, Mailly, Bouzy, and Ambonnay; the Vallée de la Marne (valley of the Marne) near Epernay, with its growths from Avenay, Ay, Mareuil, Hautvillers, Cumières, Damery, Pierry, and Vinay; and the Côte des Blanc (Great White Hillside) southeast of Epernay, noted for the white grapes of Avize, Cramant, Oger, Le Mesnil, etc., that produce the world-renowned Blanc de Blancs champagnes.

Throughout these three portions of the delimited champagne region the vineyards cling to the flanks of the hills as they have for more than a thousand years. Cultivated the year round by the most meticulous methods, the vines require constant personal care from the viticulturists. Each vinegrower owns an average of two acres. The joint holdings of these proud, independent, hard-working growers comprise 88 per cent of the total cultivated area. The remaining 12 per cent of the acreage is in the hands of the 146 champagne firms that use their own grapes, combined with those that they purchase from the independent growers, in the production of their champagnes.

To understand why champagne is so delicious and to comprehend fully the elements of its cost, one must follow the meticulous steps that go into its production.

Methods of cultivating the vines of champagne are quite different from those practiced elsewhere. The unpredictability of the weather, the geological formation of the chalky soil, and the fact that the quantity of harvest is government-regulated, all make it necessary for the vignerons to put forth relentless efforts to produce their grapes. Formerly, though the vines were carefully tended, they gave the impression of growing at random as they were planted *en foule* (in crowds). But since the reorganization of the vineyards, they look extremely orderly. The plants are grown in rows that are set a little over three feet apart. In each row the vines are planted at a distance of 60 or 80 centimeters (approximately 24 or 32 inches) apart. Each field regularly contains about ten thousand such vines to a hectare (2.471 acres).

In the early winter the vinedresser's work consists of constant tilling and fertilizing of the soil. Around January or February he

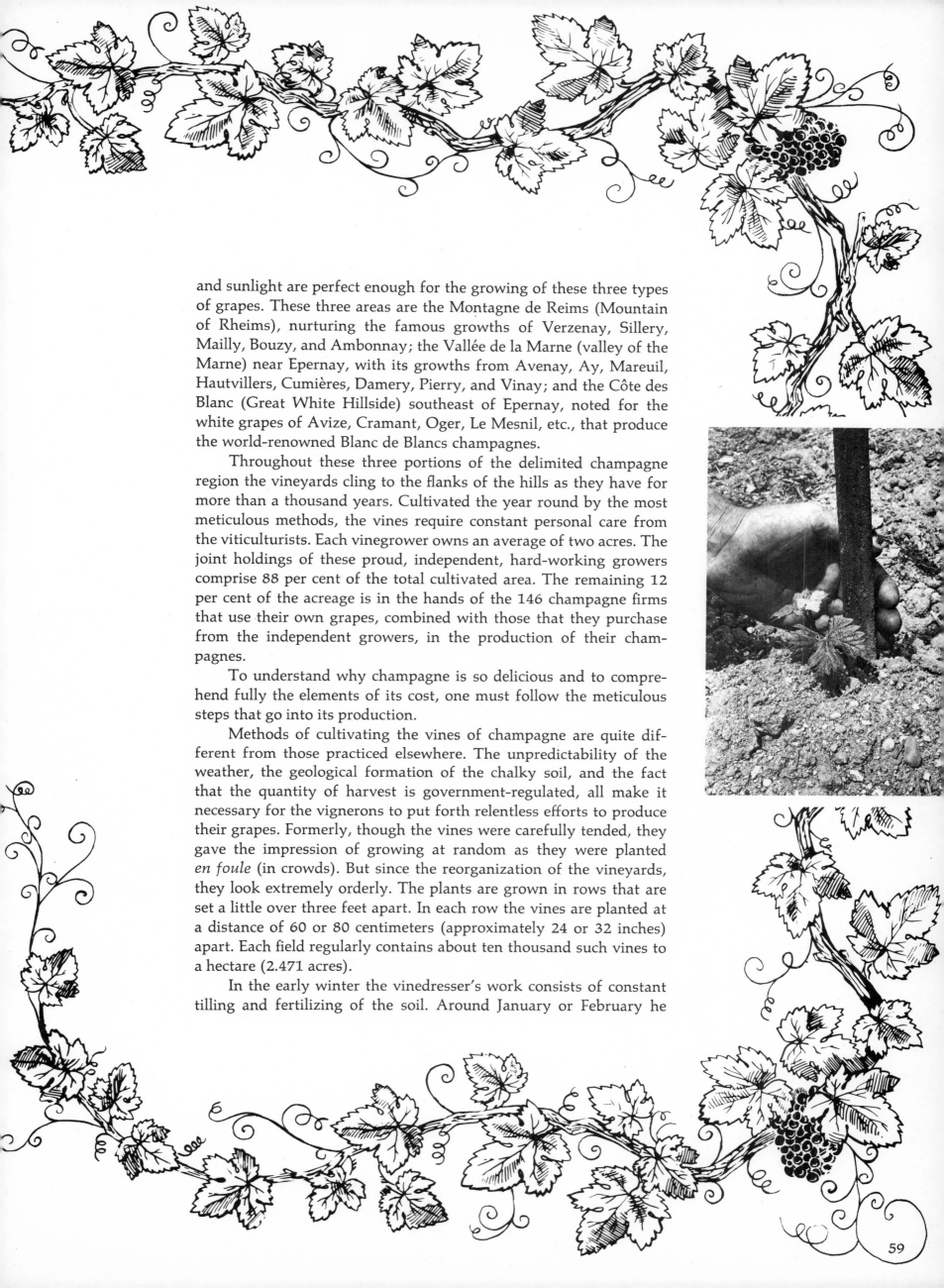

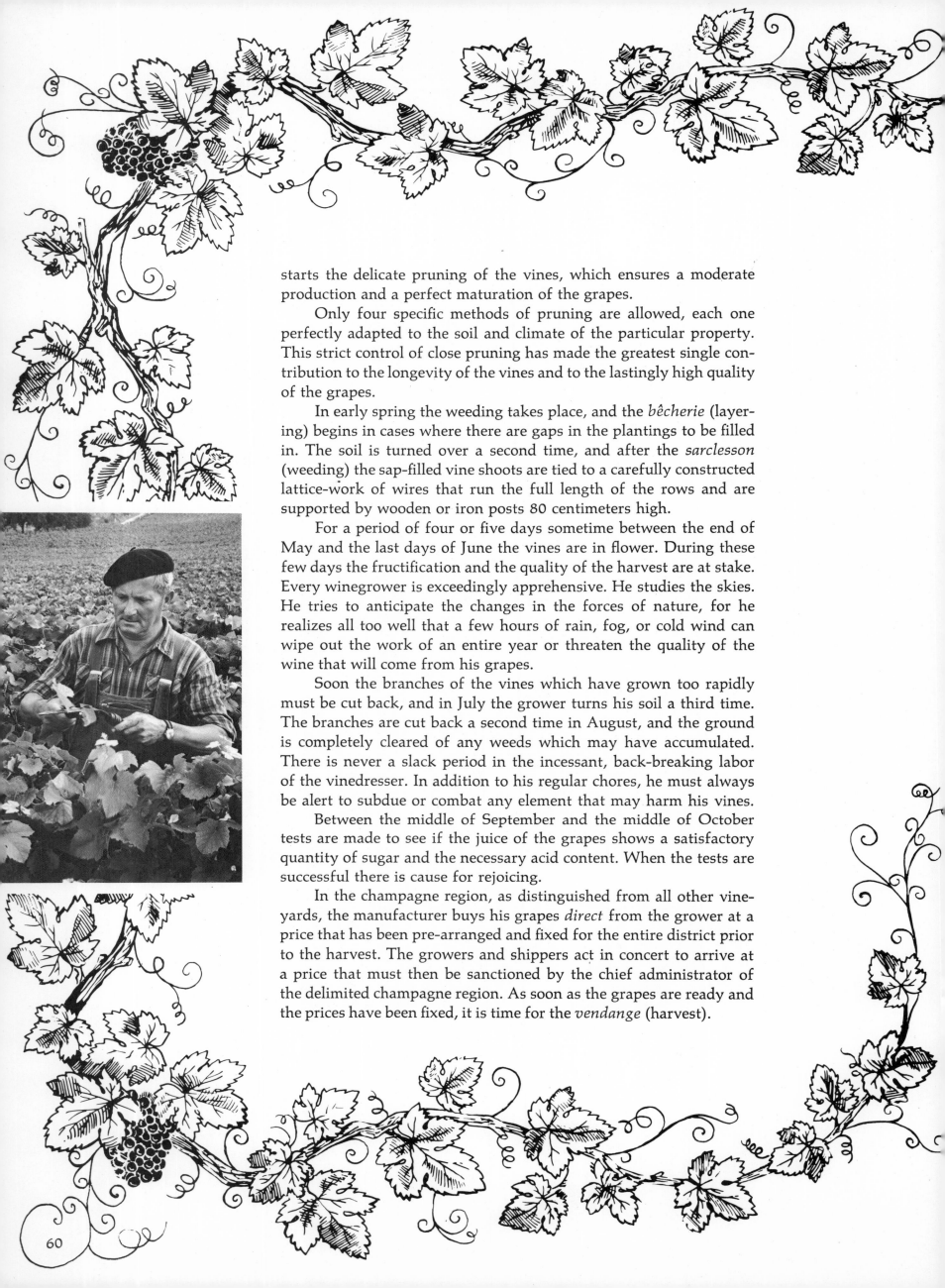

starts the delicate pruning of the vines, which ensures a moderate production and a perfect maturation of the grapes.

Only four specific methods of pruning are allowed, each one perfectly adapted to the soil and climate of the particular property. This strict control of close pruning has made the greatest single contribution to the longevity of the vines and to the lastingly high quality of the grapes.

In early spring the weeding takes place, and the *bêcherie* (layering) begins in cases where there are gaps in the plantings to be filled in. The soil is turned over a second time, and after the *sarclesson* (weeding) the sap-filled vine shoots are tied to a carefully constructed lattice-work of wires that run the full length of the rows and are supported by wooden or iron posts 80 centimeters high.

For a period of four or five days sometime between the end of May and the last days of June the vines are in flower. During these few days the fructification and the quality of the harvest are at stake. Every winegrower is exceedingly apprehensive. He studies the skies. He tries to anticipate the changes in the forces of nature, for he realizes all too well that a few hours of rain, fog, or cold wind can wipe out the work of an entire year or threaten the quality of the wine that will come from his grapes.

Soon the branches of the vines which have grown too rapidly must be cut back, and in July the grower turns his soil a third time. The branches are cut back a second time in August, and the ground is completely cleared of any weeds which may have accumulated. There is never a slack period in the incessant, back-breaking labor of the vinedresser. In addition to his regular chores, he must always be alert to subdue or combat any element that may harm his vines.

Between the middle of September and the middle of October tests are made to see if the juice of the grapes shows a satisfactory quantity of sugar and the necessary acid content. When the tests are successful there is cause for rejoicing.

In the champagne region, as distinguished from all other vineyards, the manufacturer buys his grapes *direct* from the grower at a price that has been pre-arranged and fixed for the entire district prior to the harvest. The growers and shippers act in concert to arrive at a price that must then be sanctioned by the chief administrator of the delimited champagne region. As soon as the grapes are ready and the prices have been fixed, it is time for the *vendange* (harvest).

HOW CHAMPAGNE IS MADE

The entire champagne region comes alive during the vendange. Extra workers arrive from all over France to join the Champenois in *hordons* (groups) of workers who band together for the early morning work. There is a spirited sense of movement everywhere as the workers gather their tools.

In the vineyards the "gatherers" cut the branches heavy laden with fruit and strip the grapes off quickly. They lay the grapes in baskets which are picked up by "carriers" who empty the grapes into even larger wicker tubs. Then the clusters of grapes are spread out on woven reed tables (*clayettes*) and the *épluchage* (plucking) begins. "Pickers" examine each grape. Those that are green, overripe, or spoiled are eliminated immediately with scissors called *épinette*. The best grapes are set aside in *mannequins:* large baskets holding roughly 154½ or 176½ pounds. The full mannequins are hefted by "loaders" into specially fabricated carts equipped with springs that protect the grapes from being jostled. As the grapes make their journey to the wine press, every effort is made to prevent the skins of the fruit from being bruised or broken. Long exposure to strong sunlight is absolutely avoided while the grapes are in transit lest premature fermentation occur that might tinge the wine with color. Ordinarily, once the grapes are delivered to the press, the winegrower's arduous work is done unless he is also a "manipulator" who conducts the vinification of his own grapes. In most instances, however, it is the wine shipper or producer who performs the delicate operations that convert the grapes into champagne.

At the *vendangeoirs* (pressing houses) the difficult task of procuring the must—the juice of the grapes—is carried on. Special presses possessing a large surface in proportion to their height permit the juice to flow quickly from the mass of the residue. Speed is essential to avoid any coloration of the must. At all costs the juice of the black grape must be prevented from becoming tinted by prolonged contact with the skins and residue. If this should happen the wine loses both delicacy and bouquet.

A *marc* or about eight thousand pounds of grapes is placed on the surface of the press. In successive, rapid pressings about 2,666 liters—thirteen casks each pressing—is extracted. Of these thirteen casks the first ten are obtained by two or three rapid turns of the wine-press screw in an operation which lasts from an hour and a half to two hours altogether. The juice of this rapid pressing is used to make the *vins de cuvée* (wines of the marriage blend), but the last three casks of juice are called the *tailles*. Each cask of the tailles takes an hour and a half in the press to procure. The juice of the tailles is used to make wines that are darker in color and not as fine as the vins de cuvée. Because they are more ordinary in taste, they are called *vins de suite* (wines which follow). The rest of the juice which still remains in the residue is extracted after several more long hours in the press. The juice of this pressing is called the *rebêche*. It is not permitted by law to bear the name champagne and is used only to make an ordinary wine which has no appelation at all.

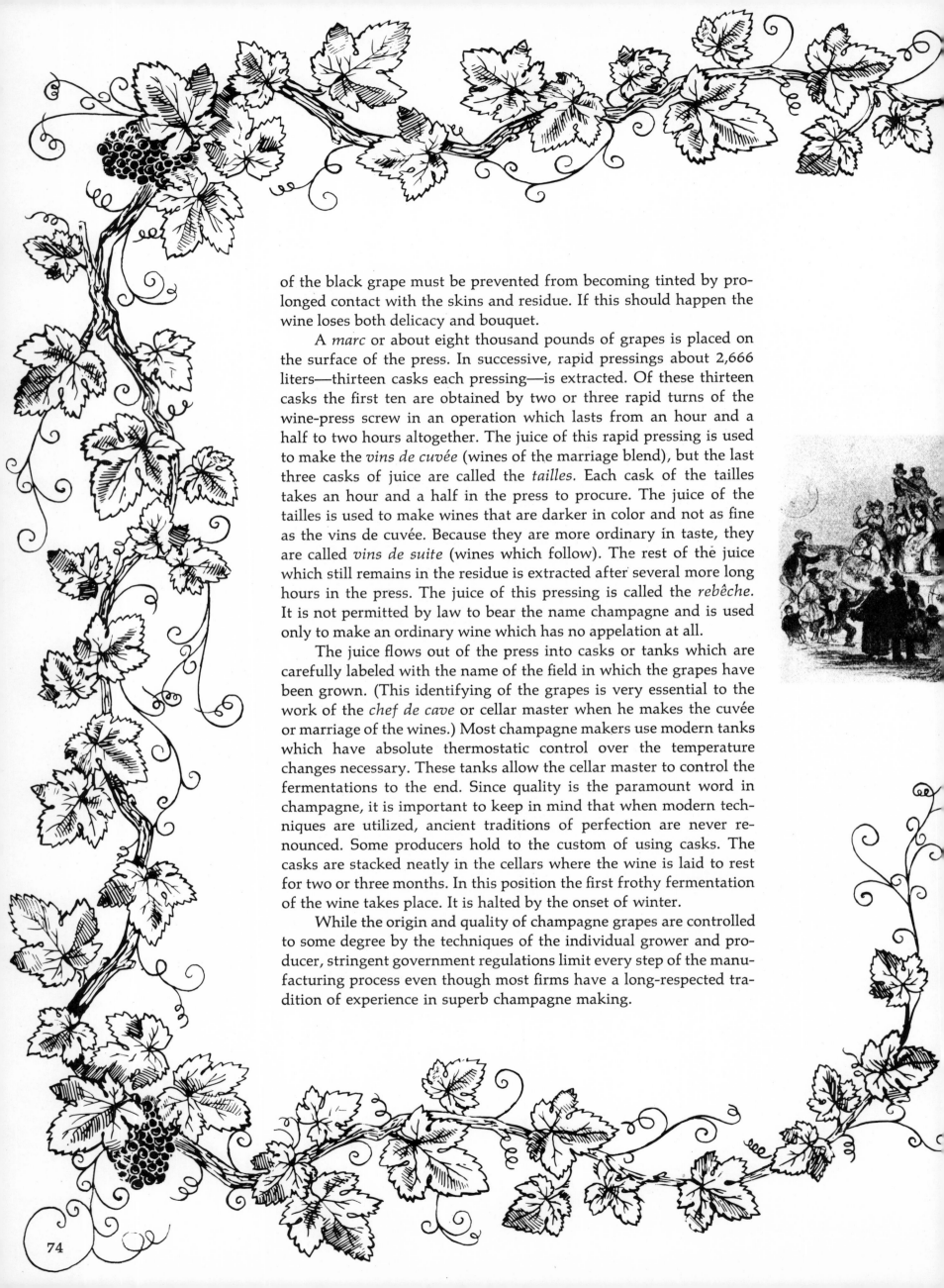

The juice flows out of the press into casks or tanks which are carefully labeled with the name of the field in which the grapes have been grown. (This identifying of the grapes is very essential to the work of the *chef de cave* or cellar master when he makes the cuvée or marriage of the wines.) Most champagne makers use modern tanks which have absolute thermostatic control over the temperature changes necessary. These tanks allow the cellar master to control the fermentations to the end. Since quality is the paramount word in champagne, it is important to keep in mind that when modern techniques are utilized, ancient traditions of perfection are never renounced. Some producers hold to the custom of using casks. The casks are stacked neatly in the cellars where the wine is laid to rest for two or three months. In this position the first frothy fermentation of the wine takes place. It is halted by the onset of winter.

While the origin and quality of champagne grapes are controlled to some degree by the techniques of the individual grower and producer, stringent government regulations limit every step of the manufacturing process even though most firms have a long-respected tradition of experience in superb champagne making.

74

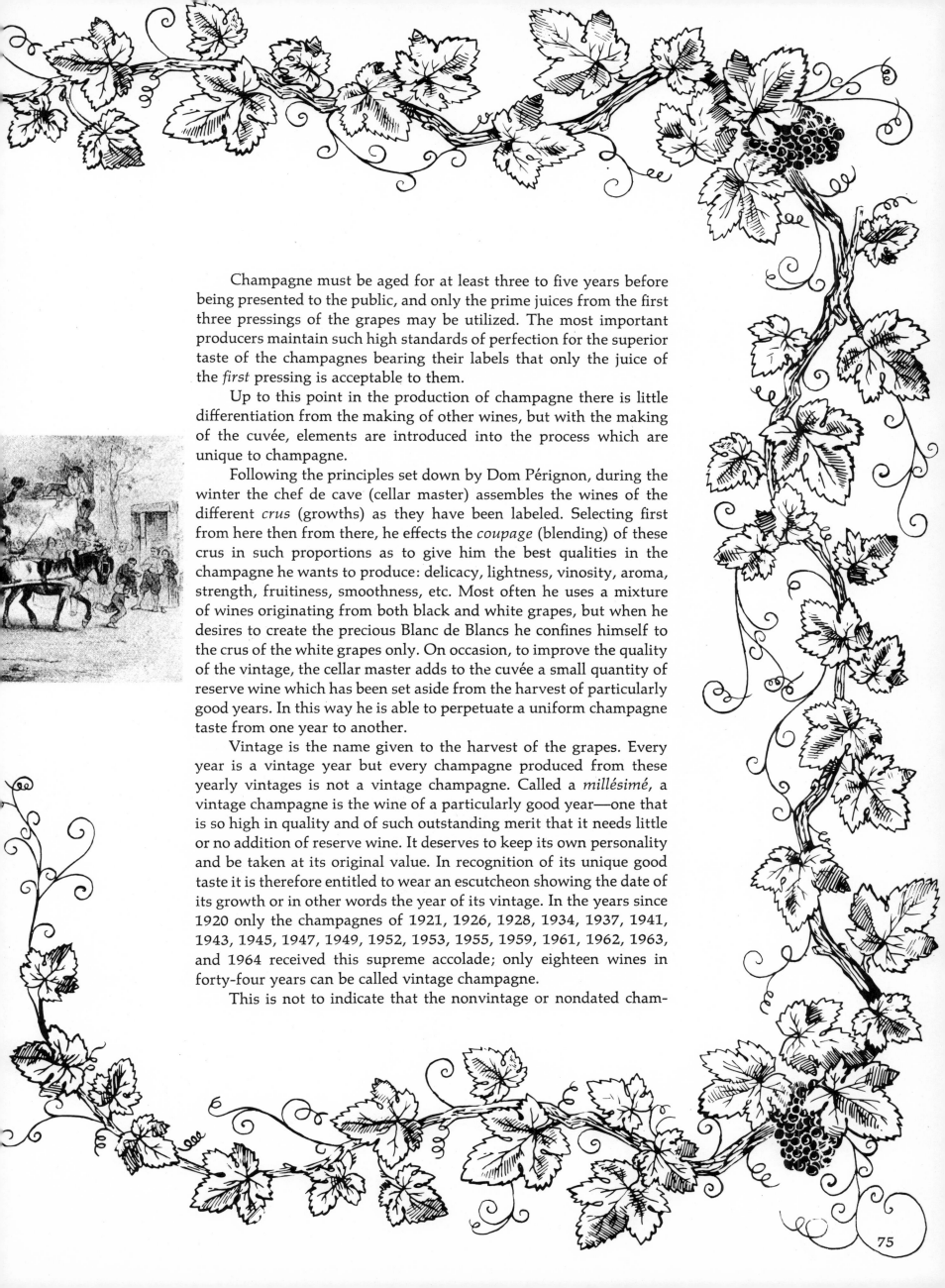

Champagne must be aged for at least three to five years before being presented to the public, and only the prime juices from the first three pressings of the grapes may be utilized. The most important producers maintain such high standards of perfection for the superior taste of the champagnes bearing their labels that only the juice of the *first* pressing is acceptable to them.

Up to this point in the production of champagne there is little differentiation from the making of other wines, but with the making of the cuvée, elements are introduced into the process which are unique to champagne.

Following the principles set down by Dom Pérignon, during the winter the chef de cave (cellar master) assembles the wines of the different *crus* (growths) as they have been labeled. Selecting first from here then from there, he effects the *coupage* (blending) of these crus in such proportions as to give him the best qualities in the champagne he wants to produce: delicacy, lightness, vinosity, aroma, strength, fruitiness, smoothness, etc. Most often he uses a mixture of wines originating from both black and white grapes, but when he desires to create the precious Blanc de Blancs he confines himself to the crus of the white grapes only. On occasion, to improve the quality of the vintage, the cellar master adds to the cuvée a small quantity of reserve wine which has been set aside from the harvest of particularly good years. In this way he is able to perpetuate a uniform champagne taste from one year to another.

Vintage is the name given to the harvest of the grapes. Every year is a vintage year but every champagne produced from these yearly vintages is not a vintage champagne. Called a *millésimé*, a vintage champagne is the wine of a particularly good year—one that is so high in quality and of such outstanding merit that it needs little or no addition of reserve wine. It deserves to keep its own personality and be taken at its original value. In recognition of its unique good taste it is therefore entitled to wear an escutcheon showing the date of its growth or in other words the year of its vintage. In the years since 1920 only the champagnes of 1921, 1926, 1928, 1934, 1937, 1941, 1943, 1945, 1947, 1949, 1952, 1953, 1955, 1959, 1961, 1962, 1963, and 1964 received this supreme accolade; only eighteen wines in forty-four years can be called vintage champagne.

This is not to indicate that the nonvintage or nondated cham-

pagnes are not superb. They are indeed. They are all good wines but they are always meant to have, as closely as possible, the same type and style of taste year after year. In contrast to this principle, vintage champagnes vary greatly from one another and from year to year. Many champagne lovers prefer nonvintage cuvées because their quality and taste are so consistent. This preference is a recognition of the art of the cellar master that is passed down from father to son. It is also an acknowledgment of the integrity of the champagne makers, who create for their customers a product which can be depended upon no matter what the year may be.

When the cellar master has completed his preliminary work—which depends upon the manufacturer's method—the clear wines are drawn off the casks or tanks, and the growths which he has chosen are blended in vats equipped with mixers that guarantee a perfect marriage of the wines. The blend is fined and the transparent liquid is ready to be bottled.

Bottling must take place in the springtime, and the shape and size of the champagne bottle is very important. It must be heavier and stronger than other wine bottles, for it is the real home of champagne for all its life, and in some cases that life may be five, ten, or even twenty-five years. The bottle must be able to stand the strain of the *prise de mousse* (pressure of carbonic acid gas) generated during fermentation. In early times champagne bottles were made of hand-blown glass. Today they are fabricated by automatic American machines each of which produces 23,000 bottles per day. The bottles are so strong that breakage in the cellars has been reduced to less than 1 per cent. Bottle sizes most often used to bottle champagne include the quarter bottle of 6½ fluid ounces, the half bottle of 13 fluid ounces, the bottle of 26 fluid ounces, and the magnum of 52 fluid ounces or 2 bottles. Champagne is bottled above ground in the *cellier* (storeroom), and then it is lowered to cold galleries underground where the temperature remains a constant 8 to 10 degrees centigrade. Piled up on their sides, the bottles are watched very carefully. Glass and corks are checked frequently so that any bottle which is defective in any way may be eliminated. While the bottles repose, secondary fermentation of the champagne sets in and the sugar that remained in the wine when winter halted its first fermentation is transformed into carbonic acid gas. This gas is imprisoned in the bottle and re-

mains in a state of suspension in the liquid until the cork is drawn from the bottle and the sparkling bubbles created by the gas rush to the top. This second fermentation takes place at a very slow pace during which a fine light opaqueness occurs and a sediment begins to form.

According to law, all champagne must remain in the cellars for at least a year. During this interval the bottles are given a little shake from time to time and the sediment becomes heavier, clinging to the lower face of the bottle until the wine itself is clear and transparent. The bottles are then placed neck downwards in racks called *pupitres*. These racks are arranged on a slope which can be modified by the skilled workmen who are in charge of the process of collecting all this sediment called *remuage* (riddling). Jealously guarding the secrets of their movements, these experts twist the bottles every day from one side to another as they lie in the racks. As they do so, they give each bottle a slight shake, resting it an eighth of an inch or so to the left or right and judging the progress of its circular turn by the white mark painted on the bottom of the bottle. Expert *remueurs* (riddlers) are able to move about 30,000 bottles per day. As they work, the sediment in the wine slides down and slowly collects in the necks of the bottles against the corks. The racks are gradually tilted during a period of six to twelve weeks until finally the bottles are *sur points* (standing straight up on their heads). They remain in this position, stored in the cold cellars, awaiting the *dégorgement* (spitting out of the sediment) for an indefinite period of time. Most often this will be for three, four, or five years, but the interval may be longer if the cellar master thinks this is necessary in order to obtain the best possible champagne.

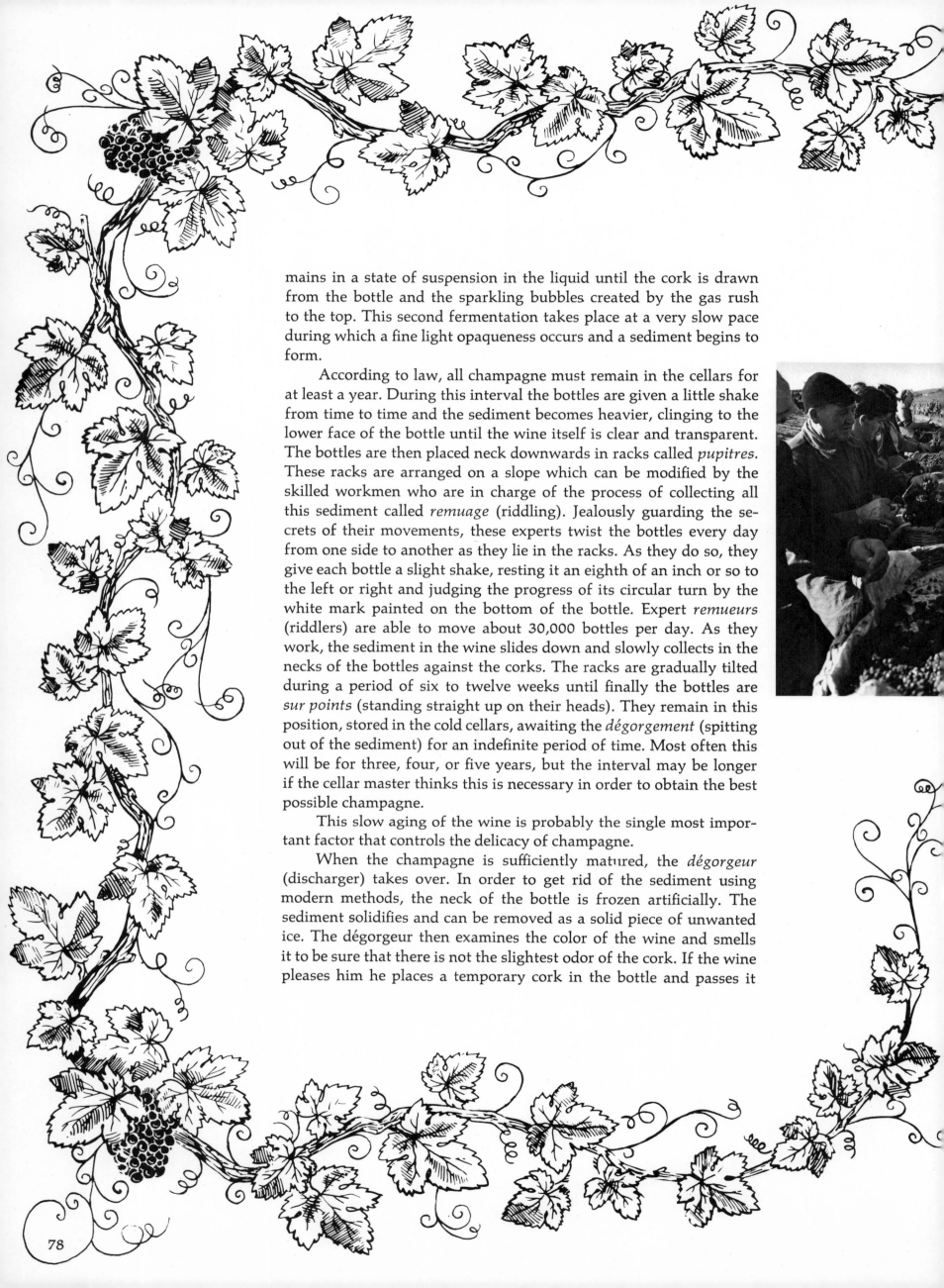

This slow aging of the wine is probably the single most important factor that controls the delicacy of champagne.

When the champagne is sufficiently matured, the *dégorgeur* (discharger) takes over. In order to get rid of the sediment using modern methods, the neck of the bottle is frozen artificially. The sediment solidifies and can be removed as a solid piece of unwanted ice. The dégorgeur then examines the color of the wine and smells it to be sure that there is not the slightest odor of the cork. If the wine pleases him he places a temporary cork in the bottle and passes it

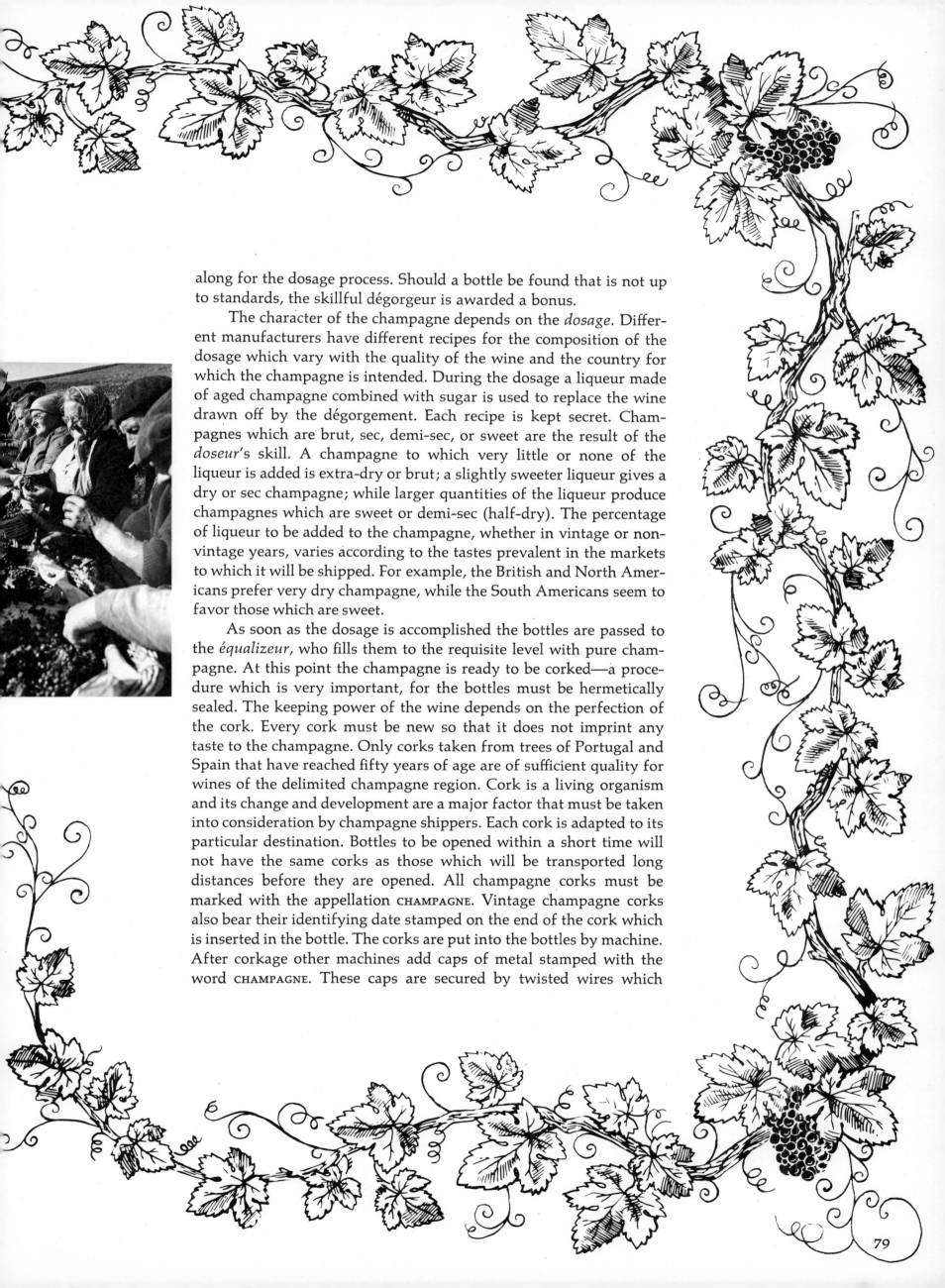

along for the dosage process. Should a bottle be found that is not up to standards, the skillful dégorgeur is awarded a bonus.

The character of the champagne depends on the *dosage*. Different manufacturers have different recipes for the composition of the dosage which vary with the quality of the wine and the country for which the champagne is intended. During the dosage a liqueur made of aged champagne combined with sugar is used to replace the wine drawn off by the dégorgement. Each recipe is kept secret. Champagnes which are brut, sec, demi-sec, or sweet are the result of the *doseur*'s skill. A champagne to which very little or none of the liqueur is added is extra-dry or brut; a slightly sweeter liqueur gives a dry or sec champagne; while larger quantities of the liqueur produce champagnes which are sweet or demi-sec (half-dry). The percentage of liqueur to be added to the champagne, whether in vintage or non-vintage years, varies according to the tastes prevalent in the markets to which it will be shipped. For example, the British and North Americans prefer very dry champagne, while the South Americans seem to favor those which are sweet.

As soon as the dosage is accomplished the bottles are passed to the *équalizeur*, who fills them to the requisite level with pure champagne. At this point the champagne is ready to be corked—a procedure which is very important, for the bottles must be hermetically sealed. The keeping power of the wine depends on the perfection of the cork. Every cork must be new so that it does not imprint any taste to the champagne. Only corks taken from trees of Portugal and Spain that have reached fifty years of age are of sufficient quality for wines of the delimited champagne region. Cork is a living organism and its change and development are a major factor that must be taken into consideration by champagne shippers. Each cork is adapted to its particular destination. Bottles to be opened within a short time will not have the same corks as those which will be transported long distances before they are opened. All champagne corks must be marked with the appellation CHAMPAGNE. Vintage champagne corks also bear their identifying date stamped on the end of the cork which is inserted in the bottle. The corks are put into the bottles by machine. After corkage other machines add caps of metal stamped with the word CHAMPAGNE. These caps are secured by twisted wires which protect the corks from being blown off by the pressure inside the bottles.

Carefully washed and labeled with the word CHAMPAGNE, the vintage year (if appropriate), the name, and the coat of arms of the manufacturer, the bottled champagne is ready to make its public debut.

Every minute detail of champagne making, from the growing of the special grapes to the labeling and shipping, takes more time and skill and demands higher standards of quality and control than does the manufacture of any other wine. This meticulous work is based on centuries of tradition. It is this careful adherence to the methods of the past that makes the champagnes we drink taste like the magic nectar of the gods, and it is this quality of magic that has made champagne the unquestionably superior wine of festivity, celebration, and elegance.

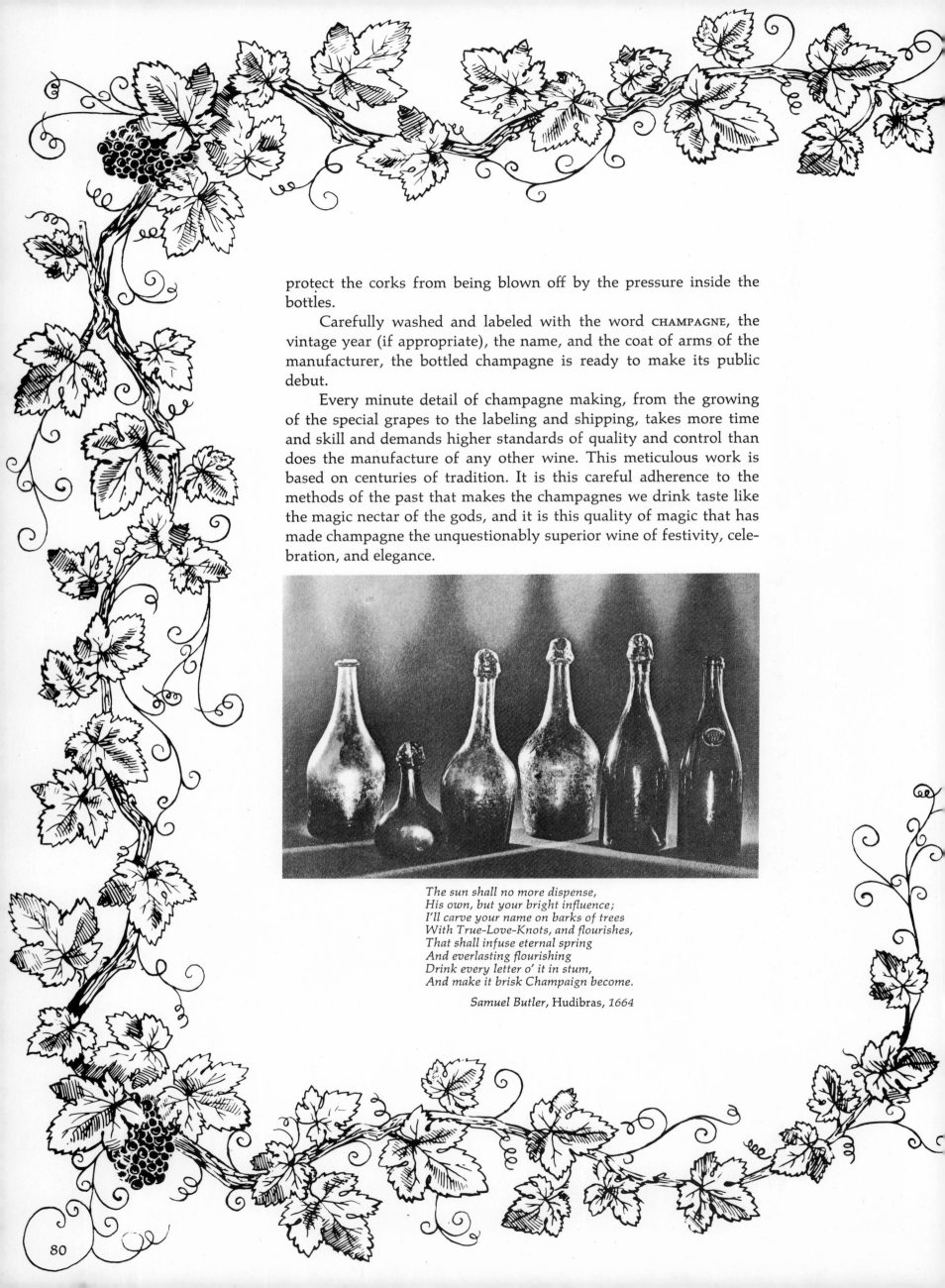

The sun shall no more dispense,
His own, but your bright influence;
I'll carve your name on barks of trees
With True-Love-Knots, and flourishes,
That shall infuse eternal spring
And everlasting flourishing
Drink every letter o' it in stum,
And make it brisk Champaign become.

Samuel Butler, Hudibras, 1664

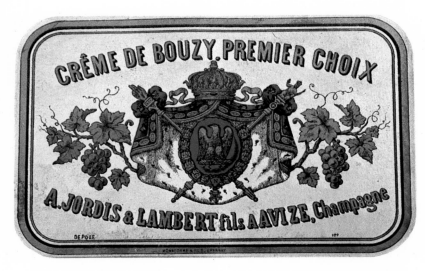

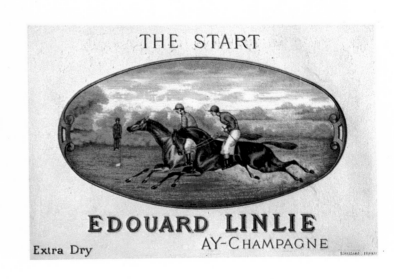

CHAMPENOISE

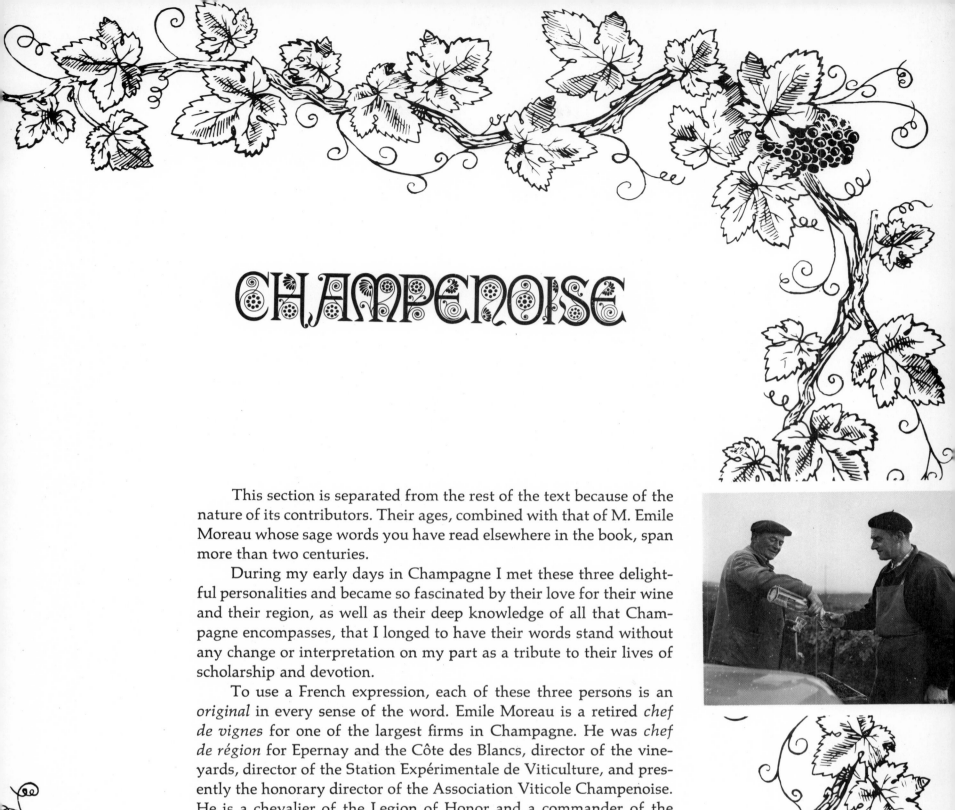

This section is separated from the rest of the text because of the nature of its contributors. Their ages, combined with that of M. Emile Moreau whose sage words you have read elsewhere in the book, span more than two centuries.

During my early days in Champagne I met these three delightful personalities and became so fascinated by their love for their wine and their region, as well as their deep knowledge of all that Champagne encompasses, that I longed to have their words stand without any change or interpretation on my part as a tribute to their lives of scholarship and devotion.

To use a French expression, each of these three persons is an *original* in every sense of the word. Emile Moreau is a retired *chef de vignes* for one of the largest firms in Champagne. He was *chef de région* for Epernay and the Côte des Blancs, director of the vineyards, director of the Station Expérimentale de Viticulture, and presently the honorary director of the Association Viticole Champenoise. He is a chevalier of the Legion of Honor and a commander of the Mérite Agricole. His ardent interests, his passionate spirit of life glows through his every comment whether his attention is apparently sparked by the beauty of a passing young woman or by the serenity of a small village—all is ever fresh and lovely to the practiced eye of this absolute authority on the vine. To say nothing of how that eye lights up when he savors a pleasantly chilled glass of champagne! The dignity and gentility of Emile Moreau are so striking that one is inspired to reach one's full potential in his presence.

In contrast, spending time in the company of René Dumont was like just letting go and swinging your feet on the edge of a dock with

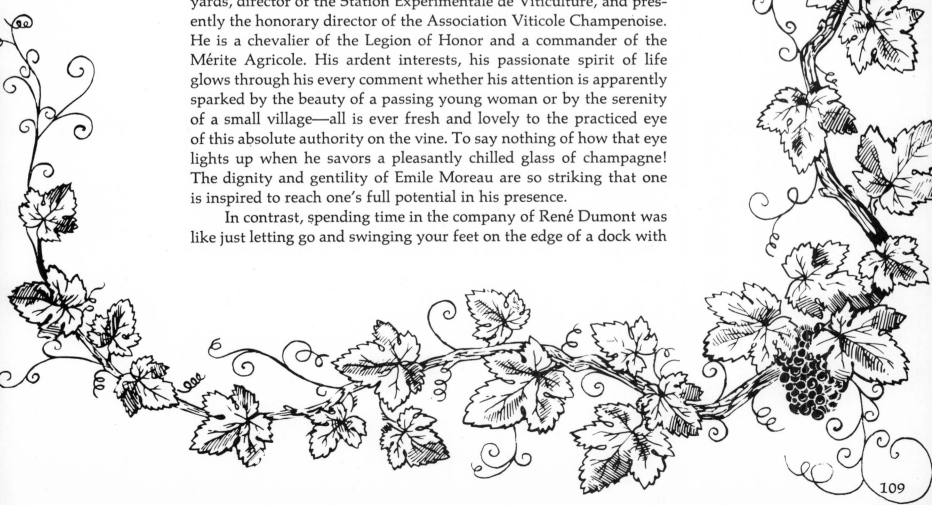

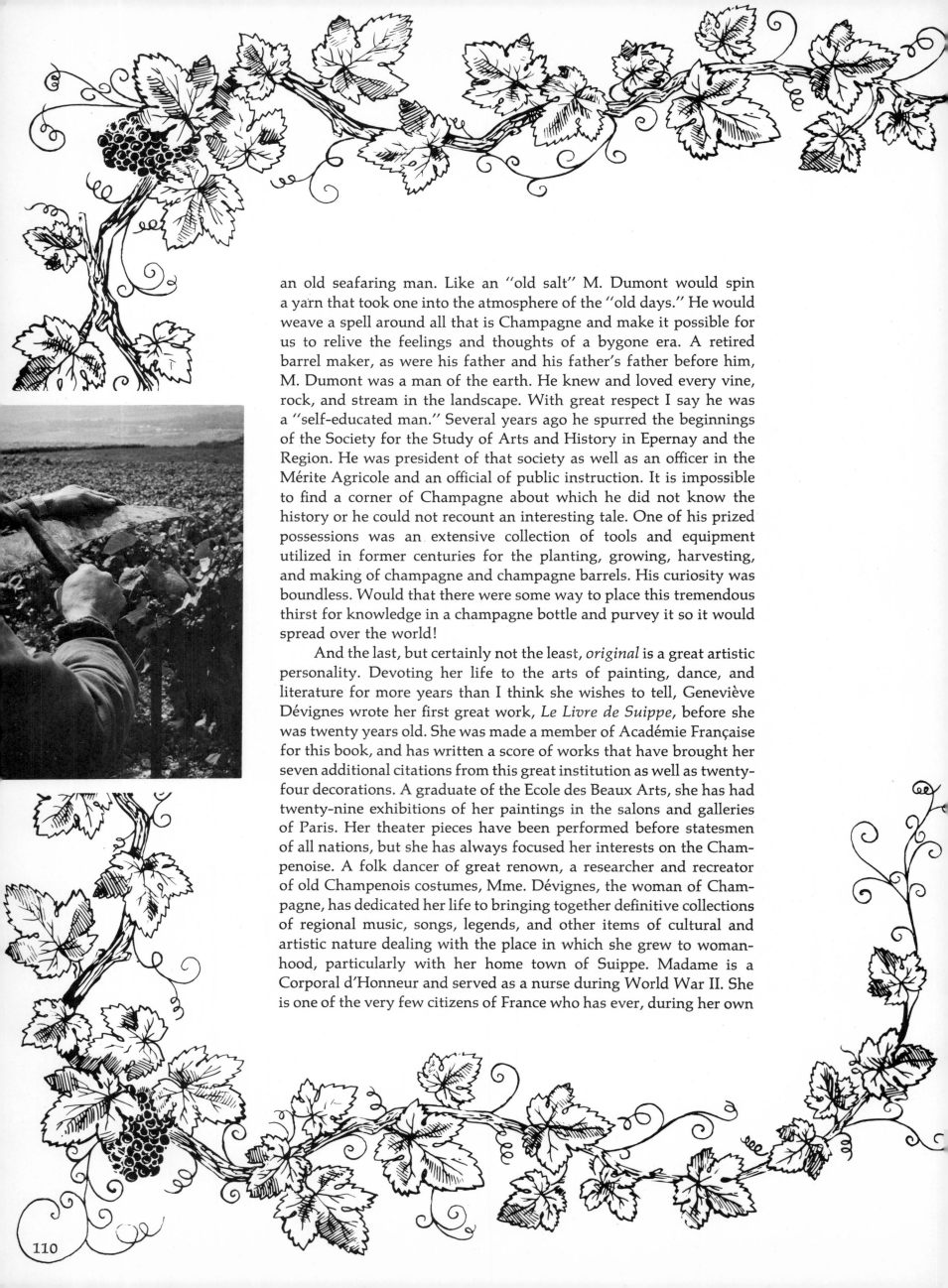

an old seafaring man. Like an "old salt" M. Dumont would spin a yarn that took one into the atmosphere of the "old days." He would weave a spell around all that is Champagne and make it possible for us to relive the feelings and thoughts of a bygone era. A retired barrel maker, as were his father and his father's father before him, M. Dumont was a man of the earth. He knew and loved every vine, rock, and stream in the landscape. With great respect I say he was a "self-educated man." Several years ago he spurred the beginnings of the Society for the Study of Arts and History in Epernay and the Region. He was president of that society as well as an officer in the Mérite Agricole and an official of public instruction. It is impossible to find a corner of Champagne about which he did not know the history or he could not recount an interesting tale. One of his prized possessions was an extensive collection of tools and equipment utilized in former centuries for the planting, growing, harvesting, and making of champagne and champagne barrels. His curiosity was boundless. Would that there were some way to place this tremendous thirst for knowledge in a champagne bottle and purvey it so it would spread over the world!

And the last, but certainly not the least, *original* is a great artistic personality. Devoting her life to the arts of painting, dance, and literature for more years than I think she wishes to tell, Geneviève Dévignes wrote her first great work, *Le Livre de Suippe*, before she was twenty years old. She was made a member of Académie Française for this book, and has written a score of works that have brought her seven additional citations from this great institution as well as twenty-four decorations. A graduate of the Ecole des Beaux Arts, she has had twenty-nine exhibitions of her paintings in the salons and galleries of Paris. Her theater pieces have been performed before statesmen of all nations, but she has always focused her interests on the Champenoise. A folk dancer of great renown, a researcher and recreator of old Champenois costumes, Mme. Dévignes, the woman of Champagne, has dedicated her life to bringing together definitive collections of regional music, songs, legends, and other items of cultural and artistic nature dealing with the place in which she grew to womanhood, particularly with her home town of Suippe. Madame is a Corporal d'Honneur and served as a nurse during World War II. She is one of the very few citizens of France who has ever, during her own

lifetime , had the distinct pleasure of strolling down a street bearing her own name.

The creative urge and the joie de vivre of Mme. Dévignes is in no way dimmed. Presently she is hard at work on a mountain of manuscripts that lie about her charming apartment. She is the living personification of the Champenois spirit of "perfection and elegance" that is reflected in its wine.

Full of hope, a deep desire for knowledge, and the will to see the new dawn of each day, these three splendid humans serve to remind us of the strength, vigor, and beauty, the dedication to truth and quality, that is characteristic of Champagne.

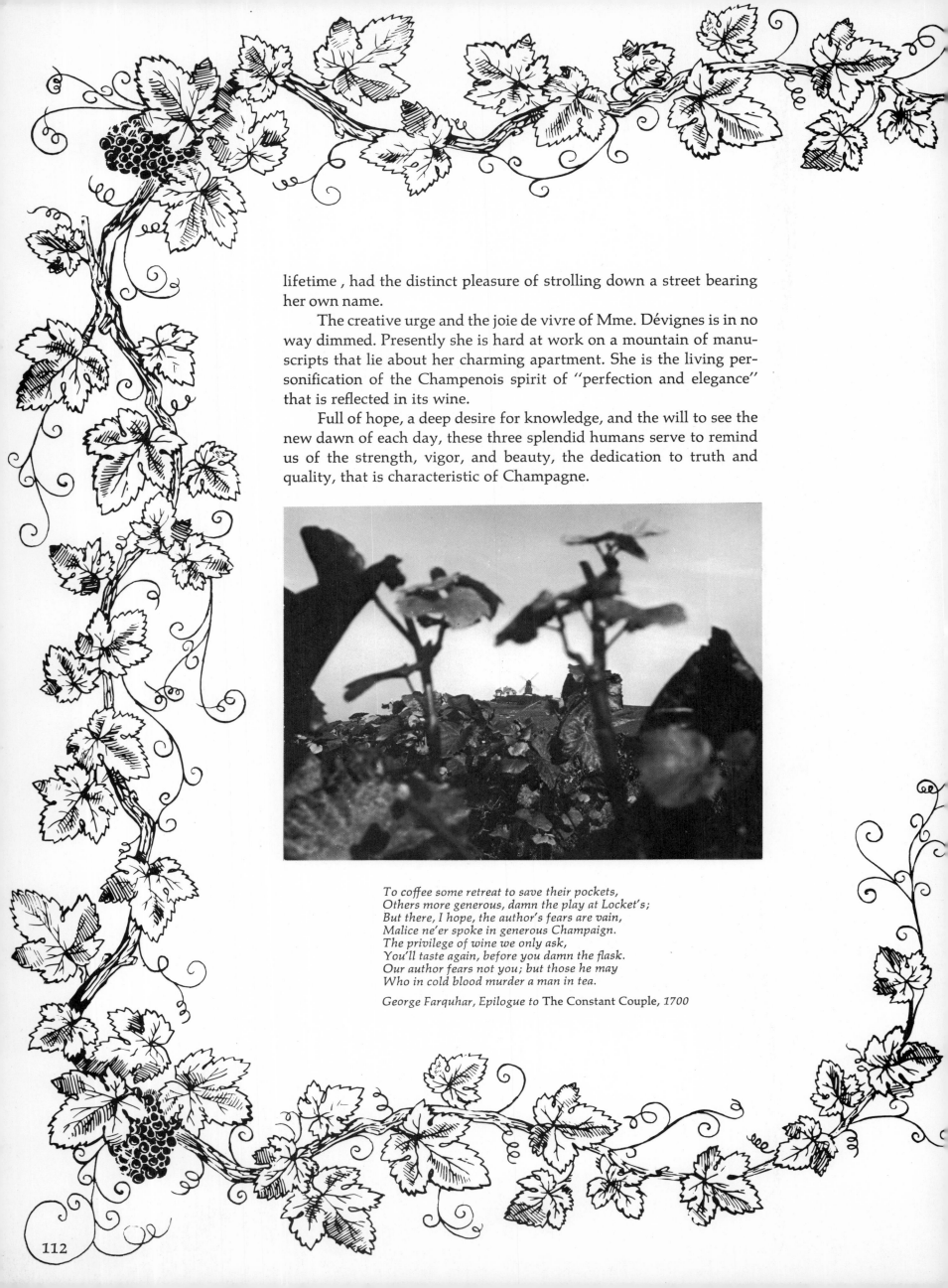

To coffee some retreat to save their pockets,
Others more generous, damn the play at Locket's;
But there, I hope, the author's fears are vain,
Malice ne'er spoke in generous Champaign.
The privilege of wine we only ask,
You'll taste again, before you damn the flask.
Our author fears not you; but those he may
Who in cold blood murder a man in tea.

George Farquhar, Epilogue to The Constant Couple, *1700*

GENESIS AND CHARACTERISTICS OF THE VINE ON THE THREE COTES OF THE MARNE AND IN THE AUBE

Interview with M. Emile Moreau

Of the origin of vines in Champagne

We know of the existence of vines in very ancient times. We find traces of them in the Tertiary period in the region of Sézanne. However, those vines produced inedible grapes. During the Quaternary period there were several varieties of wild vines yielding grapes that could be squeezed to make a palatable juice. These vines grew at the edge of the forests, very often wrapping their tendrils around the branches of the nearby trees. The Gauls used to pick those grapes, probably without sorting them from other berries, and made some sort of drinkable beverage.

Then came the Romans in the middle of the first century B.C. Julius Caesar's soldiers came from wine-making families, or at the very least they had marched through the Mediterranean region where vines had been under cultivation for many years. The Romans must have been surprised to discover that the Gauls were ignorant of all the use they could have made of the various vines indigenous to their country. They very much wanted to have a supply "on location," so to speak, of all the wine they needed for their legions, so as to avoid costly and difficult transportation. They encouraged the Gauls in a methodical cultivation of their vines. There is little doubt that our

rink thy flask of Champaign,
Twill serve you for paint and love potion.

champagne vines were in existence before the Roman invasion, but they were not taken care of. It was the Romans or, to be exact, the Roman legionaries—some of whom were no doubt liberated war prisoners from the different wine-producing regions of the Mediterranean shores—who taught our forebears to tend their vines in a productive way. It goes without saying that some of the natives became specialized in this sort of culture and that some parts of the country called *monts-à-vins* were set aside for it. Vines were planted on the slopes of well-exposed hills with the proper kind of soil, whereas the plains were reserved for the culture of cereals.

Originally there must have been three different places where vines were grown: the Montagne de Reims, the Vallée de la Marne, the Montagne de Vertus. The best-cared-for vineyards were those of important people of the Roman and later of the Gallo-Roman society; those vineyards stretched out into the country surrounding the cities.

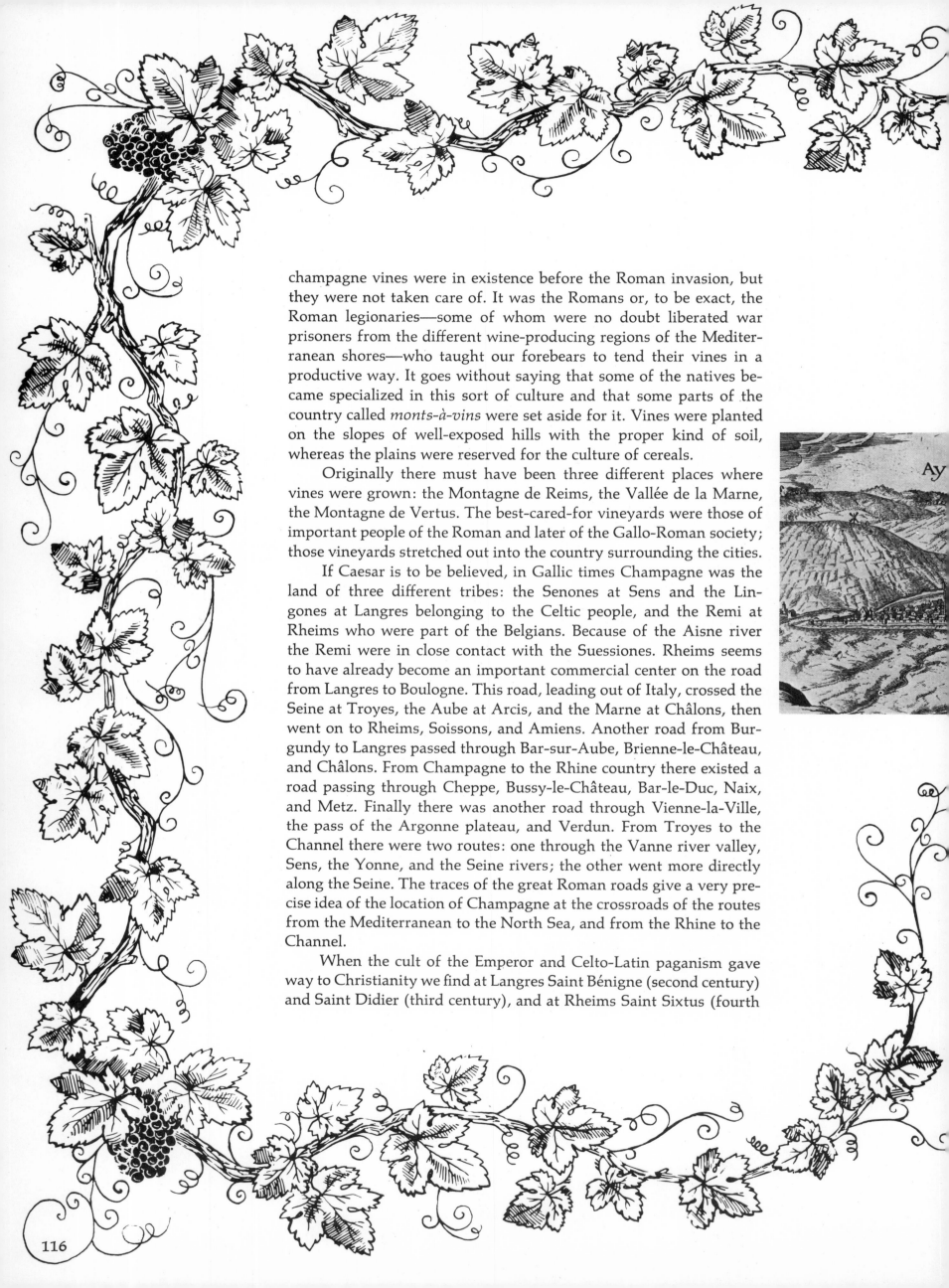

If Caesar is to be believed, in Gallic times Champagne was the land of three different tribes: the Senones at Sens and the Lingones at Langres belonging to the Celtic people, and the Remi at Rheims who were part of the Belgians. Because of the Aisne river the Remi were in close contact with the Suessiones. Rheims seems to have already become an important commercial center on the road from Langres to Boulogne. This road, leading out of Italy, crossed the Seine at Troyes, the Aube at Arcis, and the Marne at Châlons, then went on to Rheims, Soissons, and Amiens. Another road from Burgundy to Langres passed through Bar-sur-Aube, Brienne-le-Château, and Châlons. From Champagne to the Rhine country there existed a road passing through Cheppe, Bussy-le-Château, Bar-le-Duc, Naix, and Metz. Finally there was another road through Vienne-la-Ville, the pass of the Argonne plateau, and Verdun. From Troyes to the Channel there were two routes: one through the Vanne river valley, Sens, the Yonne, and the Seine rivers; the other went more directly along the Seine. The traces of the great Roman roads give a very precise idea of the location of Champagne at the crossroads of the routes from the Mediterranean to the North Sea, and from the Rhine to the Channel.

When the cult of the Emperor and Celto-Latin paganism gave way to Christianity we find at Langres Saint Bénigne (second century) and Saint Didier (third century), and at Rheims Saint Sixtus (fourth

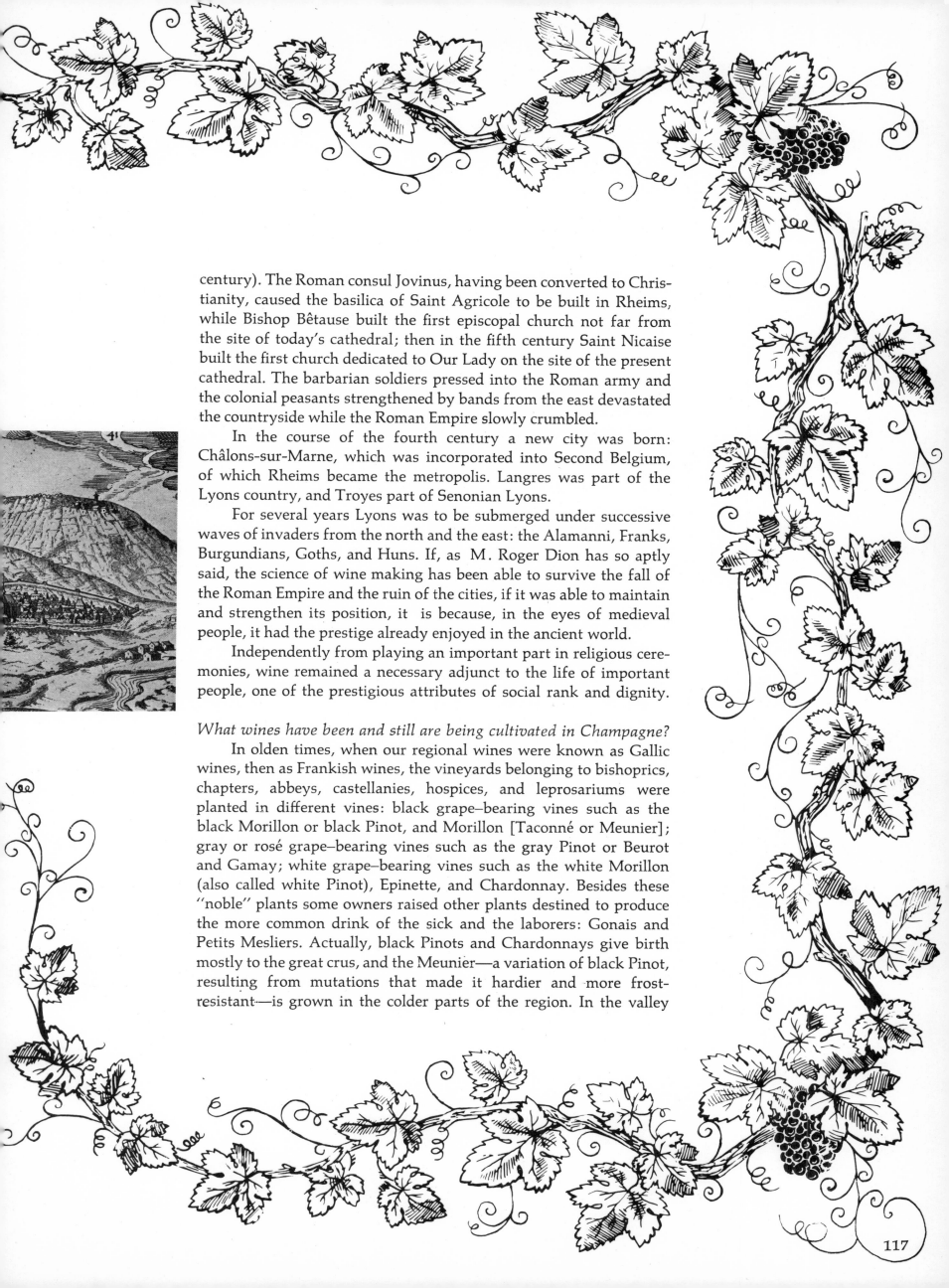

century). The Roman consul Jovinus, having been converted to Christianity, caused the basilica of Saint Agricole to be built in Rheims, while Bishop Bêtause built the first episcopal church not far from the site of today's cathedral; then in the fifth century Saint Nicaise built the first church dedicated to Our Lady on the site of the present cathedral. The barbarian soldiers pressed into the Roman army and the colonial peasants strengthened by bands from the east devastated the countryside while the Roman Empire slowly crumbled.

In the course of the fourth century a new city was born: Châlons-sur-Marne, which was incorporated into Second Belgium, of which Rheims became the metropolis. Langres was part of the Lyons country, and Troyes part of Senonian Lyons.

For several years Lyons was to be submerged under successive waves of invaders from the north and the east: the Alamanni, Franks, Burgundians, Goths, and Huns. If, as M. Roger Dion has so aptly said, the science of wine making has been able to survive the fall of the Roman Empire and the ruin of the cities, if it was able to maintain and strengthen its position, it is because, in the eyes of medieval people, it had the prestige already enjoyed in the ancient world.

Independently from playing an important part in religious ceremonies, wine remained a necessary adjunct to the life of important people, one of the prestigious attributes of social rank and dignity.

What wines have been and still are being cultivated in Champagne?

In olden times, when our regional wines were known as Gallic wines, then as Frankish wines, the vineyards belonging to bishoprics, chapters, abbeys, castellanies, hospices, and leprosariums were planted in different vines: black grape–bearing vines such as the black Morillon or black Pinot, and Morillon [Taconné or Meunier]; gray or rosé grape–bearing vines such as the gray Pinot or Beurot and Gamay; white grape–bearing vines such as the white Morillon (also called white Pinot), Epinette, and Chardonnay. Besides these "noble" plants some owners raised other plants destined to produce the more common drink of the sick and the laborers: Gonais and Petits Mesliers. Actually, black Pinots and Chardonnays give birth mostly to the great crus, and the Meunier—a variation of black Pinot, resulting from mutations that made it hardier and more frost-resistant—is grown in the colder parts of the region. In the valley of the Marne or the Aisne some small vineyards are still planted in Petits Mesliers (no more than twenty hectares). In the Aube country around Baroville we still have a few vineyards planted in Arbanne vines (no more than three hectares—produced, so they say, by the monks of the Abbey of Clairvaux). It is quite sure that within a very short space of time only black Pinot or Meunier and Chardonnay will be found in Champagne.

Very early, three centers of wine making had been established in the heart of Champagne: the Montagne de Reims, the Vallée de la Marne, and the Montagne de Vertus. Between these last two places there appeared for a time the Côte des Blancs, thus named because the vinegrowers of this region specialized in the culture of Chardonnay.

What had been started by the Romans was pursued and intensified by the religious dignitaries of the diocese of Rheims, Châlons, and Troyes. Their efforts were all the more successful because the vineyards they were interested in were close to their residence and boasted of rich abbeys and dynamic monks.

What kinds of wines were produced by the region which was to give birth to champagne wine?

Originally, in the valleys of the Marne and the Aisne, red and rosé wines obtained from colored grapes, and white wines obtained from white grapes. In the valley of the Aube we had either red or white wines, and sometimes rosé wines, a specialty of the Ricey region.

At the start of the eighteenth century the success encountered by Dom Pérignon's white wines, which he had obtained through a patiently worked-out technique, caused the red wines to be discriminated against. The Benedictine monks of Hautvillers and Pierry kept on manufacturing them, but only in small quantity, only in very good years, or when the grapes ripened quickly and it was difficult to obtain perfectly white wine. However, the surplus of white wine from 1720 to 1730 brought on such a drop in prices that the wine makers in the not so famous parts of the region went back to the production of red wine which they could be sure of selling.

Can you conceive that once upon a time red champagne wine was a favorite? At the time there arose some problems with Burgundy since our wines were very similar to theirs.

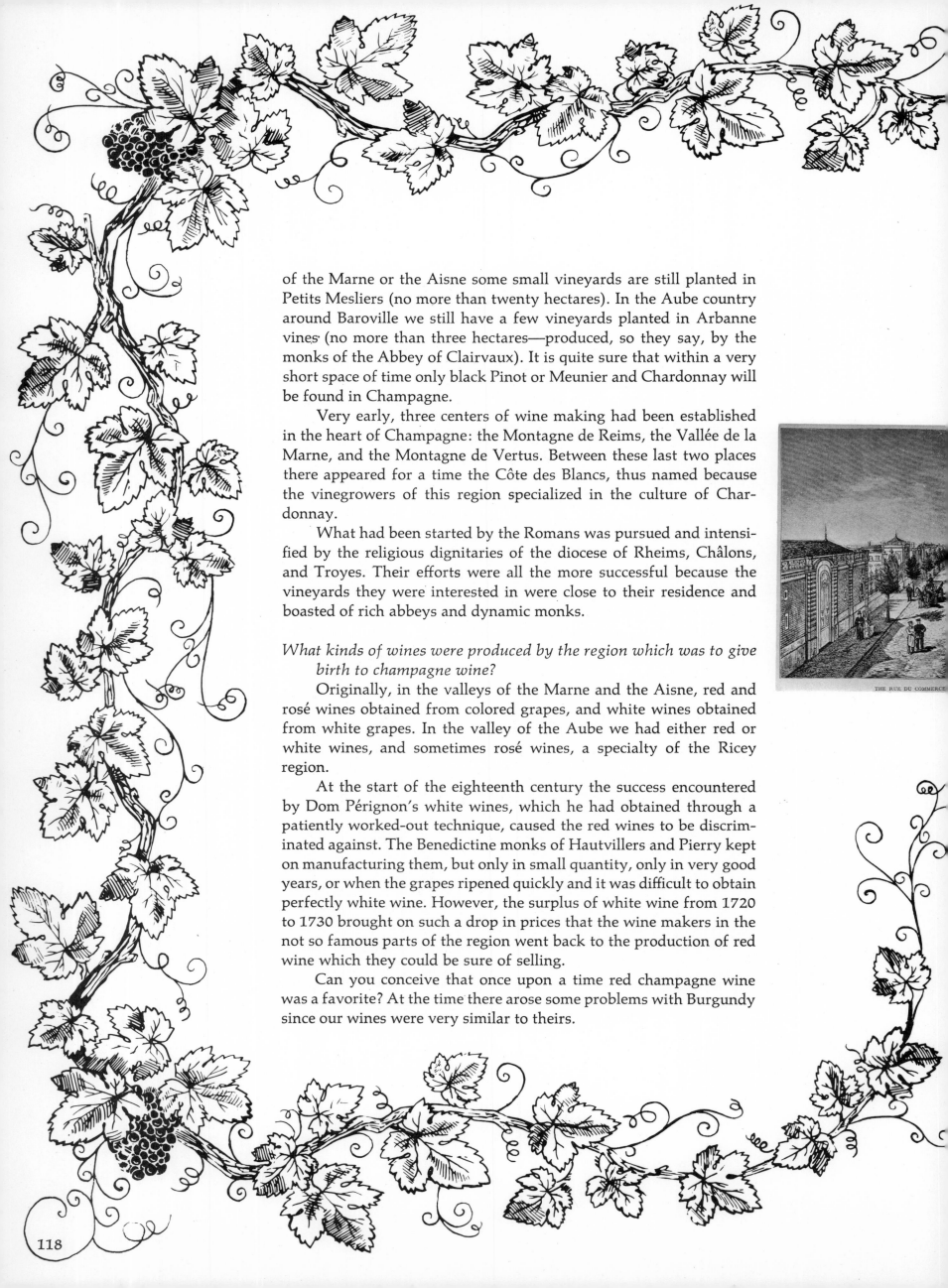

THE RUE DU COMMERCE

118

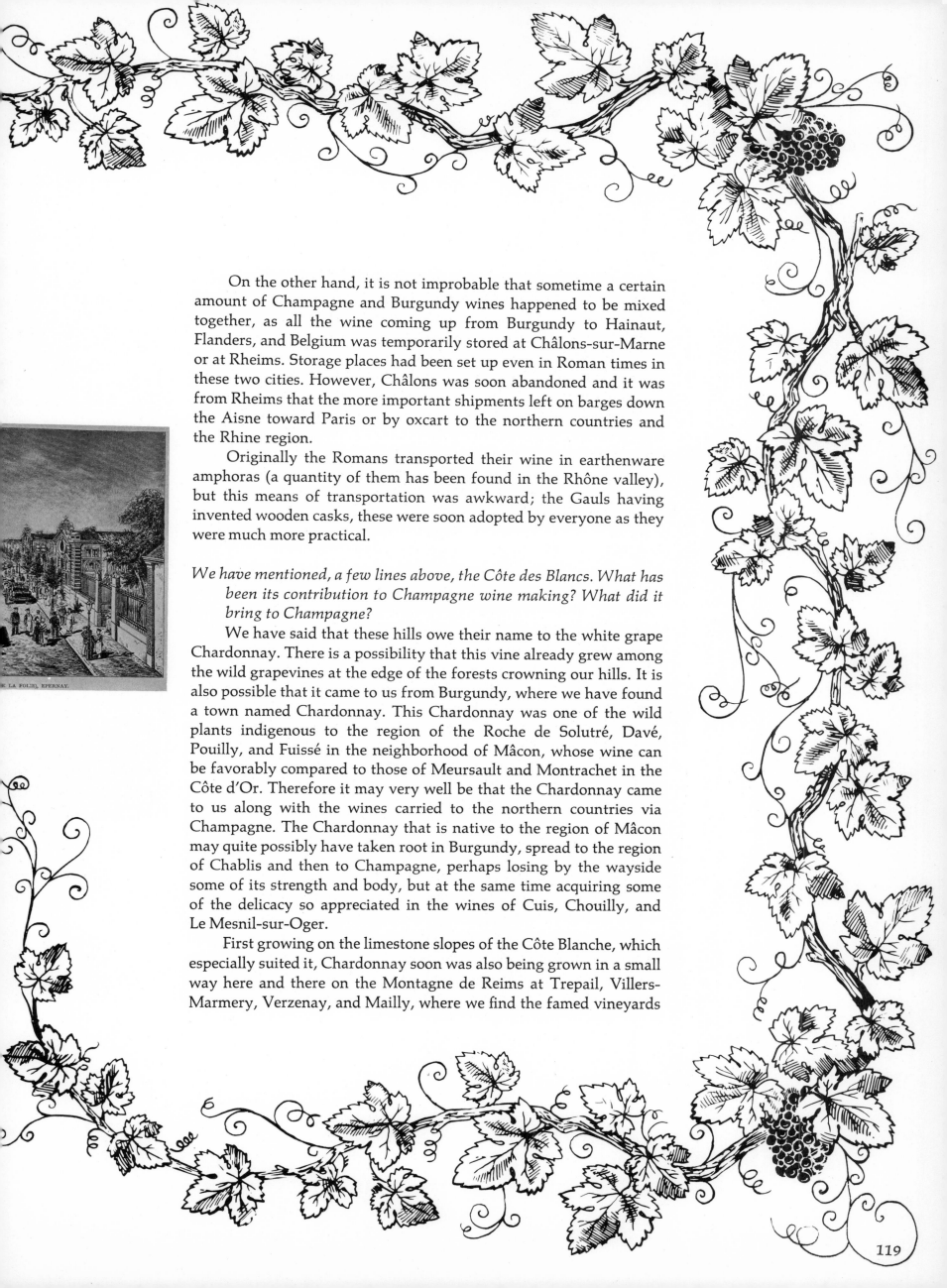

On the other hand, it is not improbable that sometime a certain amount of Champagne and Burgundy wines happened to be mixed together, as all the wine coming up from Burgundy to Hainaut, Flanders, and Belgium was temporarily stored at Châlons-sur-Marne or at Rheims. Storage places had been set up even in Roman times in these two cities. However, Châlons was soon abandoned and it was from Rheims that the more important shipments left on barges down the Aisne toward Paris or by oxcart to the northern countries and the Rhine region.

Originally the Romans transported their wine in earthenware amphoras (a quantity of them has been found in the Rhône valley), but this means of transportation was awkward; the Gauls having invented wooden casks, these were soon adopted by everyone as they were much more practical.

We have mentioned, a few lines above, the Côte des Blancs. What has been its contribution to Champagne wine making? What did it bring to Champagne?

We have said that these hills owe their name to the white grape Chardonnay. There is a possibility that this vine already grew among the wild grapevines at the edge of the forests crowning our hills. It is also possible that it came to us from Burgundy, where we have found a town named Chardonnay. This Chardonnay was one of the wild plants indigenous to the region of the Roche de Solutré, Davé, Pouilly, and Fuissé in the neighborhood of Mâcon, whose wine can be favorably compared to those of Meursault and Montrachet in the Côte d'Or. Therefore it may very well be that the Chardonnay came to us along with the wines carried to the northern countries via Champagne. The Chardonnay that is native to the region of Mâcon may quite possibly have taken root in Burgundy, spread to the region of Chablis and then to Champagne, perhaps losing by the wayside some of its strength and body, but at the same time acquiring some of the delicacy so appreciated in the wines of Cuis, Chouilly, and Le Mesnil-sur-Oger.

First growing on the limestone slopes of the Côte Blanche, which especially suited it, Chardonnay soon was also being grown in a small way here and there on the Montagne de Reims at Trepail, Villers-Marmery, Verzenay, and Mailly, where we find the famed vineyards of Chardonnay, and also on the hills of Nogent-l'Abbesse and on the famous property of the Maréchal d'Estrée and that of the Marquis de Sillery. These last vines were tended with lavish care by the Brulart family and the famous team of the Ordre des Coteaux. In the Marne valley black Pinot is king as well as throughout the Côtes de Bourgogne. Naturally it became the parent vine of the different variations and mutations created by the vineyard owners, who like true artists were seeking quality. One member of my family, Gustave Moreau, thus created the famous black Pinot of Ay, a town of which he became mayor. It was made with small grapes that had only one fault: the crop never went over 4000 kilos to the hectare; very often it was closer to 2500 or 3000 kilos. These people were true *amateurs* (devotees). Black Pinots were also to be found in Vertus, Bouzy, Trepail, etc. From the same Meunier comes the selection of Vignon de Chavenay with its impressive regular yield.

Were there famous vineyards north of the Montagne de Reims?

Yes, there were vineyards on the hill of Laon where Hugues Capet mentions a very extensive property which was to become the wine capital in the twelfth century. In the ninth century the abbeys of Flanders and Hainaut were already the proprietors of some vineyards in the lower reaches of the Aisne valley; the wines they made were for their own use. The abbey of Saint-Amand near Valenciennes owned some vineyards in the neighborhood of Coucy-le-Château, and that of Saint-Bavon of Ghent had some near Soissons. The monastery of Lobbes in Hainaut grew some vines in Laonnois, and that of Saint-Ghislain near Mons was cultivating grapes at Allemand in Soissonnais. However, it developed that Laon was obliged to make use of the costly route by land for the exportation of its wine, and that Soissons, to satisfy the wine merchants in charge of the Paris trade, had to give preference to the winegrowers whose produce was more noted for abundance than excellence. The demand of the capital for cheap ordinary wine fatally encouraged people to grow vines which would yield in quantity if not in quality. Little by little the better wines disappeared. The same thing happened to the wines of Coucy-le-Château, which in the reign of Henry IV were "among all the wines of France the most excellent, just as among the Champagne wines those of Ay have first rank." (La Framboisière.)

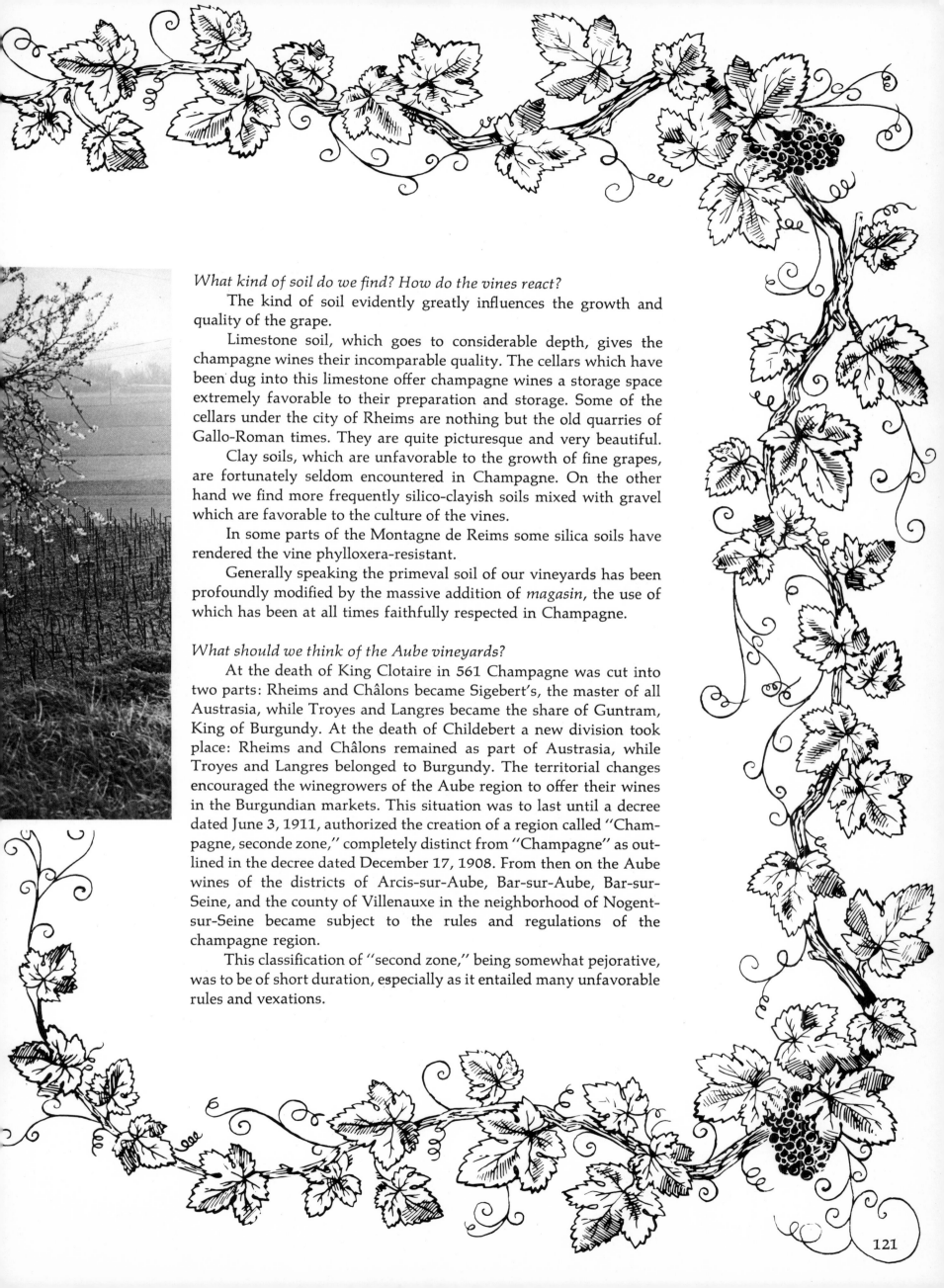

What kind of soil do we find? How do the vines react?

The kind of soil evidently greatly influences the growth and quality of the grape.

Limestone soil, which goes to considerable depth, gives the champagne wines their incomparable quality. The cellars which have been dug into this limestone offer champagne wines a storage space extremely favorable to their preparation and storage. Some of the cellars under the city of Rheims are nothing but the old quarries of Gallo-Roman times. They are quite picturesque and very beautiful.

Clay soils, which are unfavorable to the growth of fine grapes, are fortunately seldom encountered in Champagne. On the other hand we find more frequently silico-clayish soils mixed with gravel which are favorable to the culture of the vines.

In some parts of the Montagne de Reims some silica soils have rendered the vine phylloxera-resistant.

Generally speaking the primeval soil of our vineyards has been profoundly modified by the massive addition of *magasin*, the use of which has been at all times faithfully respected in Champagne.

What should we think of the Aube vineyards?

At the death of King Clotaire in 561 Champagne was cut into two parts: Rheims and Châlons became Sigebert's, the master of all Austrasia, while Troyes and Langres became the share of Guntram, King of Burgundy. At the death of Childebert a new division took place: Rheims and Châlons remained as part of Austrasia, while Troyes and Langres belonged to Burgundy. The territorial changes encouraged the winegrowers of the Aube region to offer their wines in the Burgundian markets. This situation was to last until a decree dated June 3, 1911, authorized the creation of a region called "Champagne, seconde zone," completely distinct from "Champagne" as outlined in the decree dated December 17, 1908. From then on the Aube wines of the districts of Arcis-sur-Aube, Bar-sur-Aube, Bar-sur-Seine, and the county of Villenauxe in the neighborhood of Nogent-sur-Seine became subject to the rules and regulations of the champagne region.

This classification of "second zone," being somewhat pejorative, was to be of short duration, especially as it entailed many unfavorable rules and vexations.

The Aube region was once a very important wine-producing country. The Gamay wine (which was judged "disgraceful" by Philip the Bold circa 1395) became very favorably known in this region as well as in Beaujolais, central France, and Lorraine. But the Aube winegrowers had also Pinot wines. They were the Ricey wines (a variation of black Pinot, which Senator Lesaché did his best to bring back to their former honorable rank). They were marvelous wines. In any case the Ricey hills and also the hills close by had begun to produce a really well-known and very good rosé wine.

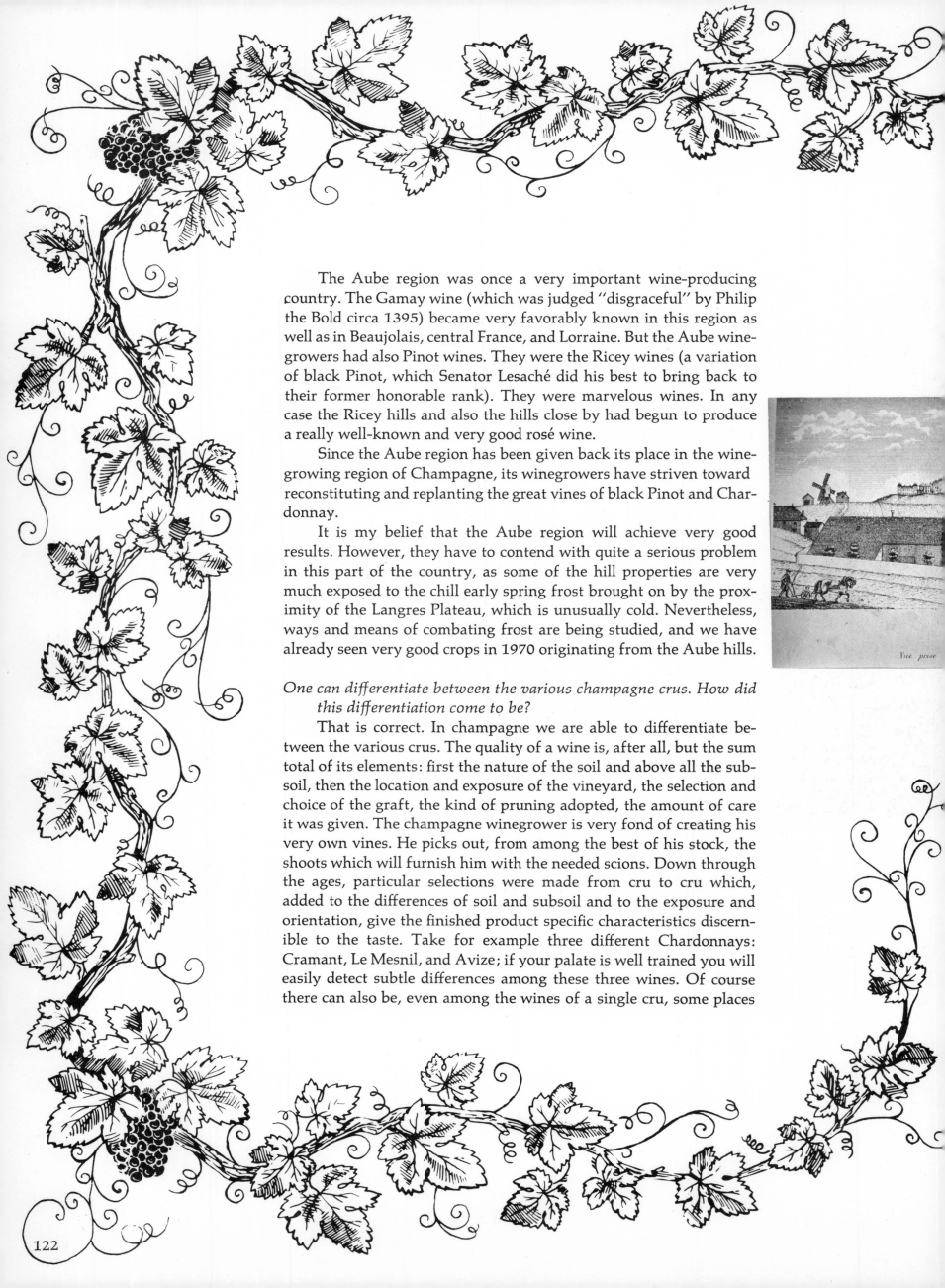

Since the Aube region has been given back its place in the winegrowing region of Champagne, its winegrowers have striven toward reconstituting and replanting the great vines of black Pinot and Chardonnay.

It is my belief that the Aube region will achieve very good results. However, they have to contend with quite a serious problem in this part of the country, as some of the hill properties are very much exposed to the chill early spring frost brought on by the proximity of the Langres Plateau, which is unusually cold. Nevertheless, ways and means of combating frost are being studied, and we have already seen very good crops in 1970 originating from the Aube hills.

One can differentiate between the various champagne crus. How did this differentiation come to be?

That is correct. In champagne we are able to differentiate between the various crus. The quality of a wine is, after all, but the sum total of its elements: first the nature of the soil and above all the subsoil, then the location and exposure of the vineyard, the selection and choice of the graft, the kind of pruning adopted, the amount of care it was given. The champagne winegrower is very fond of creating his very own vines. He picks out, from among the best of his stock, the shoots which will furnish him with the needed scions. Down through the ages, particular selections were made from cru to cru which, added to the differences of soil and subsoil and to the exposure and orientation, give the finished product specific characteristics discernible to the taste. Take for example three different Chardonnays: Cramant, Le Mesnil, and Avize; if your palate is well trained you will easily detect subtle differences among these three wines. Of course there can also be, even among the wines of a single cru, some places which will not produce wines as fine or delicate as the others. Generally speaking, the progressive organizations of Champagne together with the Institut National des Appellations d'Origine des Vins et Eaux-de-Vie have endeavored to list only the very best locations of each cru. We have mentioned only the region of Chardonnay, but the same would be true of the others planted in black Pinot or Meunier. The wine dealers, the successors of the *negotiatores vinarii* of Roman and Gallo-Roman times, were already distinguishing among the different wines of Champagne. For many years the custom was to price the wines according to the price quoted for the wine of Ay. This method was in use up to 1910. In 1911 a scale of prices was adopted ranging from 47 to 100 per cent for three fourths of the wine-growing counties; the grapes of the lesser crus were paid one fourth of the price quoted for Ay. In 1920 this scale was completed and improved, upgrading by 10 per cent the wines valued below 80 per cent of the price for Ay, and by 5 per cent some of the others. In 1937 the Aube wines and those of the Aisne valley were quoted at 50 per cent. The minimum then became 58 per cent, and later on the differences became even slighter: the Aube wines were quoted at 70 per cent, those of the Aisne valley at 75 per cent. The price of the kilo of grapes is supposed to be officially fixed each year before the start of the grape-picking season. The date of the latter is chosen by the services of the Comité Interprofessionnel du Vin de Champagne (C.I.V.C.) after due deliberation in the course of a meeting presided over by the regional prefect.

Were there specialties in the Champagne winegrowing region? What was the evolution of these specialties?

Evidently some of the people who had grown black Pinot were led to produce red wines which compared sometimes very favorably with Burgundian wines. It is my belief that in the years gone by the Burgundians must have produced good years, considering that Burgundy enjoys a much better climate than Champagne from the point of view of winegrowing. However, there was a time when Champagne was very highly prized for its red wines. There is no doubt that from time to time, thanks to particularly favorable weather conditions, Champagne has been able to produce quite remarkable red wines.

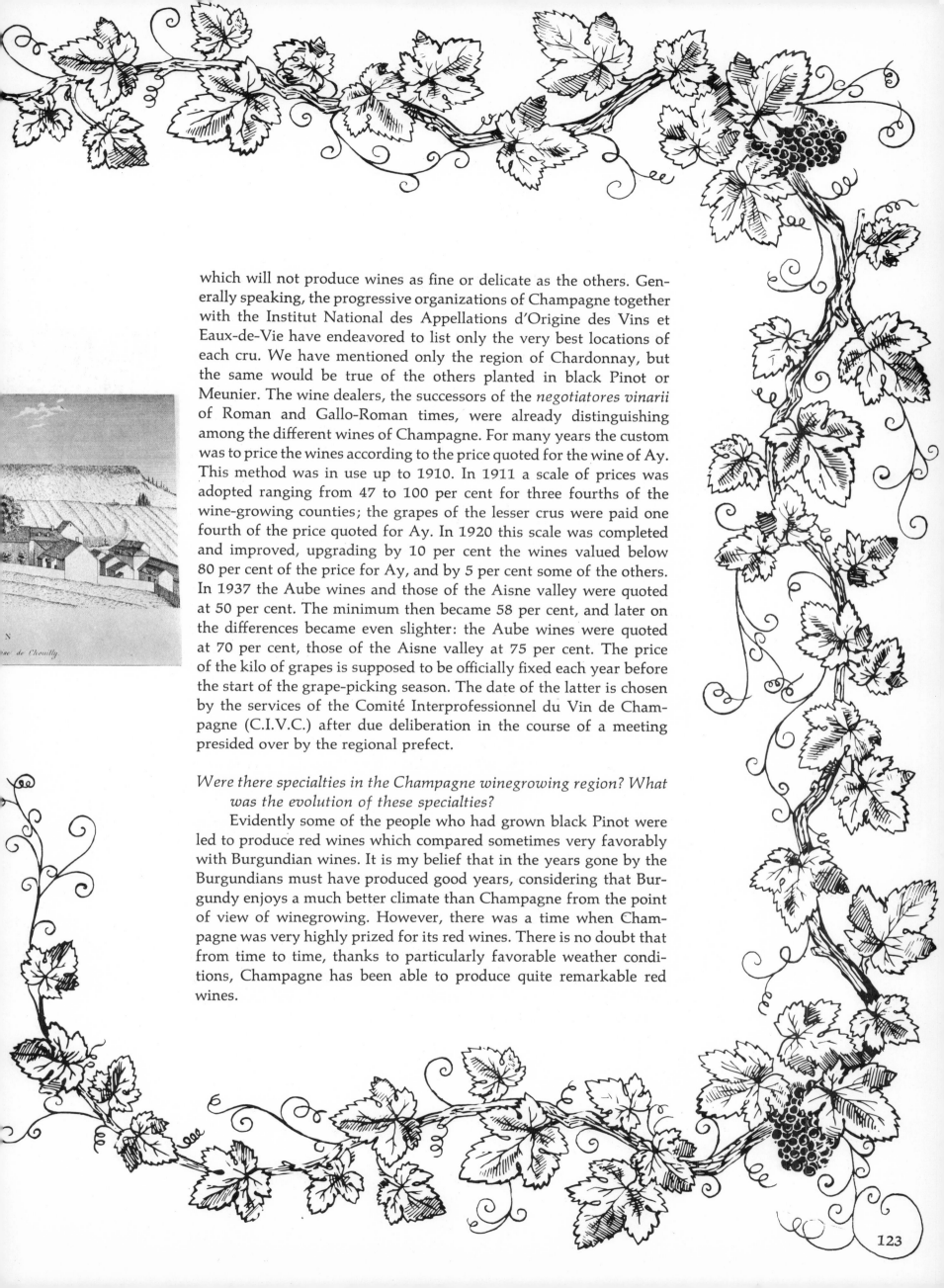

N
se de Chouilly.

Moreau-Berillon tells us that before the French Revolution red Champagne wines were marketed in Thiérache, Brie, Flanders, Picardy, etc. However, a great part of the crop was for home use or the wayside inns. At the end of the eighteenth century and at the start of the nineteenth our red wine, if Julliard is to be believed, was bottled after only one year's settling in the casks, and could be kept as long as ten or twelve years, depending upon the temperature of the year in which the grapes had matured, the way the wine had been made, and the cellar in which it had been stored.

Our red wines were divided into four different classes: *First class:* Verzy, Verzenay, Mailly. They had a lovely color, some body, headiness, and above all a great subtlety of fragrance and bouquet. The Bouzy was endowed with the same qualities but had also its own particular delicate flavor. The Saint-Thierry had the color and bouquet of burgundy and the lightness of champagne.

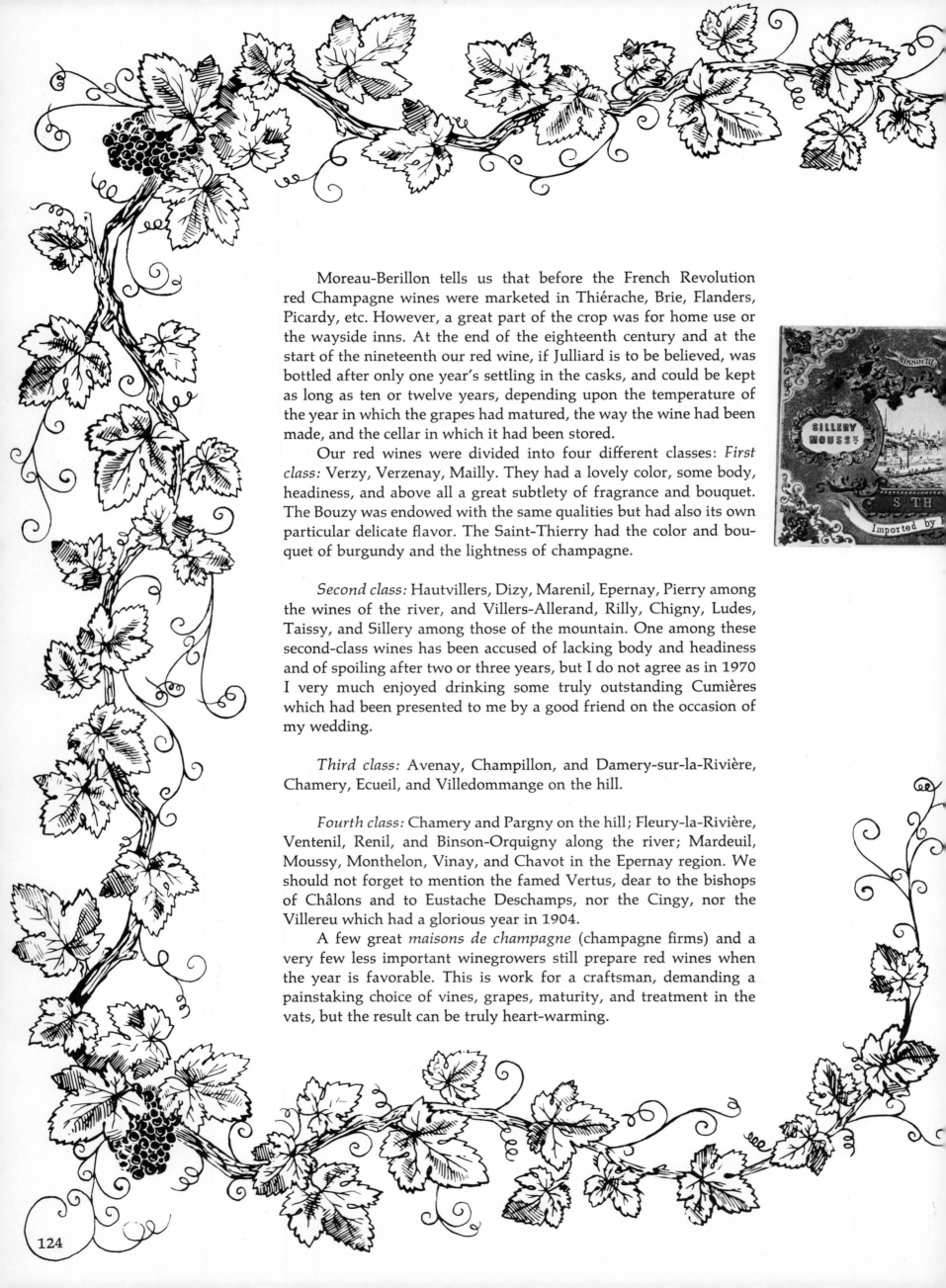

Second class: Hautvillers, Dizy, Marenil, Epernay, Pierry among the wines of the river, and Villers-Allerand, Rilly, Chigny, Ludes, Taissy, and Sillery among those of the mountain. One among these second-class wines has been accused of lacking body and headiness and of spoiling after two or three years, but I do not agree as in 1970 I very much enjoyed drinking some truly outstanding Cumières which had been presented to me by a good friend on the occasion of my wedding.

Third class: Avenay, Champillon, and Damery-sur-la-Rivière, Chamery, Ecueil, and Villedommange on the hill.

Fourth class: Chamery and Pargny on the hill; Fleury-la-Rivière, Ventenil, Renil, and Binson-Orquigny along the river; Mardeuil, Moussy, Monthelon, Vinay, and Chavot in the Epernay region. We should not forget to mention the famed Vertus, dear to the bishops of Châlons and to Eustache Deschamps, nor the Cingy, nor the Villereu which had a glorious year in 1904.

A few great *maisons de champagne* (champagne firms) and a very few less important winegrowers still prepare red wines when the year is favorable. This is work for a craftsman, demanding a painstaking choice of vines, grapes, maturity, and treatment in the vats, but the result can be truly heart-warming.

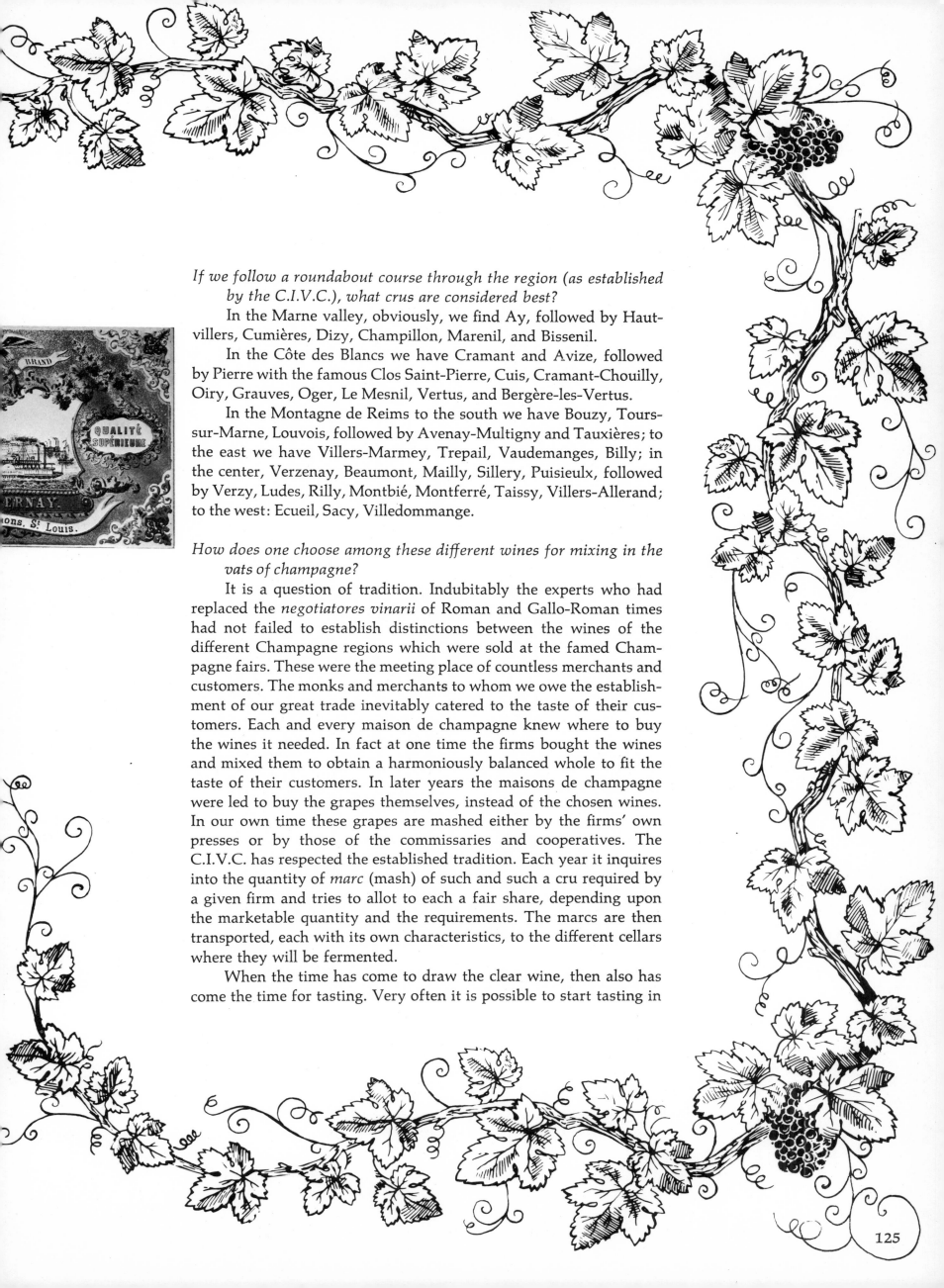

If we follow a roundabout course through the region (as established by the C.I.V.C.), what crus are considered best?

In the Marne valley, obviously, we find Ay, followed by Hautvillers, Cumières, Dizy, Champillon, Marenil, and Bissenil.

In the Côte des Blancs we have Cramant and Avize, followed by Pierre with the famous Clos Saint-Pierre, Cuis, Cramant-Chouilly, Oiry, Grauves, Oger, Le Mesnil, Vertus, and Bergère-les-Vertus.

In the Montagne de Reims to the south we have Bouzy, Tourssur-Marne, Louvois, followed by Avenay-Multigny and Tauxières; to the east we have Villers-Marmey, Trepail, Vaudemanges, Billy; in the center, Verzenay, Beaumont, Mailly, Sillery, Puisieulx, followed by Verzy, Ludes, Rilly, Montbié, Montferré, Taissy, Villers-Allerand; to the west: Ecueil, Sacy, Villedommange.

How does one choose among these different wines for mixing in the vats of champagne?

It is a question of tradition. Indubitably the experts who had replaced the *negotiatores vinarii* of Roman and Gallo-Roman times had not failed to establish distinctions between the wines of the different Champagne regions which were sold at the famed Champagne fairs. These were the meeting place of countless merchants and customers. The monks and merchants to whom we owe the establishment of our great trade inevitably catered to the taste of their customers. Each and every maison de champagne knew where to buy the wines it needed. In fact at one time the firms bought the wines and mixed them to obtain a harmoniously balanced whole to fit the taste of their customers. In later years the maisons de champagne were led to buy the grapes themselves, instead of the chosen wines. In our own time these grapes are mashed either by the firms' own presses or by those of the commissaries and cooperatives. The C.I.V.C. has respected the established tradition. Each year it inquires into the quantity of *marc* (mash) of such and such a cru required by a given firm and tries to allot to each a fair share, depending upon the marketable quantity and the requirements. The marcs are then transported, each with its own characteristics, to the different cellars where they will be fermented.

When the time has come to draw the clear wine, then also has come the time for tasting. Very often it is possible to start tasting in

January, February, or March, depending upon the year. It is at this time that they decide upon the quantity of wine from a given place that is to go into a particular vat in order to satisfy the requirements of a certain customer. The wines which have been tasted are very carefully graded. The first tasting sessions generally take place at the pressing, and even beside each cask. Sometimes it is done for a whole vat, which of course goes much faster. Personally I have seen it done cask by cask or rather "piece by piece." Then and only then came the tasting "assemblage by assemblage." It a highly technical performance but a very interesting one, or better yet a very fascinating one.

Is it possible to obtain strictly identical cuvées?

Just as in lovely types of blondes, redheads, or brunettes there are subtle differences of charm and personality, some cuvées with natural identical characteristics offer distinctive qualities resulting from the climatic conditions of the year, the evolution of the fermentation, etc. Consequently no two wine-making years, although presenting great similarity, can be strictly identical, and in the last analysis that is what gives each its own charming distinction.

Climatic conditions influence the crops to such an extent that it is important to take into consideration the annual weather average, which enables us to make useful predictions. These mean averages can be established (as I was taught to do by my colleague Dr. Manceau, at the weather station of Fort Chabrol) by adding the mean daily temperatures, the sum of sunlight hours, and subtracting the total rainfall. The resulting figures from March 1 to September 30, compared with those of the preceding year, permit very interesting conclusions.

One very often hears it said that the maisons de champagne ferment their wine in oak casks so they can assert that their wines are preferable to those fermented in other containers. What do you think of it?

As an old native of Champagne I have the deepest respect for the minutiae, the subtleties which have gone into making champagne wine what it is and have contributed to the spread of its fame throughout the world. But I also appreciate progress and I can see that some of the new techniques are more practical and more economical.

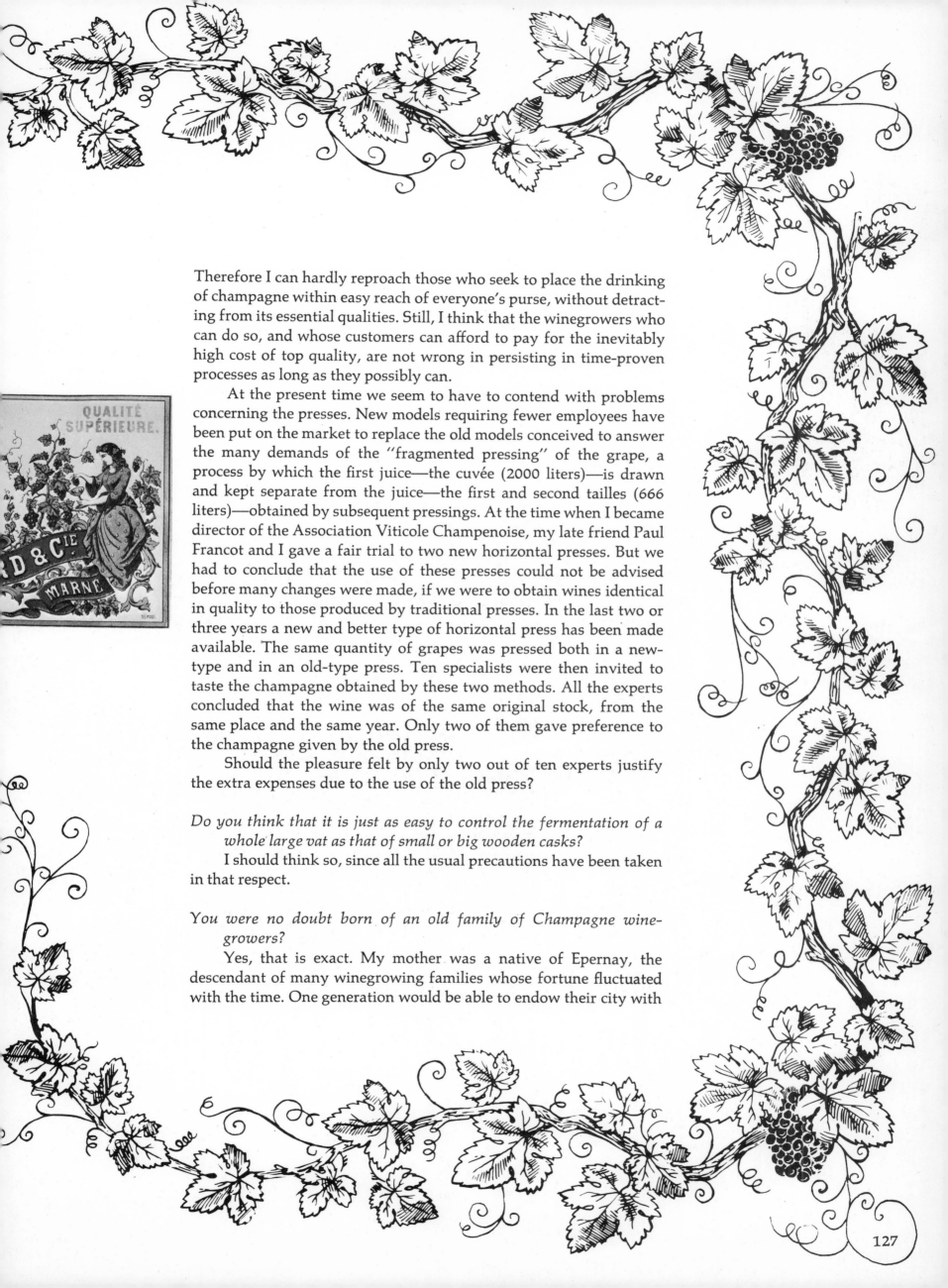

Therefore I can hardly reproach those who seek to place the drinking of champagne within easy reach of everyone's purse, without detracting from its essential qualities. Still, I think that the winegrowers who can do so, and whose customers can afford to pay for the inevitably high cost of top quality, are not wrong in persisting in time-proven processes as long as they possibly can.

At the present time we seem to have to contend with problems concerning the presses. New models requiring fewer employees have been put on the market to replace the old models conceived to answer the many demands of the "fragmented pressing" of the grape, a process by which the first juice—the cuvée (2000 liters)—is drawn and kept separate from the juice—the first and second tailles (666 liters)—obtained by subsequent pressings. At the time when I became director of the Association Viticole Champenoise, my late friend Paul Francot and I gave a fair trial to two new horizontal presses. But we had to conclude that the use of these presses could not be advised before many changes were made, if we were to obtain wines identical in quality to those produced by traditional presses. In the last two or three years a new and better type of horizontal press has been made available. The same quantity of grapes was pressed both in a new-type and in an old-type press. Ten specialists were then invited to taste the champagne obtained by these two methods. All the experts concluded that the wine was of the same original stock, from the same place and the same year. Only two of them gave preference to the champagne given by the old press.

Should the pleasure felt by only two out of ten experts justify the extra expenses due to the use of the old press?

Do you think that it is just as easy to control the fermentation of a whole large vat as that of small or big wooden casks?
I should think so, since all the usual precautions have been taken in that respect.

You were no doubt born of an old family of Champagne wine-growers?
Yes, that is exact. My mother was a native of Epernay, the descendant of many winegrowing families whose fortune fluctuated with the time. One generation would be able to endow their city with

127

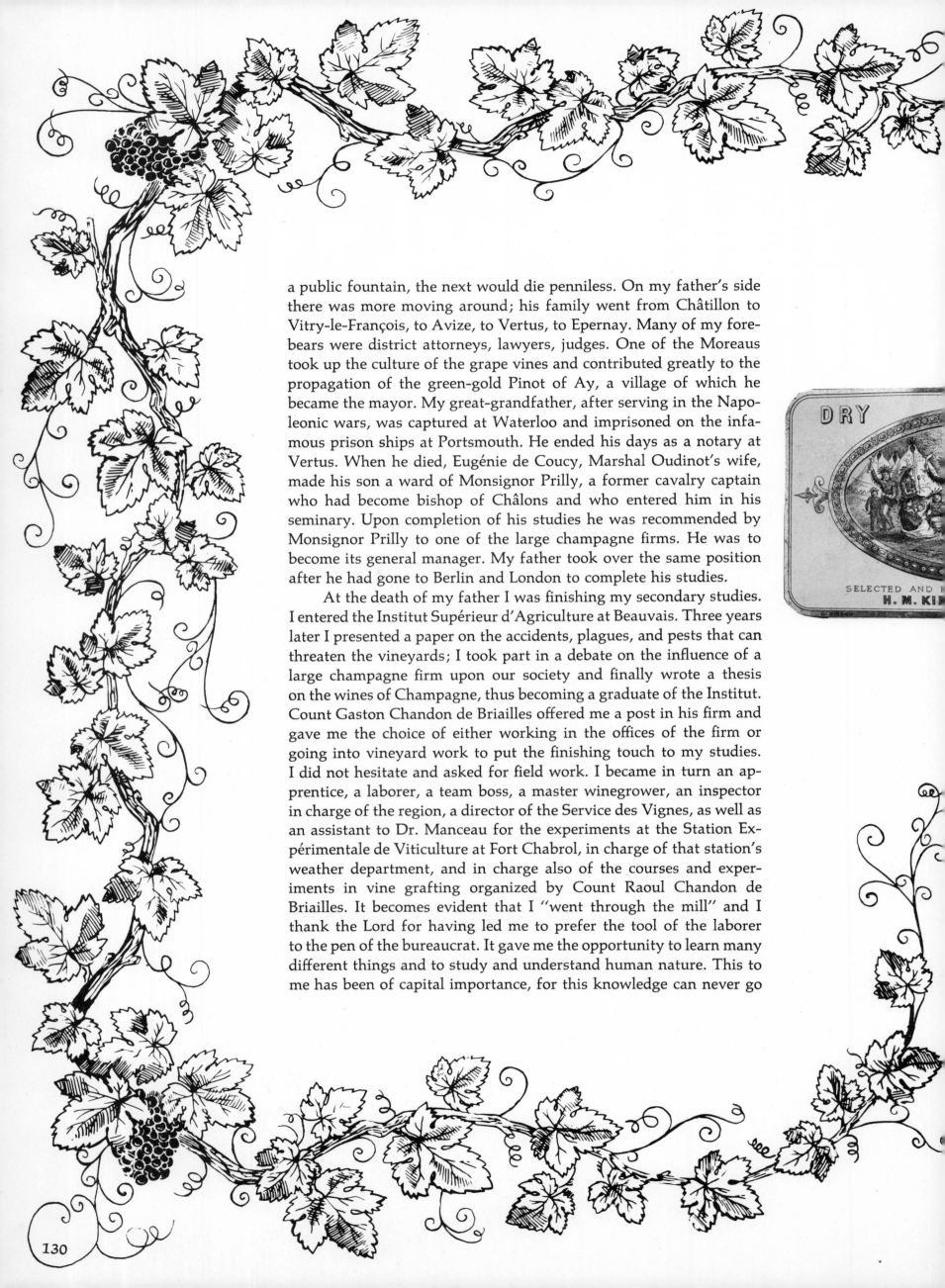

a public fountain, the next would die penniless. On my father's side there was more moving around; his family went from Châtillon to Vitry-le-François, to Avize, to Vertus, to Epernay. Many of my forebears were district attorneys, lawyers, judges. One of the Moreaus took up the culture of the grape vines and contributed greatly to the propagation of the green-gold Pinot of Ay, a village of which he became the mayor. My great-grandfather, after serving in the Napoleonic wars, was captured at Waterloo and imprisoned on the infamous prison ships at Portsmouth. He ended his days as a notary at Vertus. When he died, Eugénie de Coucy, Marshal Oudinot's wife, made his son a ward of Monsignor Prilly, a former cavalry captain who had become bishop of Châlons and who entered him in his seminary. Upon completion of his studies he was recommended by Monsignor Prilly to one of the large champagne firms. He was to become its general manager. My father took over the same position after he had gone to Berlin and London to complete his studies.

At the death of my father I was finishing my secondary studies. I entered the Institut Supérieur d'Agriculture at Beauvais. Three years later I presented a paper on the accidents, plagues, and pests that can threaten the vineyards; I took part in a debate on the influence of a large champagne firm upon our society and finally wrote a thesis on the wines of Champagne, thus becoming a graduate of the Institut. Count Gaston Chandon de Briailles offered me a post in his firm and gave me the choice of either working in the offices of the firm or going into vineyard work to put the finishing touch to my studies. I did not hesitate and asked for field work. I became in turn an apprentice, a laborer, a team boss, a master winegrower, an inspector in charge of the region, a director of the Service des Vignes, as well as an assistant to Dr. Manceau for the experiments at the Station Expérimentale de Viticulture at Fort Chabrol, in charge of that station's weather department, and in charge also of the courses and experiments in vine grafting organized by Count Raoul Chandon de Briailles. It becomes evident that I "went through the mill" and I thank the Lord for having led me to prefer the tool of the laborer to the pen of the bureaucrat. It gave me the opportunity to learn many different things and to study and understand human nature. This to me has been of capital importance, for this knowledge can never go

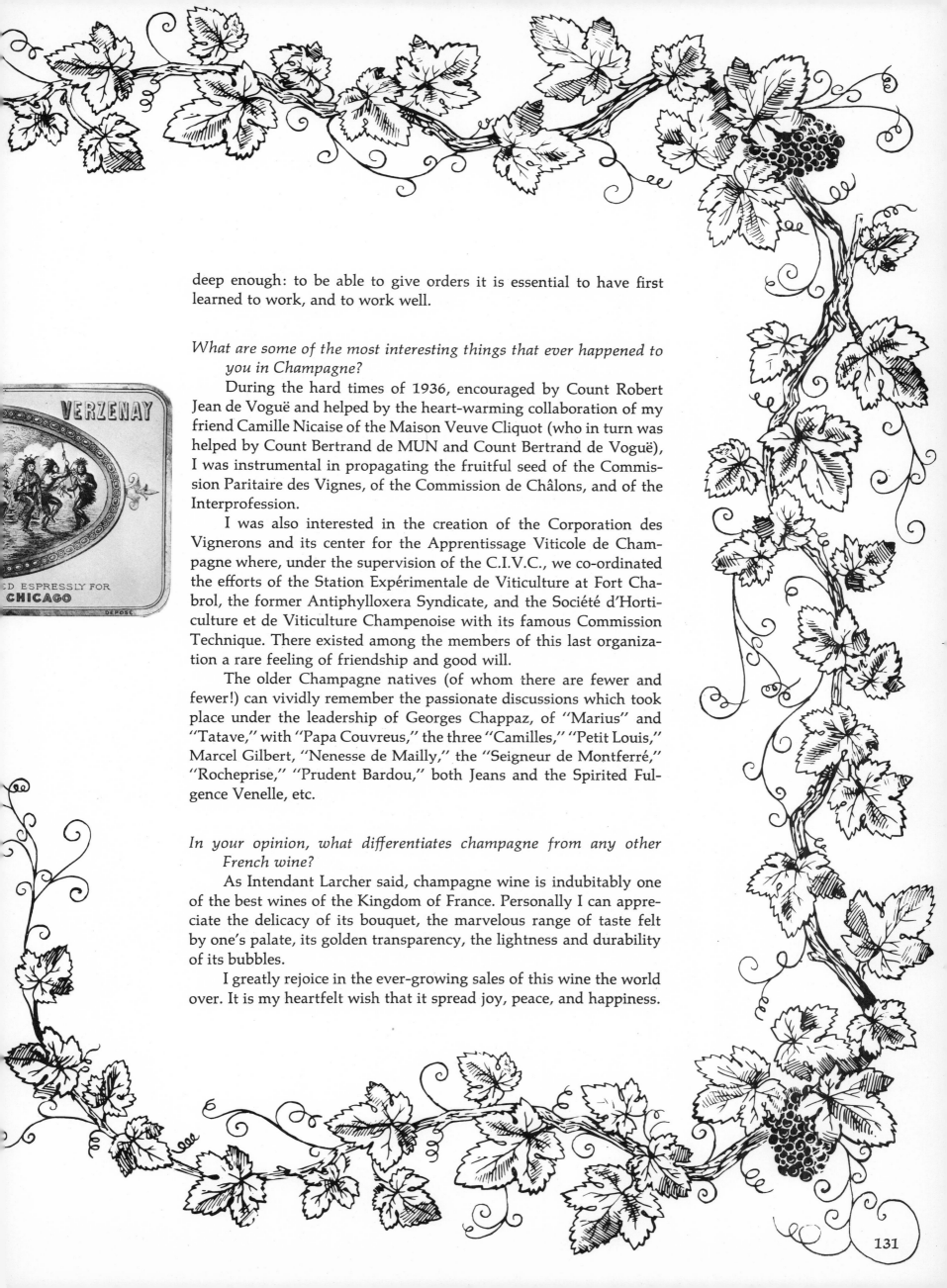

deep enough: to be able to give orders it is essential to have first learned to work, and to work well.

What are some of the most interesting things that ever happened to you in Champagne?

During the hard times of 1936, encouraged by Count Robert Jean de Voguë and helped by the heart-warming collaboration of my friend Camille Nicaise of the Maison Veuve Cliquot (who in turn was helped by Count Bertrand de MUN and Count Bertrand de Voguë), I was instrumental in propagating the fruitful seed of the Commission Paritaire des Vignes, of the Commission de Châlons, and of the Interprofession.

I was also interested in the creation of the Corporation des Vignerons and its center for the Apprentissage Viticole de Champagne where, under the supervision of the C.I.V.C., we co-ordinated the efforts of the Station Expérimentale de Viticulture at Fort Chabrol, the former Antiphylloxera Syndicate, and the Société d'Horticulture et de Viticulture Champenoise with its famous Commission Technique. There existed among the members of this last organization a rare feeling of friendship and good will.

The older Champagne natives (of whom there are fewer and fewer!) can vividly remember the passionate discussions which took place under the leadership of Georges Chappaz, of "Marius" and "Tatave," with "Papa Couvreus," the three "Camilles," "Petit Louis," Marcel Gilbert, "Nenesse de Mailly," the "Seigneur de Montferré," "Rocheprise," "Prudent Bardou," both Jeans and the Spirited Fulgence Venelle, etc.

In your opinion, what differentiates champagne from any other French wine?

As Intendant Larcher said, champagne wine is indubitably one of the best wines of the Kingdom of France. Personally I can appreciate the delicacy of its bouquet, the marvelous range of taste felt by one's palate, its golden transparency, the lightness and durability of its bubbles.

I greatly rejoice in the ever-growing sales of this wine the world over. It is my heartfelt wish that it spread joy, peace, and happiness.

Is champagne better today than in the course of years gone by?

There is not the slightest doubt that its development has been the object of painstaking research, which has sometimes ended in disaster before the glass blowers could find a way to make sufficiently strong bottles. We have only to recall the fantastic bottle breakage suffered by the unfortunate Benedictine monks of Hautvillers and Pierry, also by the early dealers in champagne. Much progress has been realized in every way. We have learned to remove the deposit that remains in the wine after fermentation; to perfect the remuage on the racks; to replace with corks the wooden *broqueleix* swathed in grease-impregnated fiber; to better our technique for removing the wine deposit; to study liquor composition; to effect a better blending for the satisfaction of our different customers; to scientifically mix for the cuvée not only different wines of the same year but also of the preceding years, so that all years of the same cru come out appreciably similar. All this has contributed to silence the reactionaries who in 1713 asserted that bubbling was but the "characteristic of inferior wine."

What is the greatest amount of champagne you have consumed on one occasion?

It would be difficult to come up with a precise figure. But allow me to tell of a memorable event. In 1936 we signed an agreement resulting in the establishment of these Commissions Paritaires soon to be adopted throughout the champagne region and through which all problems could be peacefully settled. I was a member of a board of managers from the five most important champagne firms. We started our talks at 9 a.m. in Maurice Paillard's garden; when we left at 11 p.m. we abandoned on the lawn twenty-five empty champagne bottles; for five people that represents five bottles each, but it was with perfectly clear heads that we took the way home!

During the tasting period which precedes the mixing of the wines to go into one cuvée, I believe that one does not drink all the wines that are offered. Is that true?

That is so. One has to rely on one's eye, one's nose, and then only on one's palate. Only incidentally, and to put the finishing touch to the cuvée, does one take a sip of the finished mixture. The gustative

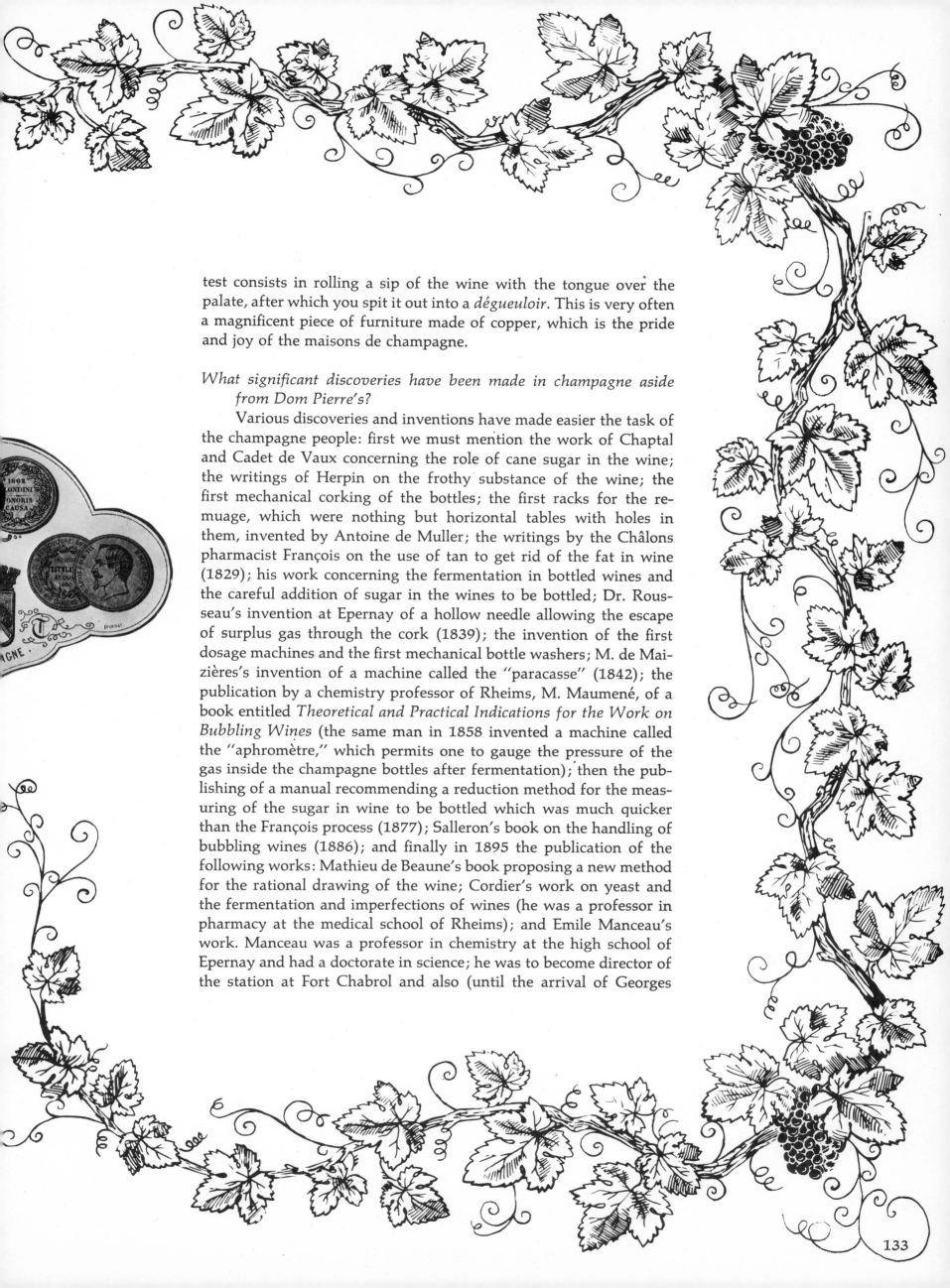

test consists in rolling a sip of the wine with the tongue over the palate, after which you spit it out into a *dégueuloir*. This is very often a magnificent piece of furniture made of copper, which is the pride and joy of the maisons de champagne.

What significant discoveries have been made in champagne aside from Dom Pierre's?

Various discoveries and inventions have made easier the task of the champagne people: first we must mention the work of Chaptal and Cadet de Vaux concerning the role of cane sugar in the wine; the writings of Herpin on the frothy substance of the wine; the first mechanical corking of the bottles; the first racks for the remuage, which were nothing but horizontal tables with holes in them, invented by Antoine de Muller; the writings by the Châlons pharmacist François on the use of tan to get rid of the fat in wine (1829); his work concerning the fermentation in bottled wines and the careful addition of sugar in the wines to be bottled; Dr. Rousseau's invention at Epernay of a hollow needle allowing the escape of surplus gas through the cork (1839); the invention of the first dosage machines and the first mechanical bottle washers; M. de Maizières's invention of a machine called the "paracasse" (1842); the publication by a chemistry professor of Rheims, M. Maumené, of a book entitled *Theoretical and Practical Indications for the Work on Bubbling Wines* (the same man in 1858 invented a machine called the "aphromètre," which permits one to gauge the pressure of the gas inside the champagne bottles after fermentation); then the publishing of a manual recommending a reduction method for the measuring of the sugar in wine to be bottled which was much quicker than the François process (1877); Salleron's book on the handling of bubbling wines (1886); and finally in 1895 the publication of the following works: Mathieu de Beaune's book proposing a new method for the rational drawing of the wine; Cordier's work on yeast and the fermentation and imperfections of wines (he was a professor in pharmacy at the medical school of Rheims); and Emile Manceau's work. Manceau was a professor in chemistry at the high school of Epernay and had a doctorate in science; he was to become director of the station at Fort Chabrol and also (until the arrival of Georges

Chappaz) director of the Station Œnologique de Champagne, which was recognized by the Department of Agriculture. He was also the publisher of *Le Vigneron Champenois*. But along with these scientists and experts who have dealt with the problems of champagne, it would be unfair not to mention those admirable artists, the heads of the famous champagne firms, the managers of the cellars, and the buyers always seeking for higher quality grapes at harvest time, who all together have ensured the reputation of our champagne wines.

We must also mention the infinitely delicate taste of the ladies of Champagne who, at the side of their relatives and of their husbands, and sometimes in their widowhood as well, have with exquisite taste and extraordinary talent been able to direct the blending of the marvelous cuvées which safeguarded the reputation of their firms.

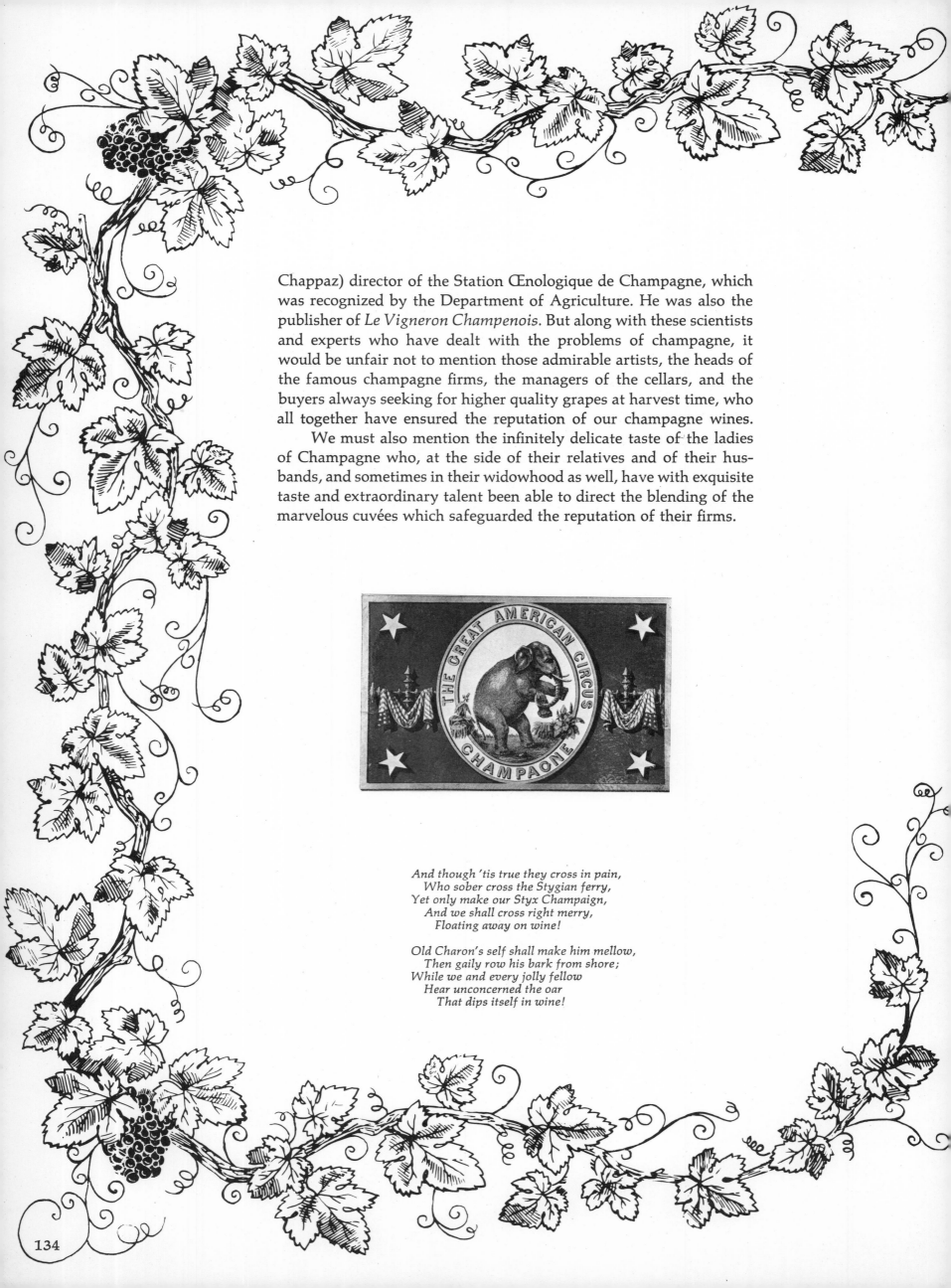

And though 'tis true they cross in pain,
Who sober cross the Stygian ferry,
Yet only make our Styx Champaign,
And we shall cross right merry,
Floating away on wine!

Old Charon's self shall make him mellow,
Then gaily row his bark from shore;
While we and every jolly fellow
Hear unconcerned the oar
That dips itself in wine!

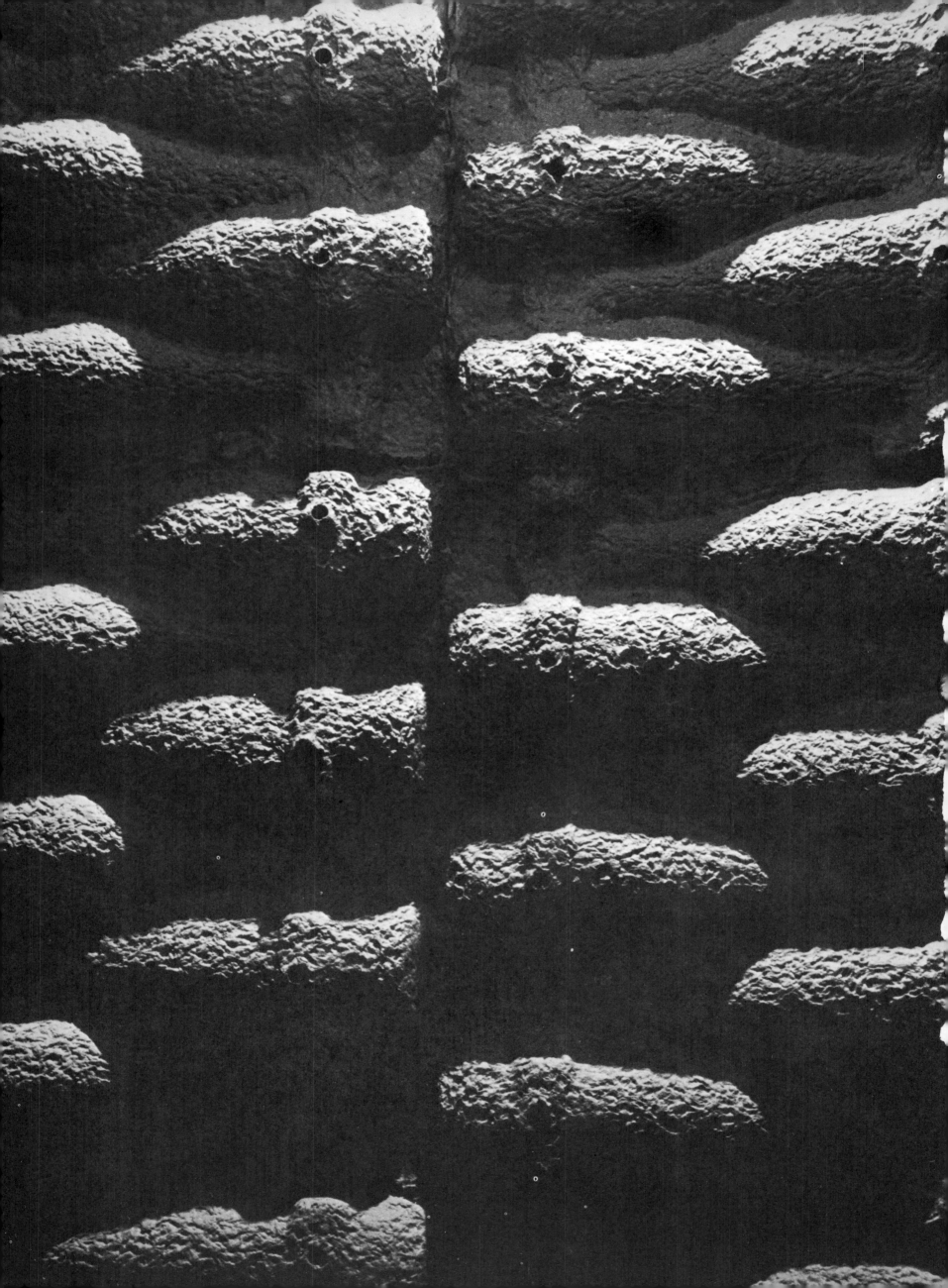

PROPRIÉTÉ DE LA MAISON J. B. CHAMONARD _ ÉPERNAY
CHAMPAGNE
De ROCHEGRÉ
ÉPERNAY
EXTRA-QUALITY
IMP. P. VERCASSON & Cie, 43, rue de Lancry, PARIS

CHAMPAGNE CHARLIE.

THE GREAT COMIC SONG WRITTEN & SUNG BY
GEORGE LEYBOURNE.

"FOR CHAMPAGNE CHARLIE IS MY NAME, CHAMPAGNE CHARLIE IS MY NAME, GOOD FOR ANY GAME AT NIGHT, MY BOYS, GOOD FOR ANY GAME AT NIGHT MY BOYS, | CHAMPAGNE CHARLIE IS MY NAME, CHAMPAGNE CHARLIE IS MY NAME GOOD FOR ANY GAME AT NIGHT, MY BOYS, WHO'LL COME AND JOIN ME IN A SPREE?

ENT. STA. HALL.

MUSIC BY
ALFRED LEE.

LONDON: C. SHEARD, 192 HIGH HOLBORN. W.C.

Pr 3/-

Messieurs !! voulez-vous conquérir les cœurs!!
CHAMPAGNE de la JARRETIÈRE
OFFREZ LE

Champagne de la Jarretière

ESTABLISHED 1858

in BOTTLE 1853

de Vita

HONI SOIT QUI MAL Y PENSE

Exiger la superbe PAIRE de JARRETIÈRES avec chaque bouteille

Imp. P VERCASSON & C.ie 43 Rue de Lancry, PARIS

CHAMPAGNE CHARLIE

Freely

The way I gained my ti-tle by a hob-by which I've got, Of

nev-er let-ting oth-ers pay how-ev-er long the shot. Who-ev-er drink at my ex-pense are

treat-ed all the same; From dukes and lords to cab-men down I make them drink cham-pagne. Oh!

Chorus
Moderately

Cham-pagne Char-lie is my name, Cham-pagne Char-lie is my

name.   Good for an - y game at night, my boys,

Good for an - y game at night, my boys.   Cham - pagne Char - lie is my

name,   Cham - pagne Char - lie is my name;

Good for an - y game at night, boys; who'll come and join me in a spree?

A bottle of Champagne
Frozen into a very vinous ice,
    Which leaves few drops of that immortal rain;
Yet in the very centre, past all price,
    About a liquid glassful will remain;
And this is stronger than the strongest grape
Could e'er express in its expanded shape:

'Tis the whole spirit brought to a quintessence;
    And thus the chilliest aspects may concentre
A hidden nectar under a cold presence.

Byron, Don Juan

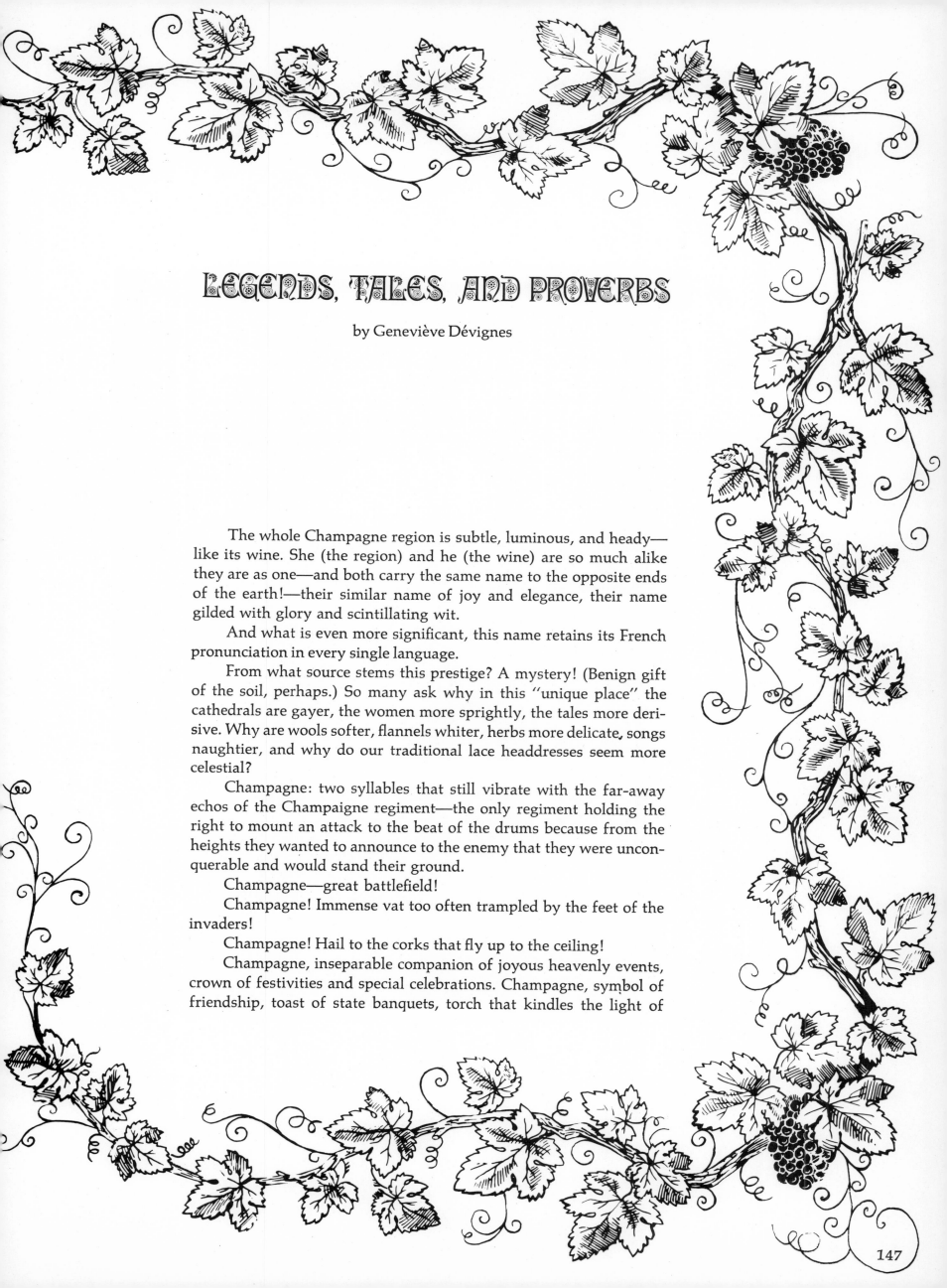

Legends, Tales, and Proverbs

by Geneviève Dévignes

The whole Champagne region is subtle, luminous, and heady—like its wine. She (the region) and he (the wine) are so much alike they are as one—and both carry the same name to the opposite ends of the earth!—their similar name of joy and elegance, their name gilded with glory and scintillating wit.

And what is even more significant, this name retains its French pronunciation in every single language.

From what source stems this prestige? A mystery! (Benign gift of the soil, perhaps.) So many ask why in this "unique place" the cathedrals are gayer, the women more sprightly, the tales more derisive. Why are wools softer, flannels whiter, herbs more delicate, songs naughtier, and why do our traditional lace headdresses seem more celestial?

Champagne: two syllables that still vibrate with the far-away echos of the Champaigne regiment—the only regiment holding the right to mount an attack to the beat of the drums because from the heights they wanted to announce to the enemy that they were unconquerable and would stand their ground.

Champagne—great battlefield!

Champagne! Immense vat too often trampled by the feet of the invaders!

Champagne! Hail to the corks that fly up to the ceiling!

Champagne, inseparable companion of joyous heavenly events, crown of festivities and special celebrations. Champagne, symbol of friendship, toast of state banquets, torch that kindles the light of triumph, ritual that launches steamships and airplanes! Remembrance of rebirth, joyful tear of anniversary, stamp of victory and peace, holy dedication of love. O Champagne! if to you are extended the hungry lips of lovers and the thirsty lips of the dying, is it not that you hold within your power the joy of life? Is it because you are, at one and the same time, my wine and my birthplace that I love you? Is it because I was, as were all who belong to me, baptized a second time in the lovely liquid which serves to sweeten the bitterness of the salt of Christianity for our newborn, that all existence seems worth while and bearable to me because of you?

Our babies in their diapers and in their cradles, tipsy at their birth, products of their native soil and of the vineyards, are enemies of vulgarity. All else that does not issue from the same stock is gross by comparison.

O Champagne! it is because of you that the motto of our minstrels and our nobles remains:

Stand in the forefront of the best
Oh my vibrant wine, my wine cloaked in the robes of state
For you are the descendant of the dawn of history!

Geneviève Dévignes

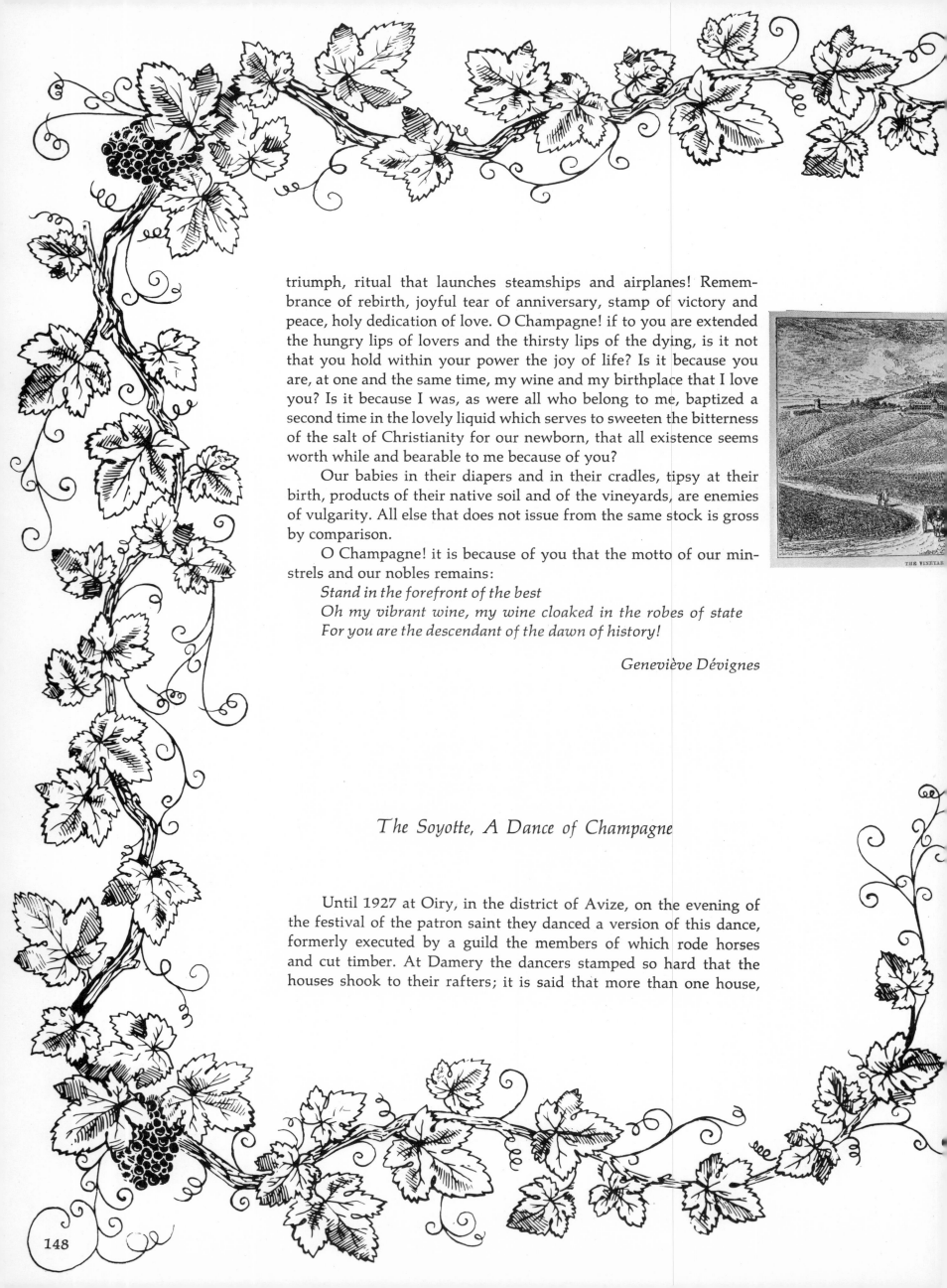

THE VINEYARD

The Soyotte, A Dance of Champagne

Until 1927 at Oiry, in the district of Avize, on the evening of the festival of the patron saint they danced a version of this dance, formerly executed by a guild the members of which rode horses and cut timber. At Damery the dancers stamped so hard that the houses shook to their rafters; it is said that more than one house,

undoubtedly dilapidated, caved in! As a result, the Soyotte was out-
lawed and forbidden.

The small revivification that I have made is executed by couples
facing each other, arms crossed, holding hands and dancing in a
quick, nimble, yet vigorous manner. It has always been most effec-
tive. I think that it is unnecessary to demonstrate the steps meticu-
lously because they are already in the process of being relearned with
ease in Champagne.

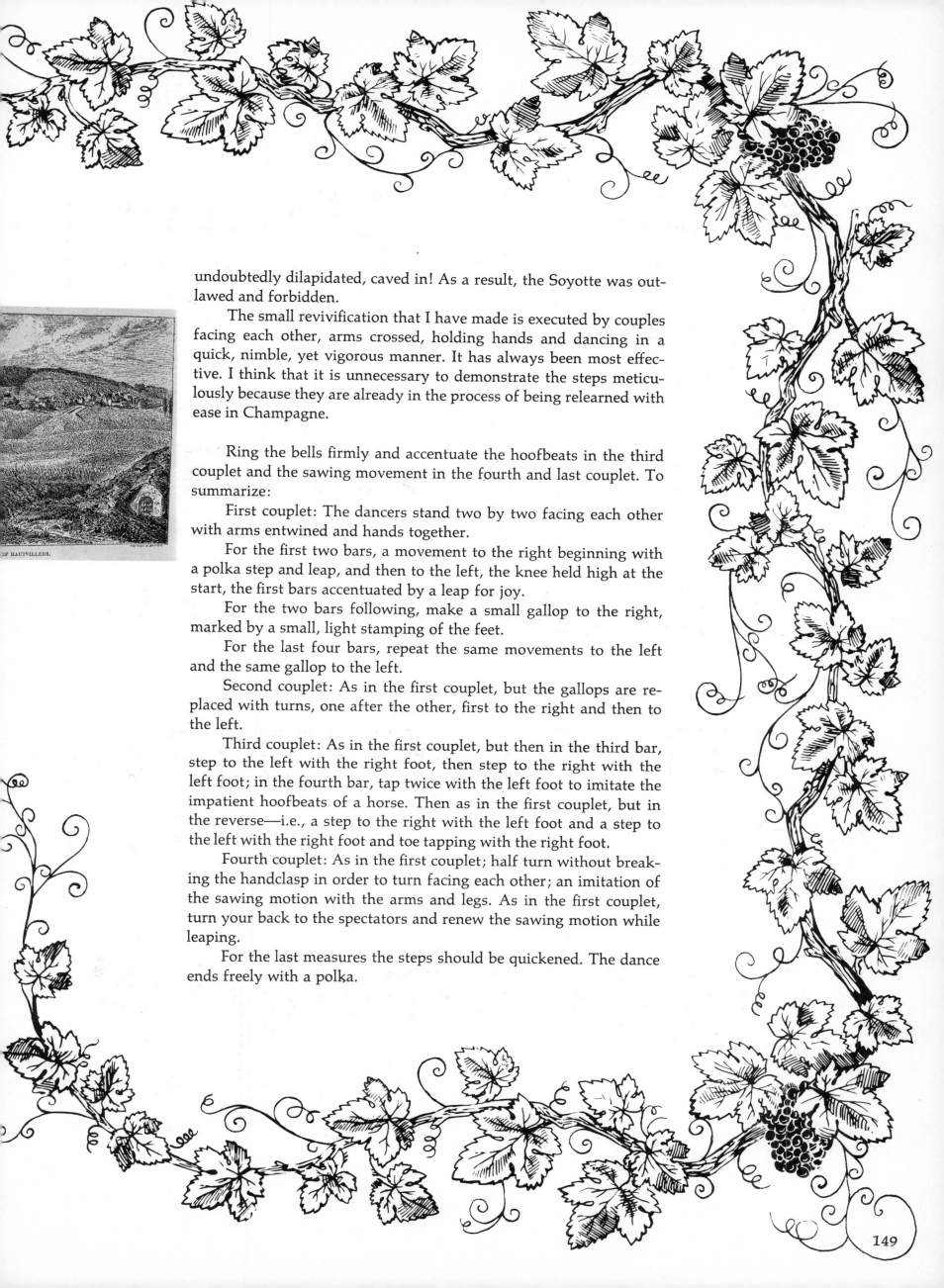

OF HAUTVILLERS.

Ring the bells firmly and accentuate the hoofbeats in the third
couplet and the sawing movement in the fourth and last couplet. To
summarize:

First couplet: The dancers stand two by two facing each other
with arms entwined and hands together.

For the first two bars, a movement to the right beginning with
a polka step and leap, and then to the left, the knee held high at the
start, the first bars accentuated by a leap for joy.

For the two bars following, make a small gallop to the right,
marked by a small, light stamping of the feet.

For the last four bars, repeat the same movements to the left
and the same gallop to the left.

Second couplet: As in the first couplet, but the gallops are replaced with turns, one after the other, first to the right and then to
the left.

Third couplet: As in the first couplet, but then in the third bar,
step to the left with the right foot, then step to the right with the
left foot; in the fourth bar, tap twice with the left foot to imitate the
impatient hoofbeats of a horse. Then as in the first couplet, but in
the reverse—i.e., a step to the right with the left foot and a step to
the left with the right foot and toe tapping with the right foot.

Fourth couplet: As in the first couplet; half turn without break-
ing the handclasp in order to turn facing each other; an imitation of
the sawing motion with the arms and legs. As in the first couplet,
turn your back to the spectators and renew the sawing motion while
leaping.

For the last measures the steps should be quickened. The dance
ends freely with a polka.

THE SOYOTTE DANCE OF CHAMPAGNE

Tempo de Polka

D'a - voir dan - sé la So - yotte Mon ru - ban S'en - vo - la!

Je suis darne et en ri - botte Mo' ca - det le r'trouv' ra!

Au pas, au

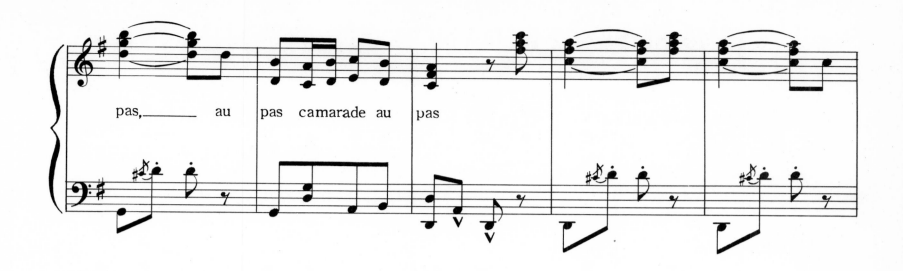

2
D'avoir dansé la soyotte
Mon bonnet s'envola!
Je suis darne et en ribotte
Mo'cadet le r'trouv'ra!

3
D'avoir dansé la soyotte
Mon sabot s'envola!
Je suis darne et en ribotte
Mo'cadet le r'trouv'ra!

THE SOYOTTE DANCE OF CHAMPAGNE

When I danced the "Soyotte",
My ribbon flew away.
I was giddy and tipsy,
But my younger sister will bring it back.

Keep step, keep step,
Keep step, fellow, keep step!

When I danced the "Soyotte"!
My bonnet flew away.
I was giddy and tipsy,
But my younger sister will bring it back.

When I danced the "Soyotte",
My shoe flew off.
I was giddy and tipsy,
But my younger sister will bring it back.

When I danced the "Soyotte",
My gentle heart fluttered away.
I was giddy and tipsy,
But my younger sister will bring it back.

The Grape That Ran Away

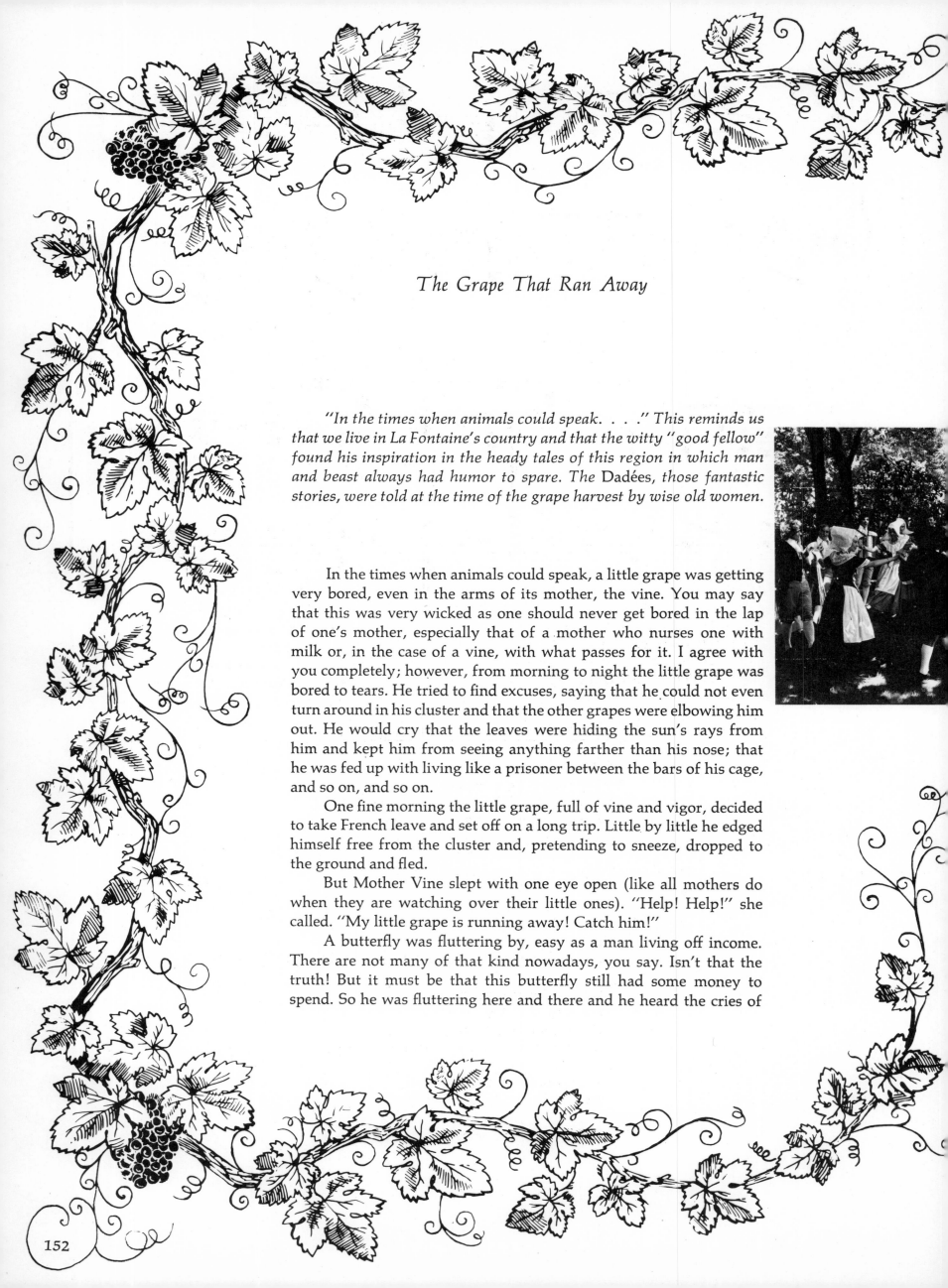

"In the times when animals could speak. . . ." This reminds us that we live in La Fontaine's country and that the witty "good fellow" found his inspiration in the heady tales of this region in which man and beast always had humor to spare. The Dadées, those fantastic stories, were told at the time of the grape harvest by wise old women.

In the times when animals could speak, a little grape was getting very bored, even in the arms of its mother, the vine. You may say that this was very wicked as one should never get bored in the lap of one's mother, especially that of a mother who nurses one with milk or, in the case of a vine, with what passes for it. I agree with you completely; however, from morning to night the little grape was bored to tears. He tried to find excuses, saying that he could not even turn around in his cluster and that the other grapes were elbowing him out. He would cry that the leaves were hiding the sun's rays from him and kept him from seeing anything farther than his nose; that he was fed up with living like a prisoner between the bars of his cage, and so on, and so on.

One fine morning the little grape, full of vine and vigor, decided to take French leave and set off on a long trip. Little by little he edged himself free from the cluster and, pretending to sneeze, dropped to the ground and fled.

But Mother Vine slept with one eye open (like all mothers do when they are watching over their little ones). "Help! Help!" she called. "My little grape is running away! Catch him!"

A butterfly was fluttering by, easy as a man living off income. There are not many of that kind nowadays, you say. Isn't that the truth! But it must be that this butterfly still had some money to spend. So he was fluttering here and there and he heard the cries of

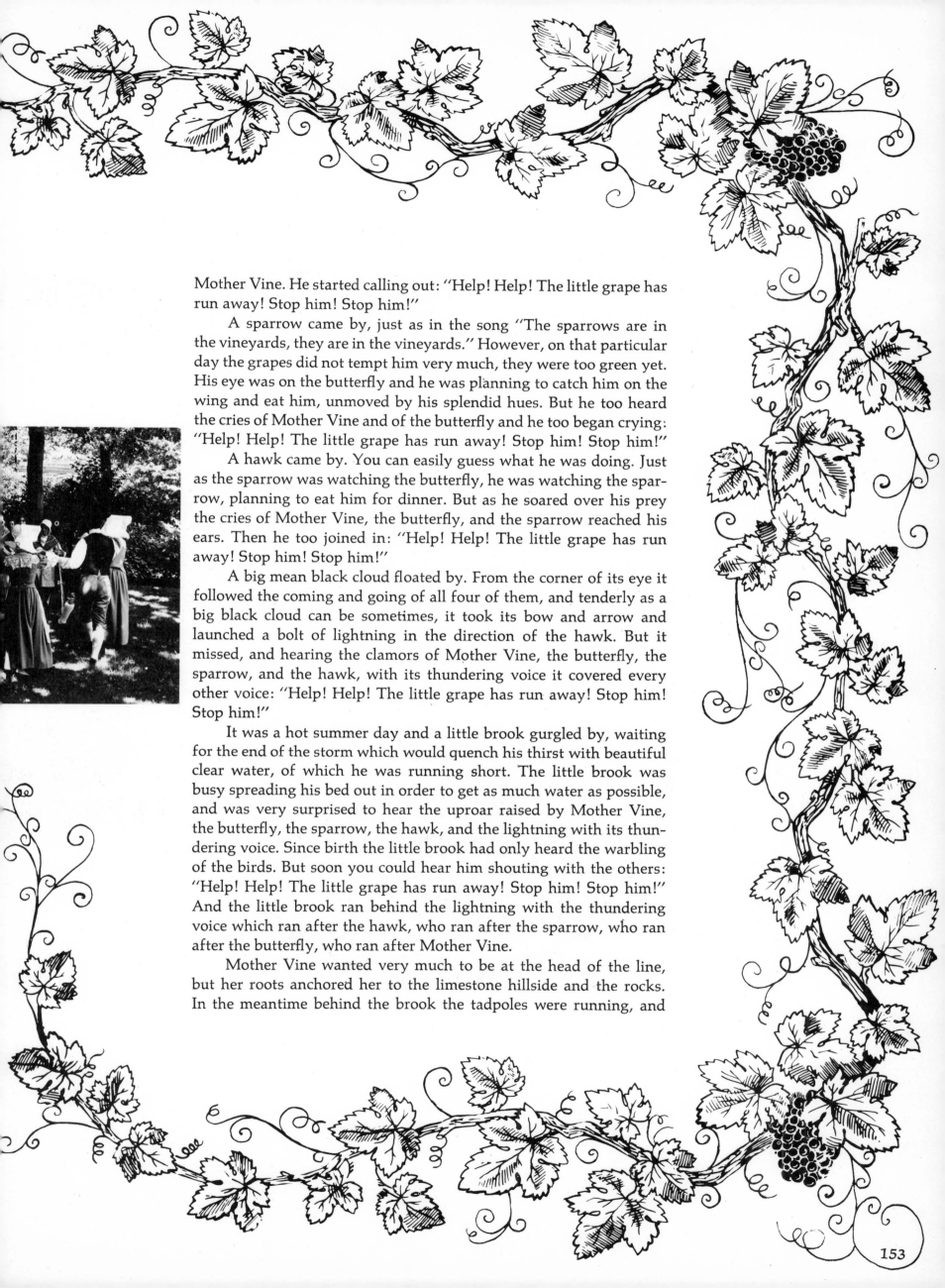

Mother Vine. He started calling out: "Help! Help! The little grape has run away! Stop him! Stop him!"

A sparrow came by, just as in the song "The sparrows are in the vineyards, they are in the vineyards." However, on that particular day the grapes did not tempt him very much, they were too green yet. His eye was on the butterfly and he was planning to catch him on the wing and eat him, unmoved by his splendid hues. But he too heard the cries of Mother Vine and of the butterfly and he too began crying: "Help! Help! The little grape has run away! Stop him! Stop him!"

A hawk came by. You can easily guess what he was doing. Just as the sparrow was watching the butterfly, he was watching the sparrow, planning to eat him for dinner. But as he soared over his prey the cries of Mother Vine, the butterfly, and the sparrow reached his ears. Then he too joined in: "Help! Help! The little grape has run away! Stop him! Stop him!"

A big mean black cloud floated by. From the corner of its eye it followed the coming and going of all four of them, and tenderly as a big black cloud can be sometimes, it took its bow and arrow and launched a bolt of lightning in the direction of the hawk. But it missed, and hearing the clamors of Mother Vine, the butterfly, the sparrow, and the hawk, with its thundering voice it covered every other voice: "Help! Help! The little grape has run away! Stop him! Stop him!"

It was a hot summer day and a little brook gurgled by, waiting for the end of the storm which would quench his thirst with beautiful clear water, of which he was running short. The little brook was busy spreading his bed out in order to get as much water as possible, and was very surprised to hear the uproar raised by Mother Vine, the butterfly, the sparrow, the hawk, and the lightning with its thundering voice. Since birth the little brook had only heard the warbling of the birds. But soon you could hear him shouting with the others: "Help! Help! The little grape has run away! Stop him! Stop him!" And the little brook ran behind the lightning with the thundering voice which ran after the hawk, who ran after the sparrow, who ran after the butterfly, who ran after Mother Vine.

Mother Vine wanted very much to be at the head of the line, but her roots anchored her to the limestone hillside and the rocks. In the meantime behind the brook the tadpoles were running, and behind them the sunfish, and behind the sunfish the trout. Behind the trout, the pike. Behind the pike, the big river drowning everything as it flowed by (it must have been the river Marne) and all of them shouted together: "Help! Help! The little grape has run away! Stop him! Stop him!"

This state of affairs could not last long! It was too much, too much of a hullabaloo, too much of an uproar in as peaceful a country as Champagne really is.

A kindhearted fairy restored peace and order: she caught the little grape and brought him back where he belonged, in the cluster in the arms of Mother Vine.

After his adventure Little Grape snickered to himself. He was once more a prisoner, but he was as proud as Lucifer to have stirred up such disorder. But he did not laugh long! September came and Little Grape, golden-ripe, felt more than ever his own importance. Someone entered the vineyard, picked the cluster from Mother Vine. And this someone was yourself, I recognized you from afar: Yes, it was you who ate the little grape. Come, my dear man, tell me tonight whether the grape was black or white.

This tale was told at Cernay-les-Reims and at Châtillon-sur-Marne, therefore in the best wine country.

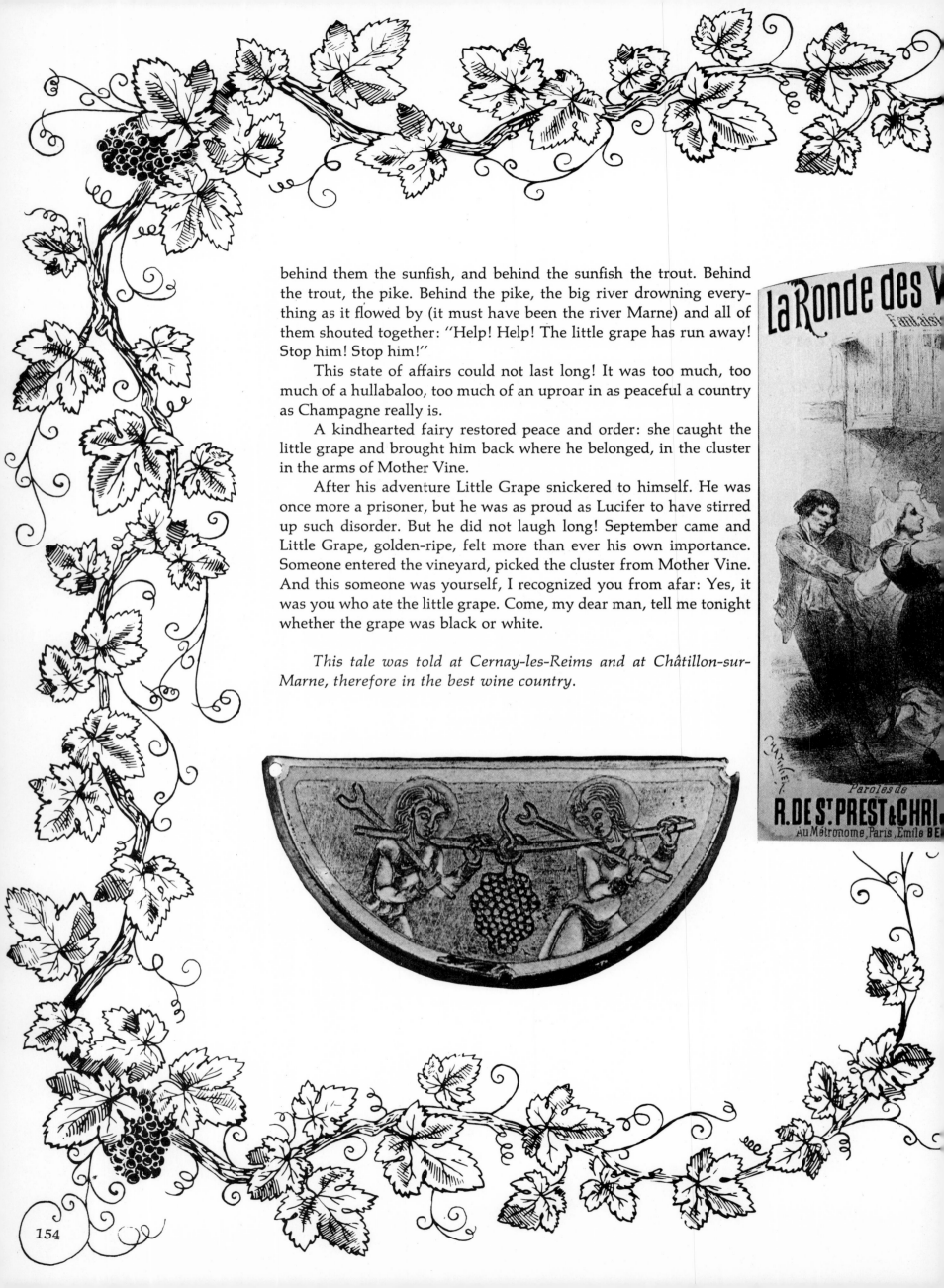

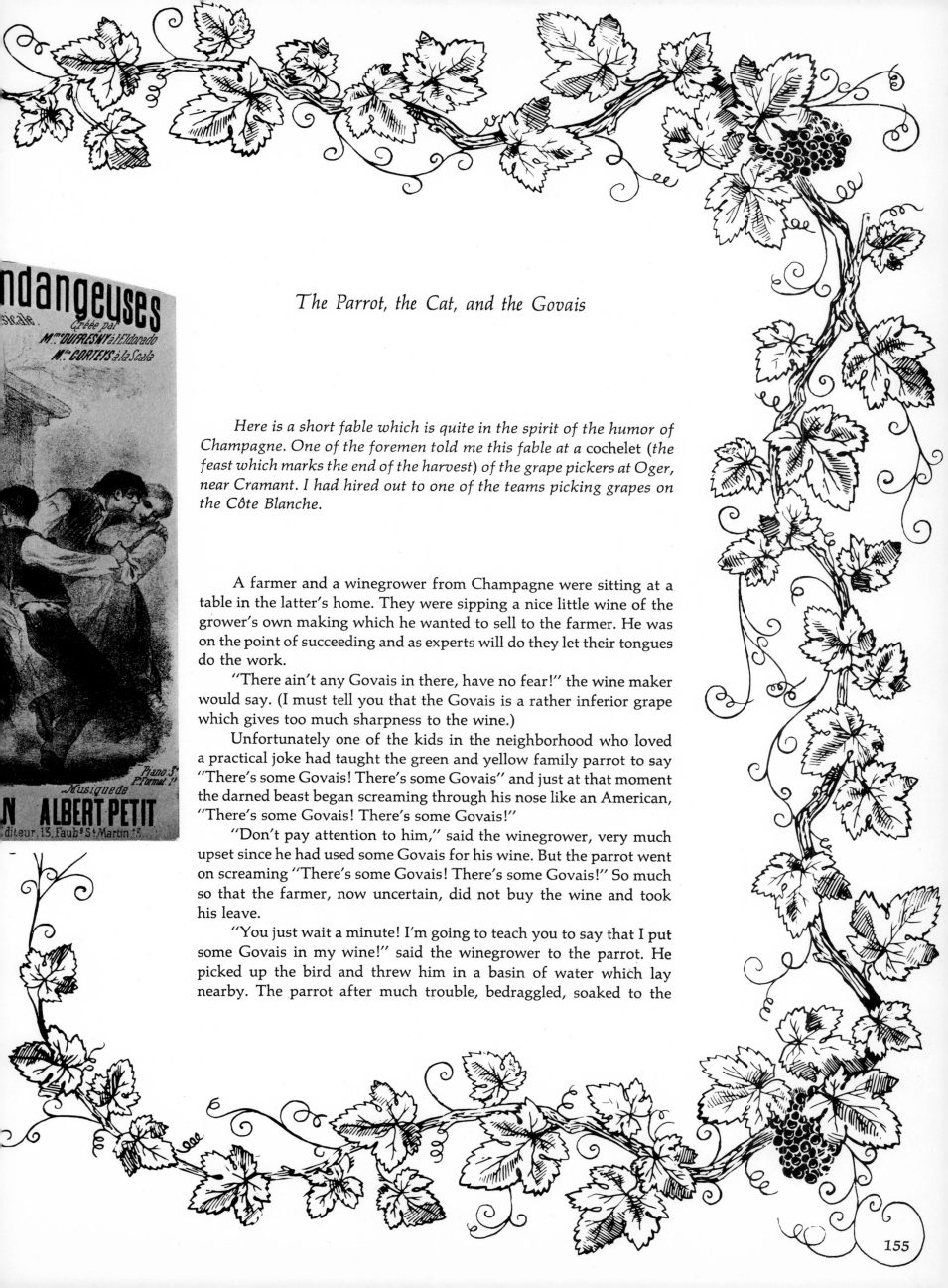

The Parrot, the Cat, and the Govais

Here is a short fable which is quite in the spirit of the humor of Champagne. One of the foremen told me this fable at a cochelet (the feast which marks the end of the harvest) of the grape pickers at Oger, near Cramant. I had hired out to one of the teams picking grapes on the Côte Blanche.

A farmer and a winegrower from Champagne were sitting at a table in the latter's home. They were sipping a nice little wine of the grower's own making which he wanted to sell to the farmer. He was on the point of succeeding and as experts will do they let their tongues do the work.

"There ain't any Govais in there, have no fear!" the wine maker would say. (I must tell you that the Govais is a rather inferior grape which gives too much sharpness to the wine.)

Unfortunately one of the kids in the neighborhood who loved a practical joke had taught the green and yellow family parrot to say "There's some Govais! There's some Govais" and just at that moment the darned beast began screaming through his nose like an American, "There's some Govais! There's some Govais!"

"Don't pay attention to him," said the winegrower, very much upset since he had used some Govais for his wine. But the parrot went on screaming "There's some Govais! There's some Govais!" So much so that the farmer, now uncertain, did not buy the wine and took his leave.

"You just wait a minute! I'm going to teach you to say that I put some Govais in my wine!" said the winegrower to the parrot. He picked up the bird and threw him in a basin of water which lay nearby. The parrot after much trouble, bedraggled, soaked to the

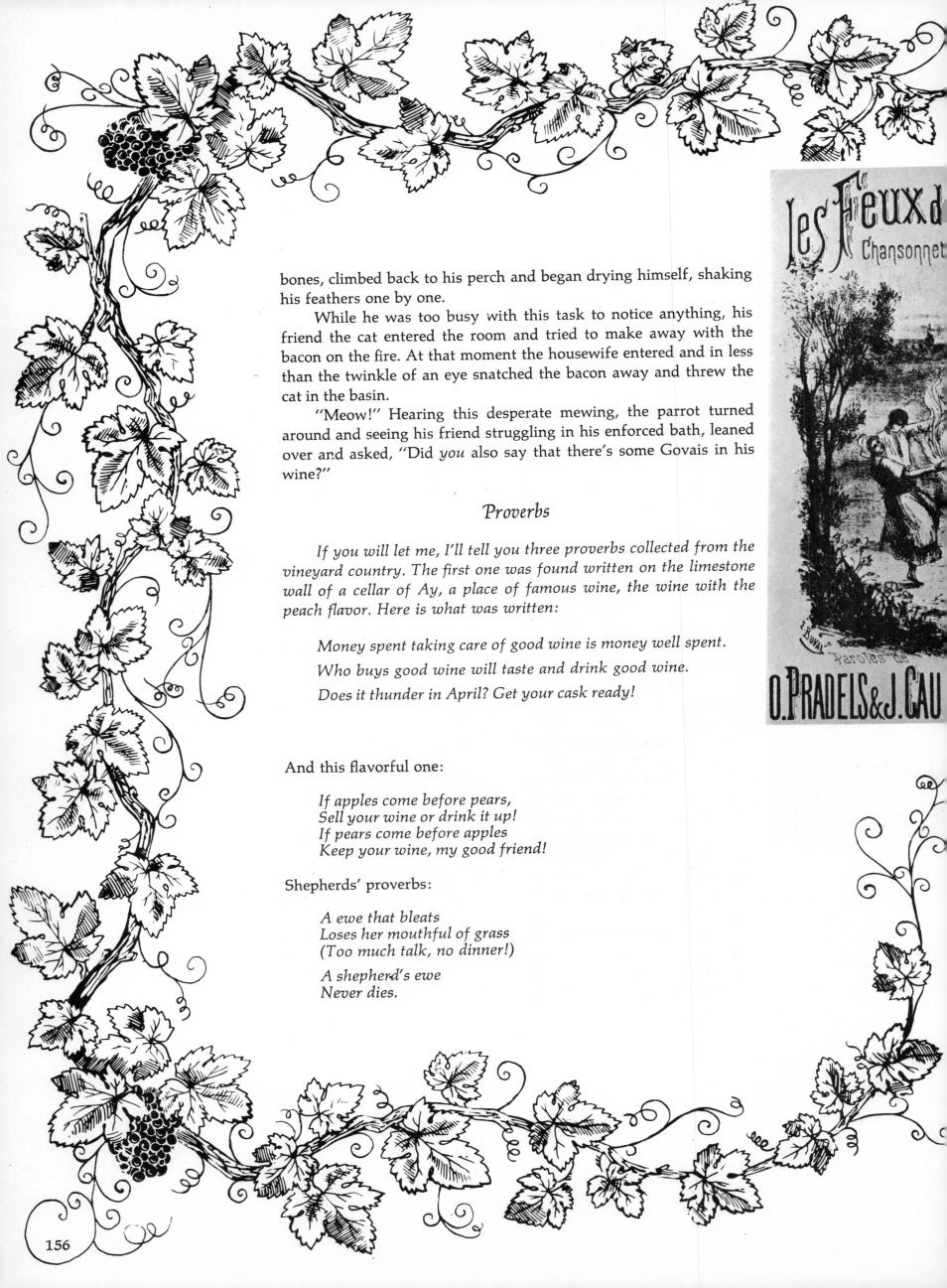

bones, climbed back to his perch and began drying himself, shaking his feathers one by one.

While he was too busy with this task to notice anything, his friend the cat entered the room and tried to make away with the bacon on the fire. At that moment the housewife entered and in less than the twinkle of an eye snatched the bacon away and threw the cat in the basin.

"Meow!" Hearing this desperate mewing, the parrot turned around and seeing his friend struggling in his enforced bath, leaned over and asked, "Did *you* also say that there's some Govais in his wine?"

Proverbs

If you will let me, I'll tell you three proverbs collected from the vineyard country. The first one was found written on the limestone wall of a cellar of Ay, a place of famous wine, the wine with the peach flavor. Here is what was written:

Money spent taking care of good wine is money well spent.

Who buys good wine will taste and drink good wine.

Does it thunder in April? Get your cask ready!

And this flavorful one:

If apples come before pears,
Sell your wine or drink it up!
If pears come before apples
Keep your wine, my good friend!

Shepherds' proverbs:

A ewe that bleats
Loses her mouthful of grass
(Too much talk, no dinner!)

A shepherd's ewe
Never dies.

Still more:

> Child who throws up
> Cures himself.
>
> Young wife and green lumber
> Will ruin the house.
>
> A fly on Saint Martin's day
> Is a better sign than a rabbit.

Excerpt from "Reims Magnifique" by Geneviève Dévignes:

Listen to these lovely lines from Count of Chevigné, who lived in Rheims in the early nineteenth century:

> Fortunate country, that of Champagne;
> The breath of exquisite wines hovers over the mountains.
> People are full of kindness, husbands full of trust,
> Women's hearts are as soft
> As the sheep in the countryside.

Here's Voltaire's opinion:

> Chloris and Egles are pouring for me
> With their own hand
> A good wine of Ay, whose captive bubble
> Sprang forth from the bottle
> And with lightning speed has thrust the cork away.

And La Fontaine has written:

> I would rather see the Turks
> Invading the country
> Than have the Germans mistreat
> Our wine.

The Song of the Wine Press

From the great plains of the Gironde
To the old Burgundian slopes,
Bronze or golden grapes, you will ripen,
Fulfilling the wishes of the winegrower,
Falling by the thousand from the vine trellises.
The wine press at the foot of the slope
Awaits your rosy sweet wine
To quench the cask's thirst.

Chorus:
Stand up, cup in hand,
And with a joyous refrain
Let's all together sing
Glory to the blessed wine press
From which love and hope
Stream round the world.
Let's sing, let's sing!
Let's sing to wine,
This king of the world!

For you, the sky full of comets
Pours hope on this French soil.
Through you will festivals be reborn
And with them the intoxication of the past.
In the air and under the boughs,
Autumn-time rings out
And the universe whispers
To bless your fertility.

Chorus:
You are the father of minstrels,
Who still make the hearts to sing.
You are the one who pours into the glasses
The courage that makes conquerors.
Return to us our glorious passions,
And under the wing of our great ancestors
Redden our tender lips,
And put some fire in our eyes!

Chorus:
Waiting for the strong men to come,
Wine press, kindle our desires
That the soul of the wine in our cellars
Respond to our yearning.
The good wine brings happy days of ecstasy
Round our table, and inspires us to sing, to laugh,
At the great banquets of love.

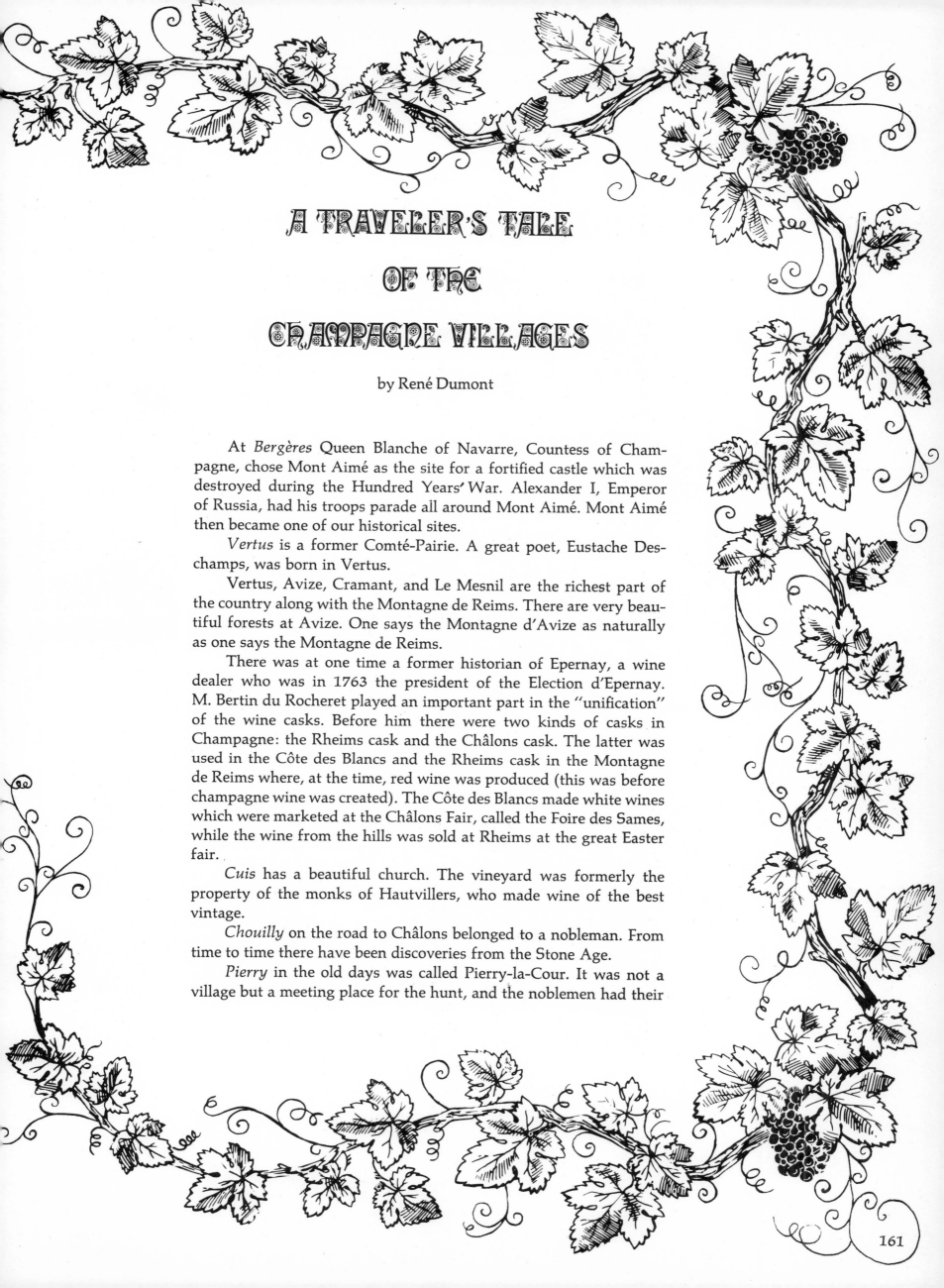

A TRAVELER'S TALE
OF THE
CHAMPAGNE VILLAGES

by René Dumont

At *Bergères* Queen Blanche of Navarre, Countess of Champagne, chose Mont Aimé as the site for a fortified castle which was destroyed during the Hundred Years' War. Alexander I, Emperor of Russia, had his troops parade all around Mont Aimé. Mont Aimé then became one of our historical sites.

Vertus is a former Comté-Pairie. A great poet, Eustache Deschamps, was born in Vertus.

Vertus, Avize, Cramant, and Le Mesnil are the richest part of the country along with the Montagne de Reims. There are very beautiful forests at Avize. One says the Montagne d'Avize as naturally as one says the Montagne de Reims.

There was at one time a former historian of Epernay, a wine dealer who was in 1763 the president of the Election d'Epernay. M. Bertin du Rocheret played an important part in the "unification" of the wine casks. Before him there were two kinds of casks in Champagne: the Rheims cask and the Châlons cask. The latter was used in the Côte des Blancs and the Rheims cask in the Montagne de Reims where, at the time, red wine was produced (this was before champagne wine was created). The Côte des Blancs made white wines which were marketed at the Châlons Fair, called the Foire des Sames, while the wine from the hills was sold at Rheims at the great Easter fair.

Cuis has a beautiful church. The vineyard was formerly the property of the monks of Hautvillers, who made wine of the best vintage.

Chouilly on the road to Châlons belonged to a nobleman. From time to time there have been discoveries from the Stone Age.

Pierry in the old days was called Pierry-la-Cour. It was not a village but a meeting place for the hunt, and the noblemen had their hunting lodges at this site. You can still find some of the manors which belonged to the aristocrats who used to come and hunt in this royal preserve. The forest belonged to the King of France, who, it is said, had expropriated it from the Duke of Enghien. Thus in the old days it was called the Forest of Enghien. As crown property it came into the hands of Napoleon I, who then sold it to Count Roy, the paymaster and peer of France whose daughter married the Marquis of Talhouët. This forest is still the property of the Marquis of Talhouët-Roy.

Pierry was also the site of the abbey of Châlons where Brother Oudard lived. Recently his tomb was discovered in the church of Pierry. Pierry was made into a parish not so very long ago, perhaps only two hundred years ago. The parish was at Saint-Julien, which was razed during the wars of religion. Then with the stones they built the church of Pierry.

As I have told you, Pierry was only the site of some hunting pavilions, the ones you can still see when you go through the countryside. I was even able to trace back the five last owners of Pierry, one of them being the famous Cazotte who was a retired navy man and lost his head during the Revolution because he believed in the royal cause. He did a lot of good at Pierry. Today's town hall used to be his castle. He also owned the château of La Marquetterie.

Moussy is a very recent place. It was not a parish. Moussy was part of Chavot, in fact not even Chavot, it was Mont Félix, which was a big commune of which Chavot, Courcourt, Vaudancourt, Mancy, and La Loge Turbane were hamlets, a part of Mont Félix. The village was built all around the church of Chavot. Now it stands alone and Chavot is farther along on the left, *Courcourt* above it and *Vaudancourt* much farther down. The church of Moussy dates from 1884; you can see that it is not very old. All this around you was hamlets with a castle on top belonging to the Count of Vermandois. Two brothers, Heribet and Herbert of Vermandois, built the castle in 954. It was destroyed at the same time as Saint-Julien during the wars of religion. We had diggings and found traces of foundations around the church. That's where the village was. At a site called Les Conardins on the edge of Pierry, there is a manor house, on your right, where a mill was set up. That is where the lands of the Conardins used to be.

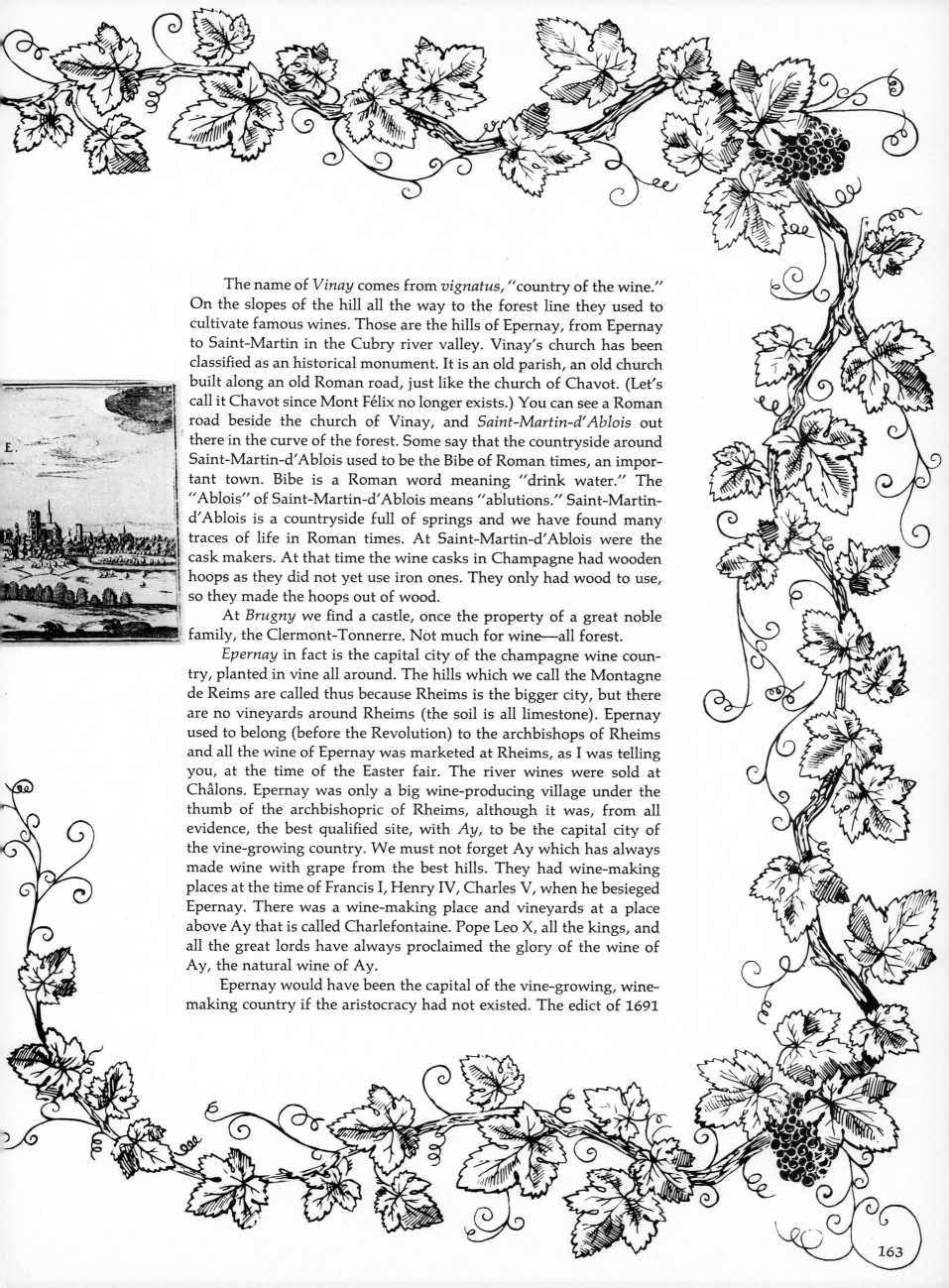

The name of *Vinay* comes from *vignatus*, "country of the wine." On the slopes of the hill all the way to the forest line they used to cultivate famous wines. Those are the hills of Epernay, from Epernay to Saint-Martin in the Cubry river valley. Vinay's church has been classified as an historical monument. It is an old parish, an old church built along an old Roman road, just like the church of Chavot. (Let's call it Chavot since Mont Félix no longer exists.) You can see a Roman road beside the church of Vinay, and *Saint-Martin-d'Ablois* out there in the curve of the forest. Some say that the countryside around Saint-Martin-d'Ablois used to be the Bibe of Roman times, an important town. Bibe is a Roman word meaning "drink water." The "Ablois" of Saint-Martin-d'Ablois means "ablutions." Saint-Martin-d'Ablois is a countryside full of springs and we have found many traces of life in Roman times. At Saint-Martin-d'Ablois were the cask makers. At that time the wine casks in Champagne had wooden hoops as they did not yet use iron ones. They only had wood to use, so they made the hoops out of wood.

At *Brugny* we find a castle, once the property of a great noble family, the Clermont-Tonnerre. Not much for wine—all forest.

Epernay in fact is the capital city of the champagne wine country, planted in vine all around. The hills which we call the Montagne de Reims are called thus because Rheims is the bigger city, but there are no vineyards around Rheims (the soil is all limestone). Epernay used to belong (before the Revolution) to the archbishops of Rheims and all the wine of Epernay was marketed at Rheims, as I was telling you, at the time of the Easter fair. The river wines were sold at Châlons. Epernay was only a big wine-producing village under the thumb of the archbishopric of Rheims, although it was, from all evidence, the best qualified site, with *Ay*, to be the capital city of the vine-growing country. We must not forget Ay which has always made wine with grape from the best hills. They had wine-making places at the time of Francis I, Henry IV, Charles V, when he besieged Epernay. There was a wine-making place and vineyards at a place above Ay that is called Charlefontaine. Pope Leo X, all the kings, and all the great lords have always proclaimed the glory of the wine of Ay, the natural wine of Ay.

Epernay would have been the capital of the vine-growing, wine-making country if the aristocracy had not existed. The edict of 1691 was abrogated and thanks to the Revolution and the wars of the Empire, wine dealers came to settle at Epernay. Today you can find very great Maisons de Champagne at Epernay.

At *Mareuil-sur-Ay* you find famous hills: Les Goisses. We have a saying, "The gentlemen of Mareuil, the people of Ay, the peasants of Avenay," and another which in speaking of wine says, "For Ay the fame, for Mareuil the good." Just small rivalries between villages. In Mareuil-sur-Ay you will find a lovely castle which belonged to the Duke of Montebello, a marshal of the First Empire.

Avenay was the site of a great convent. One finds at Avenay many mementos of that time, when the nuns were all daughters of the aristocracy. For instance we still have the church, which is one of the most beautiful in Champagne. Avenay is the birthplace of a famous family, the Paris family. Henri Paris was a well-known lawyer. Louis Paris was a member of the Académie Française, Paulin Paris a member of the Institut de France. Streets have been named for them in Rheims and Avenay. If you go to the Avenay cemetery you will discover that half the headstones bear their names.

Mutigny, which stands above Avenay, is also the site of a good vineyard. From the top of the hill you get a lovely view. Behind it stretches the forest.

At *Fontaine-sur-Ay* there are no vineyards to speak of. Fontaine owes its name to the springs that flow down from the foothills of the Montagne de Reims. In Champagne all springs are called fountains, and when you see them running down to this village you understand why we call it the capital of springs. They used to grow watercress there and sold it in the streets of Epernay, calling out, "Watercress from Fontaine!"

Louvois once had a medieval castle owned by Gaucher de Châtilloy. Then Michel le Tellier, Marquis de Louvois, Louis XIV's war minister, built on the site of this castle what remains today of his own castle. This country made up the holdings of the Louvois castle when it was Michel le Tellier's property. He had only one son, who entered a religious order and became one of the librarians of Louis XV. Therefore the land passed on to his nephew, the Marquis de Souvré, who squandered his fortune away: he used to give sumptuous receptions and was almost holding court at Louvois. The property then was taken over by the Dames de France, Sophie, Victoire, and Ade-

laïde, who were the daughters of Louis XV. They bought the Louvois holdings and were here when the Revolution caught up with them. They were well liked and well thought of here.

This is also where you will find the *Chemin des Dames* where many bitter battles were fought in 1914–1918 between the Aisne and Ailette rivers. It took its name from the fact that the Dames de France used this road when they went to visit their lady-in-waiting Mme. de Narbonne at the château of La Bove. In our own part of the country at Verzy, Villers, Marmery, Mailly, and Verzenay one finds the vineyard of the Dames de France and the woods of the Dames de France, all in memory of these three princesses. In front of the Louvois castle there is an Allée des Dames.

Tours-sur-Marne is not a Champagne name. At one time Charles the Bald, King of France, owned a castle on top of Mont Aigu, between Tours and Avenay. He presented it to the dean of Tours (in Touraine) who made a priory of it and gave it its name. They had a mill on the Marne river which was still being used not so long ago. From an archaeological point of view Tours is very interesting. We have found many burial mounds from the Stone Age, Celtic mounds which were really pits.

Now we come to *Trepail*, where there is an old church built of local stone called *burge*. I was the first and only one to discover all the quarries of burge hidden on this Montagne de Reims. It was used as a filler for the Rheims cathedral, the church of Saint-Rémi, those of Ambonnay, Bouzy, Trepail, Verzenay, Avenay—and once upon a time for the church of Verzy, which has since been demolished. Trepail has a subterranean river which is quite interesting to see. There was another one at Villers-Marmery and another at Verzy on the eastern slope of the Montagne de Reims. Trepail uses its own water; water is free of charge at Trepail.

Then we come to *Verzy*, which was the site of a Benedictine abbey. There were two of them. The first was founded by Queen Suavegotte, the wife of one of Clovis's sons, who granted large holdings to the abbey. This monastery occupied the center of the village. A nobleman from Limoges, Saint Basle, whose name was Basole in his lifetime, stopped here. He became a hermit and lived on the top of the mountain, praying to God. After a while he left for Lorraine to spread the word of God. You will find many villages in Lorraine

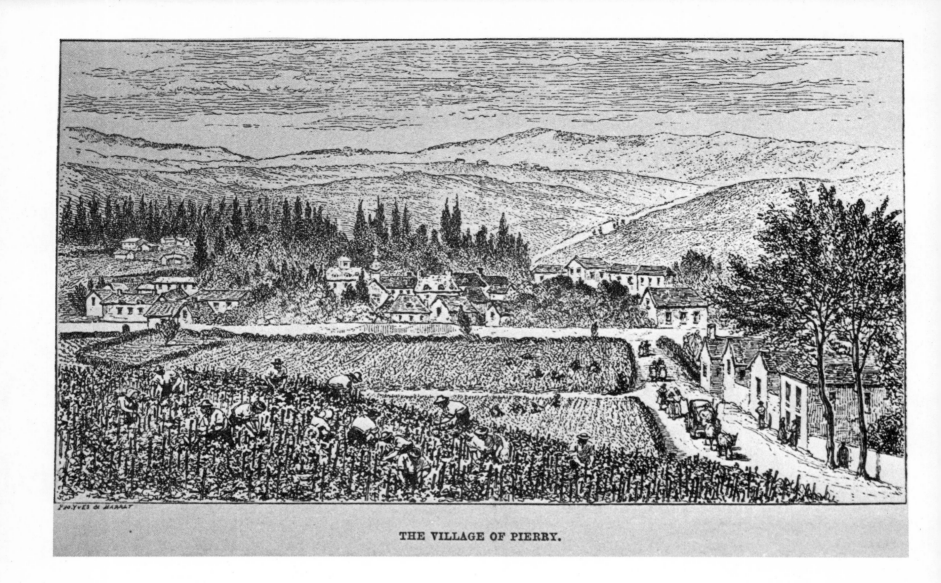

THE VILLAGE OF PIERRY.

GENERAL VIEW OF AVIZE.

THE CHAMPAGNE VINTAGE IN THE NEIGHBOURHOOD OF EPERNAY.

THE VINEYARDS OF BOUZY.

that bear his name: Dombasle-sur-Meurthe, Dombasle-en-Argonne, Dombasle-en-Xaintois, Dombasle-devant-Darney, and the Bazoilles of Lorraine. He played an important part in the evangelization of Lorraine, he and Saint Remy of Rheims. The latter has also given his name to villages: Remiremont and Domrémy, birthplace of Joan of Arc. From a religious point of view the eastern part of France, the kingdom of Austrasia, was ahead of its time because of the conversion of Clovis at Rheims.

Saint Basle came back to Verzy and died at a place called the Hermitage. Now the name has been changed to Mont Sinaï.* That is where he was buried. In memory of him Saint Nivard, who was archbishop of Rheims, built the second monastery of Verzy, on top of the mountain, alongside the road to Faux. Unfortunately this monastery was also destroyed at the time of the Revolution. It was a very important monastery built by Saint Nivard, who also founded the abbey of Hautvillers.

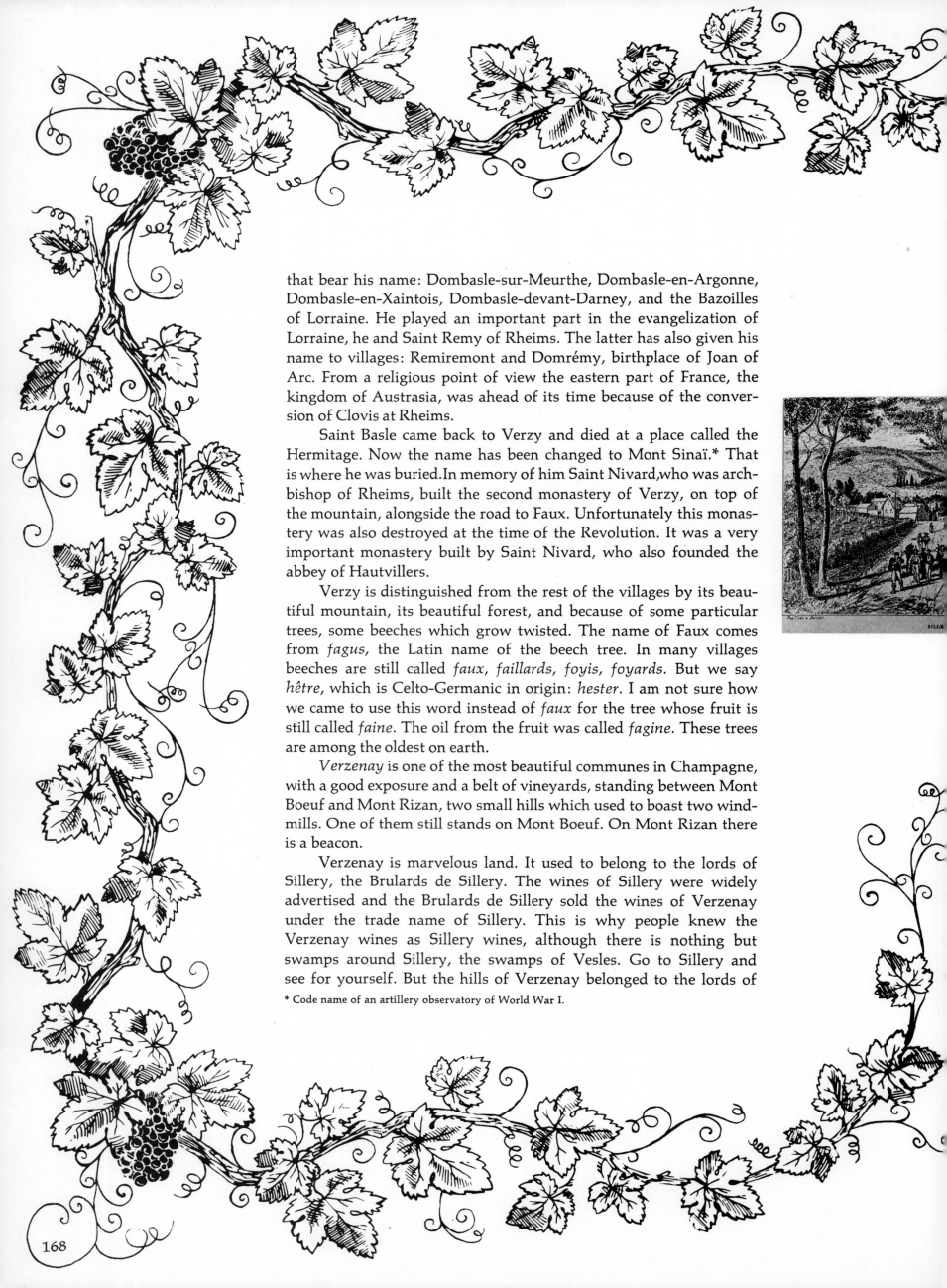

Verzy is distinguished from the rest of the villages by its beautiful mountain, its beautiful forest, and because of some particular trees, some beeches which grow twisted. The name of Faux comes from *fagus*, the Latin name of the beech tree. In many villages beeches are still called *faux, faillards, foyis, foyards*. But we say *hêtre*, which is Celto-Germanic in origin: *hester*. I am not sure how we came to use this word instead of *faux* for the tree whose fruit is still called *faine*. The oil from the fruit was called *fagine*. These trees are among the oldest on earth.

Verzenay is one of the most beautiful communes in Champagne, with a good exposure and a belt of vineyards, standing between Mont Boeuf and Mont Rizan, two small hills which used to boast two windmills. One of them still stands on Mont Boeuf. On Mont Rizan there is a beacon.

Verzenay is marvelous land. It used to belong to the lords of Sillery, the Brulards de Sillery. The wines of Sillery were widely advertised and the Brulards de Sillery sold the wines of Verzenay under the trade name of Sillery. This is why people knew the Verzenay wines as Sillery wines, although there is nothing but swamps around Sillery, the swamps of Vesles. Go to Sillery and see for yourself. But the hills of Verzenay belonged to the lords of

* Code name of an artillery observatory of World War I.

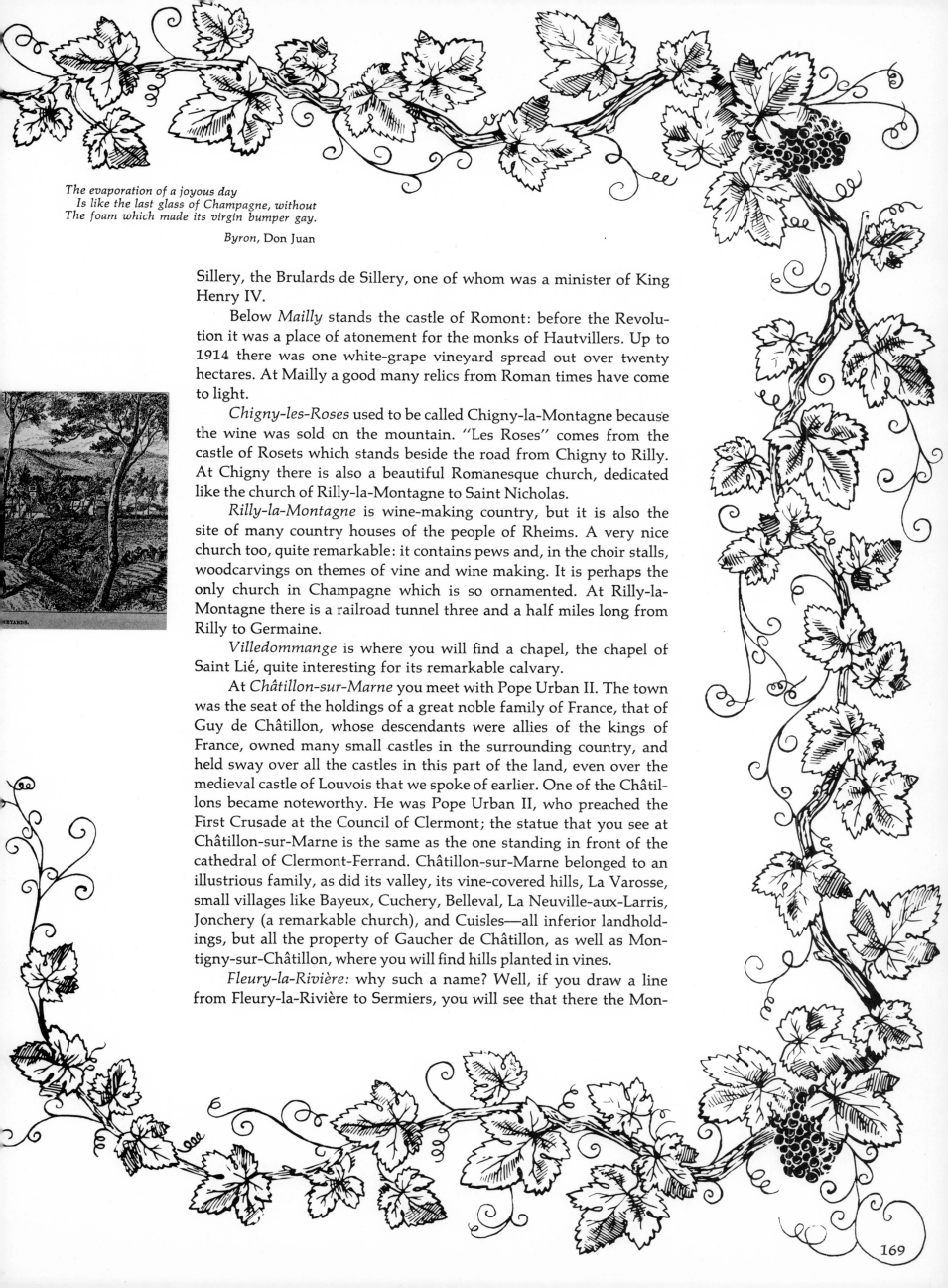

Sillery, the Brulards de Sillery, one of whom was a minister of King Henry IV.

Below *Mailly* stands the castle of Romont: before the Revolution it was a place of atonement for the monks of Hautvillers. Up to 1914 there was one white-grape vineyard spread out over twenty hectares. At Mailly a good many relics from Roman times have come to light.

Chigny-les-Roses used to be called Chigny-la-Montagne because the wine was sold on the mountain. "Les Roses" comes from the castle of Rosets which stands beside the road from Chigny to Rilly. At Chigny there is also a beautiful Romanesque church, dedicated like the church of Rilly-la-Montagne to Saint Nicholas.

Rilly-la-Montagne is wine-making country, but it is also the site of many country houses of the people of Rheims. A very nice church too, quite remarkable: it contains pews and, in the choir stalls, woodcarvings on themes of vine and wine making. It is perhaps the only church in Champagne which is so ornamented. At Rilly-la-Montagne there is a railroad tunnel three and a half miles long from Rilly to Germaine.

Villedommange is where you will find a chapel, the chapel of Saint Lié, quite interesting for its remarkable calvary.

At *Châtillon-sur-Marne* you meet with Pope Urban II. The town was the seat of the holdings of a great noble family of France, that of Guy de Châtillon, whose descendants were allies of the kings of France, owned many small castles in the surrounding country, and held sway over all the castles in this part of the land, even over the medieval castle of Louvois that we spoke of earlier. One of the Châtillons became noteworthy. He was Pope Urban II, who preached the First Crusade at the Council of Clermont; the statue that you see at Châtillon-sur-Marne is the same as the one standing in front of the cathedral of Clermont-Ferrand. Châtillon-sur-Marne belonged to an illustrious family, as did its valley, its vine-covered hills, La Varosse, small villages like Bayeux, Cuchery, Belleval, La Neuville-aux-Larris, Jonchery (a remarkable church), and Cuisles—all inferior landholdings, but all the property of Gaucher de Châtillon, as well as Montigny-sur-Châtillon, where you will find hills planted in vines.

Fleury-la-Rivière: why such a name? Well, if you draw a line from Fleury-la-Rivière to Sermiers, you will see that there the Montagne de Reims ends; you have come down into the plain. Thus they got the names "Fleury that sells along the river," and (formerly) "Sermiers-on-the-Mountain," since it sold its wines on the mountain. Both villages were once important centers because the mountain wines were red wines, and the river wines were sold at Châlons.

Venteuil owes its name to its location on the heights: windy country. Venteuil is good hill for wine, with two little hamlets, Artis and Tincourt. The same saying goes for Venteuil as for Trepail: "At Venteuil you take three drinks: one for Venteuil, one for Artis, one for Tincourt." It was at Venteuil that the 1911 revolt of the Champagne vintners started. The winegrowers were unable to sell their wine because unscrupulous wine dealers were getting their wine from the South and turning it into sparkling champagne. So one fine day, being completely disgusted and also a little starved—perhaps also after a little drinking here and there—they went down to Damery, entered a wine dealer's shop (one whom they knew to sell fraudulent wine), broke up everything in sight in the cellars, and rolled the carts down into the Marne. When the police and the troops arrived, there was no one to be seen. All had left and entrenched themselves at Venteuil. They negotiated with the horsemen of the Thirtieth Regiment of Dragoons. This was the start of the vintners' revolt; 15,000 rioters went down to Epernay to protest. The soldiers pushed them back in the direction of Ay, and at Ay they set fire to several Maisons de Champagne and to the Center of the village. There must have been some with a little too much to drink. They were led by some revolutionaries and anarchists who came down from Paris.

Damery, which stands below Venteuil, has a beautiful church. Many Gallo-Roman relics were uncovered at Damery. We even found a mint. Damery is very important for ancient finds. We call the people of Damery the *neyeux de saint*, a corruption of *noyeurs de saint*, that is to say, "the people who drown saints." There were great cherry orchards at Damery. On Saint George's day all the cherry trees froze up. As you know, the saying goes, "When the weather is fine on Saint George's day, cherries are already yours to eat." So because of the frost on Saint George's day the people of Damery were so furious they went to the church, got Saint George's statue, and threw it in the Marne. But the statue was carved of wood and the

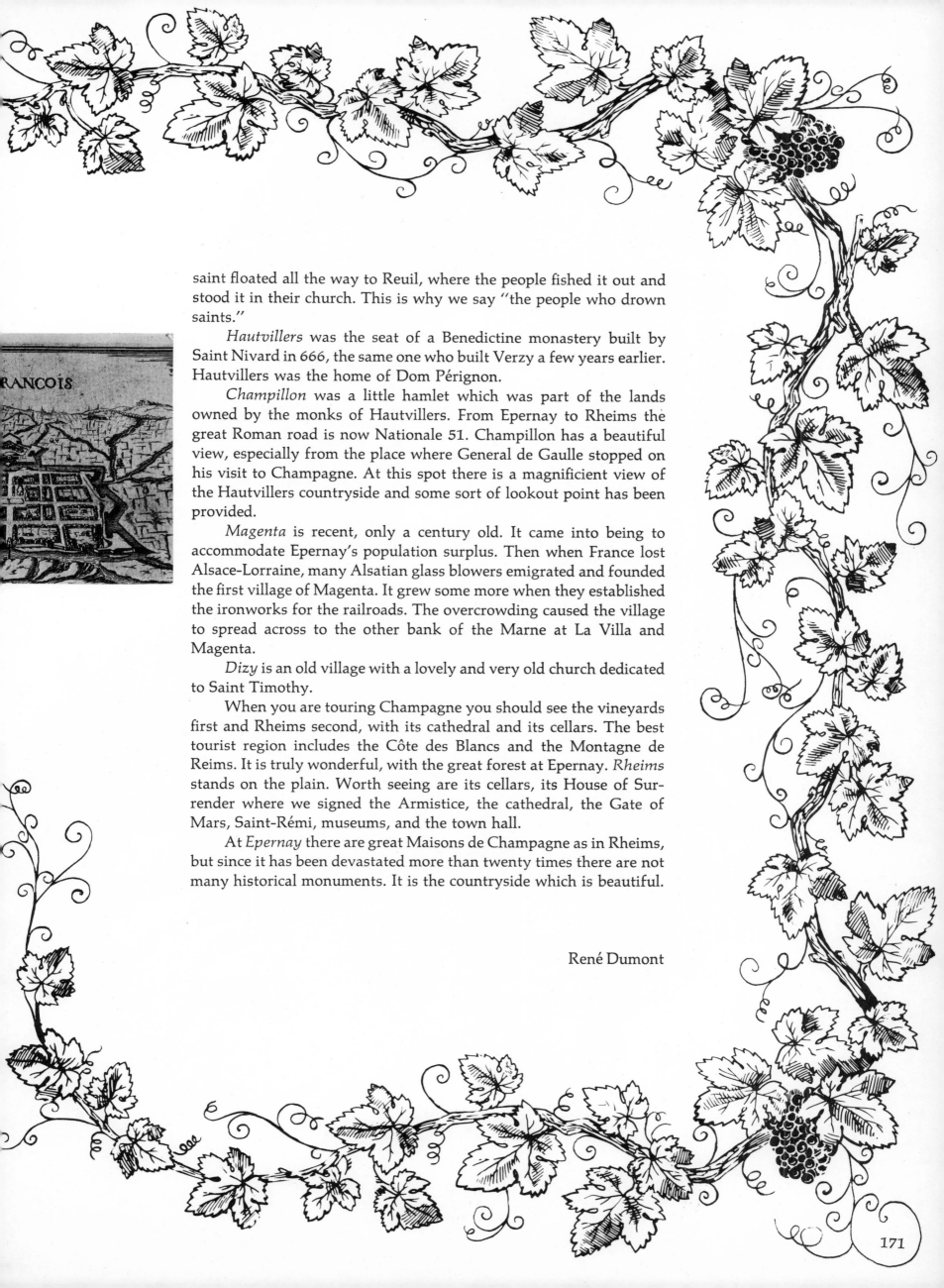

saint floated all the way to Reuil, where the people fished it out and stood it in their church. This is why we say "the people who drown saints."

Hautvillers was the seat of a Benedictine monastery built by Saint Nivard in 666, the same one who built Verzy a few years earlier. Hautvillers was the home of Dom Pérignon.

Champillon was a little hamlet which was part of the lands owned by the monks of Hautvillers. From Epernay to Rheims the great Roman road is now Nationale 51. Champillon has a beautiful view, especially from the place where General de Gaulle stopped on his visit to Champagne. At this spot there is a magnificient view of the Hautvillers countryside and some sort of lookout point has been provided.

Magenta is recent, only a century old. It came into being to accommodate Epernay's population surplus. Then when France lost Alsace-Lorraine, many Alsatian glass blowers emigrated and founded the first village of Magenta. It grew some more when they established the ironworks for the railroads. The overcrowding caused the village to spread across to the other bank of the Marne at La Villa and Magenta.

Dizy is an old village with a lovely and very old church dedicated to Saint Timothy.

When you are touring Champagne you should see the vineyards first and Rheims second, with its cathedral and its cellars. The best tourist region includes the Côte des Blancs and the Montagne de Reims. It is truly wonderful, with the great forest at Epernay. *Rheims* stands on the plain. Worth seeing are its cellars, its House of Surrender where we signed the Armistice, the cathedral, the Gate of Mars, Saint-Rémi, museums, and the town hall.

At *Epernay* there are great Maisons de Champagne as in Rheims, but since it has been devastated more than twenty times there are not many historical monuments. It is the countryside which is beautiful.

René Dumont

TRADITIONAL RECIPES

OF CHAMPAGNE

Chicken in Red Wine

Coq au Vin Bouzy

1 2½-to 3-pound frying chicken
2 cloves of garlic
1 *bouquet garni* (thyme, bay leaf, parsley)
3 large onions, quartered
4 tablespoons flour
½ bottle red Bouzy wine
2 pounds tomato purée
  salt, pepper
½ pound fresh mushrooms
3 to 4 ounces lean bacon
12 small white onions

Cut up chicken: legs, wings, back, and breast. Sauté with a little cooking oil in heavy casserole. When chicken is well browned, add garlic, *bouquet garni*, and big onions. When entire mixture is lightly browned, add the flour, red Bouzy wine, and tomato purée. Also add enough water to cover chicken. Add salt and pepper. Cover casserole and simmer slowly 60 to 90 minutes. While chicken is cooking, slice mushrooms very thin and toss into hot butter. Dice bacon, drop in boiling water, and drain. Sauté bacon in butter until lightly browned, then mix with mushrooms. Add some of chicken gravy. In a frying pan, glaze the small onions in butter, salt, and sugar. Cover pan. When onions are tender, remove lid and allow liquid to evaporate until onions are glazed brown. Arrange chicken on a serving platter garnished with the mushrooms, bacon, glazed onions, and sauce. Yield: 4 servings.

Roast Chicken in Champagne

Poularde au Champagne

1 4½-to 5-pound roasting chicken
 salt and pepper
4 ounces butter
 softened butter
1 jigger champagne brandy
½ bottle champagne
9 to 10 ounces fresh mushrooms precooked
3 egg yolks
½ pint cream

Sprinkle cavity of chicken with salt and pepper. In a large skillet, melt the butter and place chicken in it; gently turn chicken without allowing it to brown. Pour champagne brandy over chicken and ignite with a match. Add champagne, salt, and pepper. Cover and simmer slowly for 30 minutes. Slice mushrooms, which have been preboiled in salt water. Lift chicken out of skillet and thicken gravy with softened butter. Combine egg yolks and cream and add mixture to gravy without boiling it. Carve chicken, arrange on a serving platter, garnish with sliced mushrooms and sauce. Yield: 4 servings.

Salade au Lard

2 ounces salt pork
2 pounds potatoes
1 large escarole or 2 pounds dandelion greens
   salt and pepper

Dice the salt pork; cook well.
Dice the potatoes.
Place in kettle, cover with water, and add salt.
Bring to a boil.
When potatoes are tender, drain and remove.
Place potatoes in an earthenware bowl and place over a double boiler.
Add the greens, salt, pepper, and the cooked diced salt pork.
Toss the salad and serve.
Yield: 6 servings.

Boiled Dinner Champenoise

Potée Champenoise

Pork:

4 soup sausages lightly smoked (Polish sausage)
3 small ham hocks
2 to 2½ pounds spareribs
1½ pounds lean bacon
1½ pounds boneless shoulder, lightly smoked

Optional:

1 fowl (stewing chicken)
1½ pounds stewing beef

Vegetables:

bouquet garni (thyme, bay leaf, parsley)
salt and pepper
thinly sliced pieces of bread
3 leeks
2 pounds carrots
1 large head of cabbage
4 turnips
2 potatoes for each person
½ pound dry white beans

Fill a large kettle with 3 to 4 quarts of cold water; into it place all the meat, including the sausage. Start cooking. When kettle comes to a boil, skim the top, lift sausage out and set it aside on a platter. Add the *bouquet garni*, leeks, parsley, carrots, and turnips. Simmer the vegetables for two hours, the meat for three. Lift carrots and turnips out and set aside on a platter with some of the liquid. Add the cabbage to the kettle of meat and simmer for another hour. In another pan, place the potatoes with some of the meat broth and cook for 15 to 20 minutes. Cook the beans separately for 2½ hours. Warm the sausage in some of the broth. In a soup tureen, place some thinly sliced pieces of bread and pour the broth over it. To serve, drain the meat and vegetables, place vegetables on bottom of platter, and the meat, ham, and sausage on top. Yield: 8 servings.

French Pastry Dough and Grape Tart

Pâté Brisée

1 egg
   pinch of salt
8 to 9 ounces flour
3 to 4 ounces butter
½ glass water

Place the egg with salt in the middle of the flour. Handle the butter to soften it and place it with the egg; add ½ glass of water. When the flour, butter, egg, salt, and water have been thoroughly blended together, press the dough into a ball and quickly flatten it twice over the board. The dough may be prepared a day before its use. Use for pies, tarts, and quiche. Yield: 2 pies.

Tarte aux Raisins

Pâté brisée (pastry dough)
Crème pâtissière (pastry cream)
Grapes in apricot syrup

Fill a pie pan with the dough. Cover with foil and bake. When the shell is ready, spread the pastry cream into it, top with grapes and glaze with apricot syrup. Yield: 2 pies.

French Pastry Cream

Crème Pâtissière

4 egg yolks
7 ounces sugar
2 ounces flour
½ quart vanilla-flavored milk, heated

Beat the yolks and sugar together with a small wire whisk in a heavy saucepan. When the mixture has become white, add flour and slowly beat in the hot vanilla-flavored milk. Set over moderate heat, stirring slowly and continuously with the whisk until the mixture begins to boil. The pastry cream will be thickened by the flour and must cook in order that the flour give it body. There is no risk of curdling. Yield: 2 pies.

COOKING
WITH
CHAMPAGNE

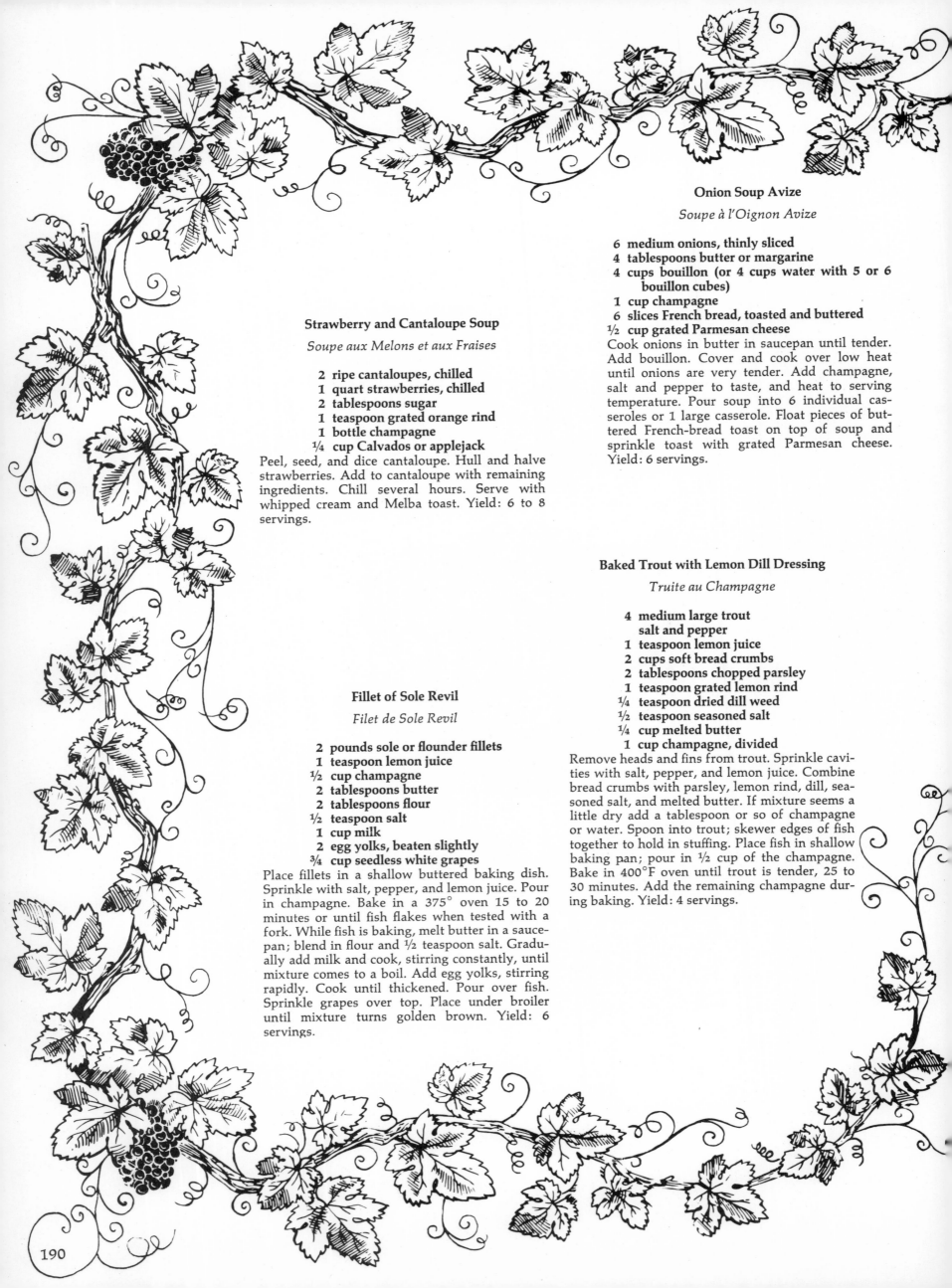

Strawberry and Cantaloupe Soup

Soupe aux Melons et aux Fraises

2 ripe cantaloupes, chilled
1 quart strawberries, chilled
2 tablespoons sugar
1 teaspoon grated orange rind
1 bottle champagne
¼ cup Calvados or applejack

Peel, seed, and dice cantaloupe. Hull and halve strawberries. Add to cantaloupe with remaining ingredients. Chill several hours. Serve with whipped cream and Melba toast. Yield: 6 to 8 servings.

Fillet of Sole Revil

Filet de Sole Revil

2 pounds sole or flounder fillets
1 teaspoon lemon juice
½ cup champagne
2 tablespoons butter
2 tablespoons flour
½ teaspoon salt
1 cup milk
2 egg yolks, beaten slightly
¾ cup seedless white grapes

Place fillets in a shallow buttered baking dish. Sprinkle with salt, pepper, and lemon juice. Pour in champagne. Bake in a 375° oven 15 to 20 minutes or until fish flakes when tested with a fork. While fish is baking, melt butter in a saucepan; blend in flour and ½ teaspoon salt. Gradually add milk and cook, stirring constantly, until mixture comes to a boil. Add egg yolks, stirring rapidly. Cook until thickened. Pour over fish. Sprinkle grapes over top. Place under broiler until mixture turns golden brown. Yield: 6 servings.

Onion Soup Avize

Soupe à l'Oignon Avize

6 medium onions, thinly sliced
4 tablespoons butter or margarine
4 cups bouillon (or 4 cups water with 5 or 6 bouillon cubes)
1 cup champagne
6 slices French bread, toasted and buttered
½ cup grated Parmesan cheese

Cook onions in butter in saucepan until tender. Add bouillon. Cover and cook over low heat until onions are very tender. Add champagne, salt and pepper to taste, and heat to serving temperature. Pour soup into 6 individual casseroles or 1 large casserole. Float pieces of buttered French-bread toast on top of soup and sprinkle toast with grated Parmesan cheese. Yield: 6 servings.

Baked Trout with Lemon Dill Dressing

Truite au Champagne

4 medium large trout
salt and pepper
1 teaspoon lemon juice
2 cups soft bread crumbs
2 tablespoons chopped parsley
1 teaspoon grated lemon rind
¼ teaspoon dried dill weed
½ teaspoon seasoned salt
¼ cup melted butter
1 cup champagne, divided

Remove heads and fins from trout. Sprinkle cavities with salt, pepper, and lemon juice. Combine bread crumbs with parsley, lemon rind, dill, seasoned salt, and melted butter. If mixture seems a little dry add a tablespoon or so of champagne or water. Spoon into trout; skewer edges of fish together to hold in stuffing. Place fish in shallow baking pan; pour in ½ cup of the champagne. Bake in 400°F oven until trout is tender, 25 to 30 minutes. Add the remaining champagne during baking. Yield: 4 servings.

Baked Salmon Supreme

Côtelettes de Saumon au Champagne

    4 slices salmon
      salt and pepper
      flour
    2 tablespoons shortening
    2 tablespoons butter
    ½ cup champagne
    1 cup sour cream
    ⅛ teaspoon dried dill weed
    ¼ cup chopped onion
    1 canned green chili, chopped

Season salmon with salt and pepper; dredge lightly in flour. Melt shortening and butter in a skillet. Add salmon and brown on both sides. Place in a casserole. Add champagne. Cover and bake in a 400°F oven 10 minutes. Combine remaining ingredients; add salt to taste. Remove cover and top salmon with sour-cream mixture. Continue baking, uncovered, until fish is done and topping glazed, about 15 minutes. Yield: 4 servings.

Deviled Scallops

Pétoncles à la Diable en Casserole

    2 pounds sea scallops
    1 bouquet garni
    1 medium onion, sliced
    1 small carrot, thinly sliced
    6 peppercorns, crushed
    1 whole clove
    1 cup champagne
    1 cup water
    6 tablespoons butter, divided
    2 tablespoons prepared mustard
    ¼ teaspoon Tabasco
    1 teaspoon Worcestershire sauce
    1 cup sliced mushrooms
    1 clove garlic, peeled
    1 cup buttered bread crumbs

Put scallops into a deep saucepan. Add *bouquet garni*, onion, carrot, peppercorns, clove, champagne, and water. Bring to a boil; reduce heat and simmer 8 to 10 minutes. Drain; reserve stock. Melt 4 tablespoons of the butter in a saucepan; blend in mustard, Tabasco, and Worcestershire sauce. Stir in 1 cup of the reserved stock; heat. Sauté mushrooms in remaining 2 tablespoons butter; add scallops and mix well. Rub a clove of garlic around inside of a 2-quart casserole; butter casserole. Add the scallops; pour sauce over all. Sprinkle with buttered bread crumbs. Bake in a 375°F oven 15 to 20 minutes. Yield: 6 servings.

Lobster Bercy

Homard Bercy

    2 2½-pound cooked lobsters
    3 tablespoons butter
    3 tablespoons olive oil
    2 shallots, minced
    2 cups champagne
    1 pint (2 cups) heavy cream, divided
    3 egg yolks
    1 tablespoon lemon juice
    1 tablespoon chopped chives

Remove meat from lobsters; reserve. Heat butter and olive oil in a deep saucepan. Add shallots and cook until lightly browned. Add lobster meat; stir until heated. Add champagne; bring to a boil. Cook, stirring occasionally, until mixture is reduced by ⅔. Add 1¾ cups cream; simmer about 5 minutes. Beat together egg yolks and remaining ¼ cup cream. Add to hot mixture, stirring rapidly. Cook until mixture thickens. Stir in lemon juice and chives. Serve over hot buttered toast points. Yield: 6 servings.

Marinated Oysters

Huîtres Marinées

    3 dozen oysters
    ½ cup champagne
    ¼ cup olive oil
    2 tablespoons lime or lemon juice
    3 tablespoons finely chopped green pepper
    1 tablespoon finely chopped onion
    1 tablespoon finely chopped chives
    1 tablespoon finely chopped parsley
    1 teaspoon Worcestershire sauce
    ⅛ teaspoon Tabasco

Open oysters, poach them in their own liquor until the edges curl. Drain oysters; add remaining ingredients to oyster liquor. Refrigerate oysters and liquor mixture, and chill. When ready to serve, place the oysters in a serving dish; pour marinade over oysters. Yield: 6 to 8 servings.

Roast Chicken with Spanish Cream Sauce

Poulet Rôti à la Crème

   1   whole 3½-pound broiler-fryer chicken
       salt and pepper
1¾   cups chicken stock, divided
   ½   cup champagne
   1   bay leaf
   ¼   teaspoon dried leaf thyme

Sprinkle chicken with salt and pepper; truss. Place in roasting pan; add 1 cup of the chicken stock and the champagne. Place in a 475°F oven. Sear 15 minutes, turning and basting occasionally. Add remaining ¾ cup stock, bay leaf, and thyme. Reduce heat to 350°F and roast 1 hour and 15 minutes. Remove from oven; cut chicken into serving pieces and keep hot. Strain stock in roasting pan and reserve. Prepare cream sauce.* Add chicken pieces; heat to serving temperature. Yield: 4 to 6 servings.

Poulet Billy-le-Grand

   2   broiler-fryer chickens, cut in serving pieces
       salt and pepper
   ⅓   cup butter
   ½   pound mushrooms, sliced
   2   large tomatoes, coarsely chopped
   1   cup champagne
   2   tablespoons brandy
   1   tablespoon finely chopped parsley
   1   tablespoon chopped chives
   1   small garlic clove, mashed

Sprinkle chicken with salt and pepper. Melt butter in a large skillet. Add larger, meatier chicken pieces first and brown on all sides. Remove. Add remaining chicken and additional butter if necessary, and brown on all sides. Return browned chicken to skillet with mushrooms and tomatoes. Cover; simmer 10 minutes. Add champagne and brandy. Cover and simmer 30 minutes or until chicken is tender. Remove chicken; keep warm. Add remaining ingredients to skillet. Cook over high heat, stirring occasionally, until liquid is reduced by half. Pour over chicken. Yield: 6 to 8 servings.

*Cream Sauce

   ¼   cup butter
   2   Spanish onions, sliced
   2   green peppers, chopped
   2   tablespoons flour
1½   cups strained stock
   1   cup heavy cream
   1   can (8 ounces) tomato sauce
   1   can (4 ounces) sliced mushrooms
   ¼   cup diced pimiento
   ½   cup sliced stuffed olives
       salt and pepper

Melt butter in a saucepan. Add onions and cook until golden. Add green peppers and cook, stirring occasionally, 5 minutes. Blend in flour. Add stock, heavy cream, and tomato sauce; bring to a boil. Add remaining ingredients. Reduce heat and simmer 20 minutes. Season to taste with salt and pepper.

Chicken Breasts Robert

Suprêmes de Volaille Robert

   3   tablespoons butter
   3   tablespoons chopped chives
   ½   teaspoon dry mustard
   ½   teaspoon sugar
   ½   cup peeled and finely chopped tomato
   1   tablespoon lemon juice
   1   cup champagne
       salt and pepper
   ½   cup seedless white grapes
   4   hot cooked chicken breasts
   ¼   cup grated Swiss cheese

Melt butter in a saucepan; add chives and cook 2 minutes. Add mustard, sugar, tomato, and lemon juice; mix well. Add champagne; bring to a boil. Season to taste with salt and pepper. Reduce heat and simmer 5 minutes. Remove from heat; stir in grapes. Place chicken in a shallow baking dish; pour in sauce. Sprinkle with grated cheese and place under broiler until lightly browned. Yield: 4 servings.

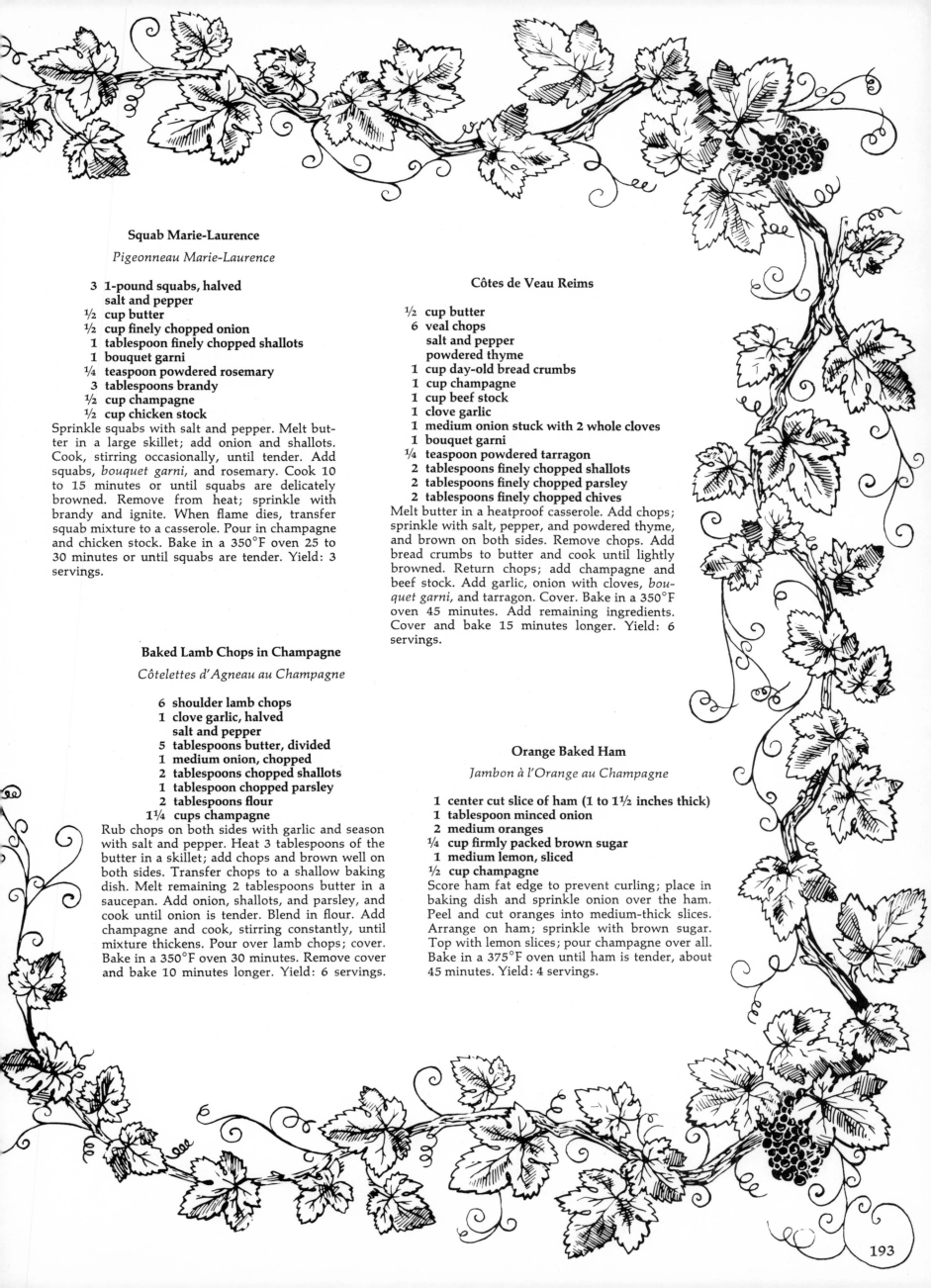

Squab Marie-Laurence

Pigeonneau Marie-Laurence

- 3 1-pound squabs, halved
  salt and pepper
- ½ cup butter
- ½ cup finely chopped onion
- 1 tablespoon finely chopped shallots
- 1 bouquet garni
- ¼ teaspoon powdered rosemary
- 3 tablespoons brandy
- ½ cup champagne
- ½ cup chicken stock

Sprinkle squabs with salt and pepper. Melt butter in a large skillet; add onion and shallots. Cook, stirring occasionally, until tender. Add squabs, *bouquet garni*, and rosemary. Cook 10 to 15 minutes or until squabs are delicately browned. Remove from heat; sprinkle with brandy and ignite. When flame dies, transfer squab mixture to a casserole. Pour in champagne and chicken stock. Bake in a 350°F oven 25 to 30 minutes or until squabs are tender. Yield: 3 servings.

Baked Lamb Chops in Champagne

Côtelettes d'Agneau au Champagne

- 6 shoulder lamb chops
- 1 clove garlic, halved
  salt and pepper
- 5 tablespoons butter, divided
- 1 medium onion, chopped
- 2 tablespoons chopped shallots
- 1 tablespoon chopped parsley
- 2 tablespoons flour
- 1¼ cups champagne

Rub chops on both sides with garlic and season with salt and pepper. Heat 3 tablespoons of the butter in a skillet; add chops and brown well on both sides. Transfer chops to a shallow baking dish. Melt remaining 2 tablespoons butter in a saucepan. Add onion, shallots, and parsley, and cook until onion is tender. Blend in flour. Add champagne and cook, stirring constantly, until mixture thickens. Pour over lamb chops; cover. Bake in a 350°F oven 30 minutes. Remove cover and bake 10 minutes longer. Yield: 6 servings.

Côtes de Veau Reims

- ½ cup butter
- 6 veal chops
  salt and pepper
  powdered thyme
- 1 cup day-old bread crumbs
- 1 cup champagne
- 1 cup beef stock
- 1 clove garlic
- 1 medium onion stuck with 2 whole cloves
- 1 bouquet garni
- ¼ teaspoon powdered tarragon
- 2 tablespoons finely chopped shallots
- 2 tablespoons finely chopped parsley
- 2 tablespoons finely chopped chives

Melt butter in a heatproof casserole. Add chops; sprinkle with salt, pepper, and powdered thyme, and brown on both sides. Remove chops. Add bread crumbs to butter and cook until lightly browned. Return chops; add champagne and beef stock. Add garlic, onion with cloves, *bouquet garni*, and tarragon. Cover. Bake in a 350°F oven 45 minutes. Add remaining ingredients. Cover and bake 15 minutes longer. Yield: 6 servings.

Orange Baked Ham

Jambon à l'Orange au Champagne

- 1 center cut slice of ham (1 to 1½ inches thick)
- 1 tablespoon minced onion
- 2 medium oranges
- ¼ cup firmly packed brown sugar
- 1 medium lemon, sliced
- ½ cup champagne

Score ham fat edge to prevent curling; place in baking dish and sprinkle onion over the ham. Peel and cut oranges into medium-thick slices. Arrange on ham; sprinkle with brown sugar. Top with lemon slices; pour champagne over all. Bake in a 375°F oven until ham is tender, about 45 minutes. Yield: 4 servings.

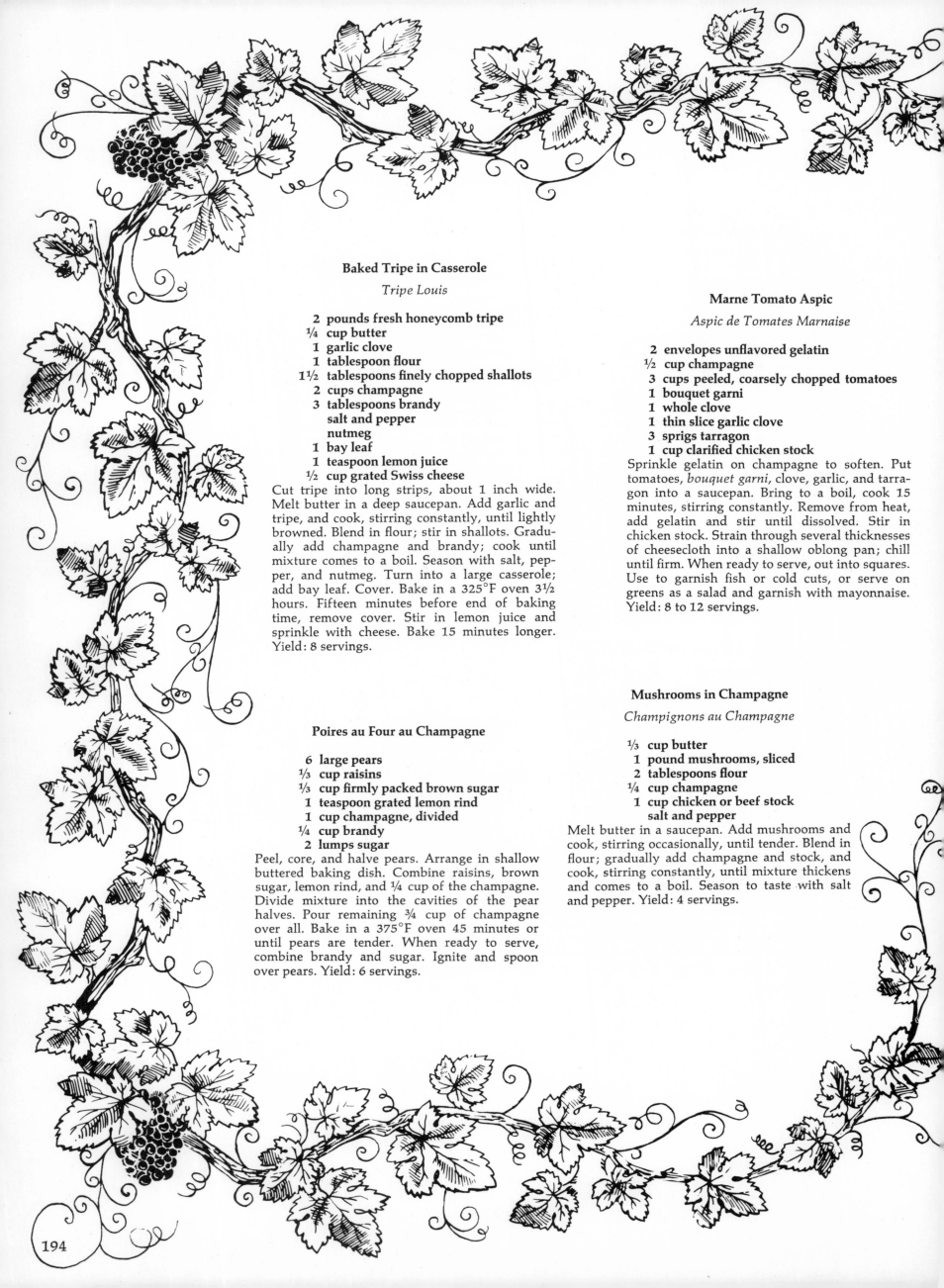

Baked Tripe in Casserole

Tripe Louis

2 pounds fresh honeycomb tripe
¼ cup butter
1 garlic clove
1 tablespoon flour
1½ tablespoons finely chopped shallots
2 cups champagne
3 tablespoons brandy
  salt and pepper
  nutmeg
1 bay leaf
1 teaspoon lemon juice
½ cup grated Swiss cheese

Cut tripe into long strips, about 1 inch wide. Melt butter in a deep saucepan. Add garlic and tripe, and cook, stirring constantly, until lightly browned. Blend in flour; stir in shallots. Gradually add champagne and brandy; cook until mixture comes to a boil. Season with salt, pepper, and nutmeg. Turn into a large casserole; add bay leaf. Cover. Bake in a 325°F oven 3½ hours. Fifteen minutes before end of baking time, remove cover. Stir in lemon juice and sprinkle with cheese. Bake 15 minutes longer. Yield: 8 servings.

Poires au Four au Champagne

6 large pears
⅓ cup raisins
⅓ cup firmly packed brown sugar
1 teaspoon grated lemon rind
1 cup champagne, divided
¼ cup brandy
2 lumps sugar

Peel, core, and halve pears. Arrange in shallow buttered baking dish. Combine raisins, brown sugar, lemon rind, and ¼ cup of the champagne. Divide mixture into the cavities of the pear halves. Pour remaining ¾ cup of champagne over all. Bake in a 375°F oven 45 minutes or until pears are tender. When ready to serve, combine brandy and sugar. Ignite and spoon over pears. Yield: 6 servings.

Marne Tomato Aspic

Aspic de Tomates Marnaise

2 envelopes unflavored gelatin
½ cup champagne
3 cups peeled, coarsely chopped tomatoes
1 bouquet garni
1 whole clove
1 thin slice garlic clove
3 sprigs tarragon
1 cup clarified chicken stock

Sprinkle gelatin on champagne to soften. Put tomatoes, *bouquet garni*, clove, garlic, and tarragon into a saucepan. Bring to a boil, cook 15 minutes, stirring constantly. Remove from heat, add gelatin and stir until dissolved. Stir in chicken stock. Strain through several thicknesses of cheesecloth into a shallow oblong pan; chill until firm. When ready to serve, out into squares. Use to garnish fish or cold cuts, or serve on greens as a salad and garnish with mayonnaise. Yield: 8 to 12 servings.

Mushrooms in Champagne

Champignons au Champagne

⅓ cup butter
1 pound mushrooms, sliced
2 tablespoons flour
¼ cup champagne
1 cup chicken or beef stock
  salt and pepper

Melt butter in a saucepan. Add mushrooms and cook, stirring occasionally, until tender. Blend in flour; gradually add champagne and stock, and cook, stirring constantly, until mixture thickens and comes to a boil. Season to taste with salt and pepper. Yield: 4 servings.

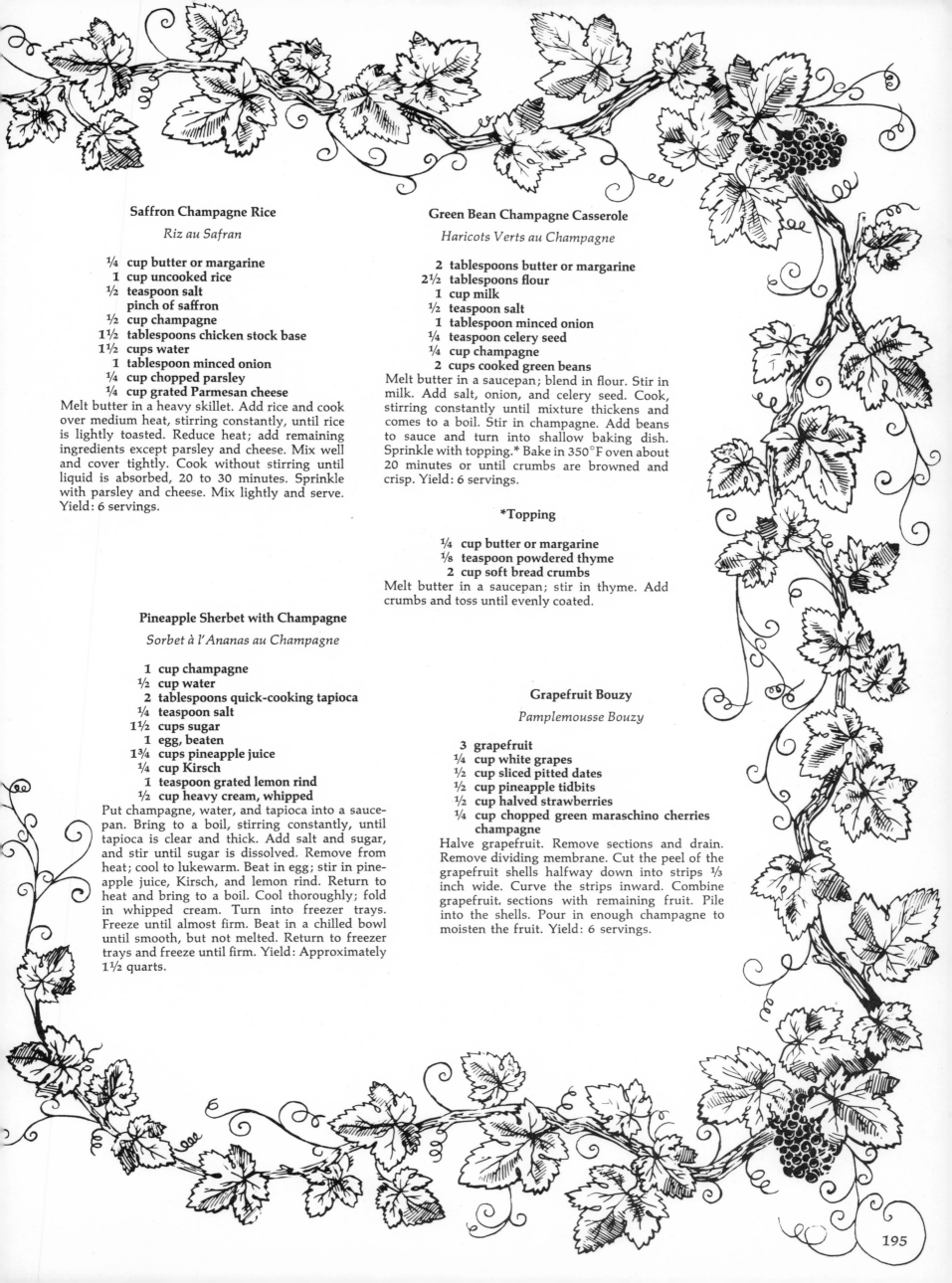

Saffron Champagne Rice

Riz au Safran

¼ cup butter or margarine
1 cup uncooked rice
½ teaspoon salt
pinch of saffron
½ cup champagne
1½ tablespoons chicken stock base
1½ cups water
1 tablespoon minced onion
¼ cup chopped parsley
¼ cup grated Parmesan cheese

Melt butter in a heavy skillet. Add rice and cook over medium heat, stirring constantly, until rice is lightly toasted. Reduce heat; add remaining ingredients except parsley and cheese. Mix well and cover tightly. Cook without stirring until liquid is absorbed, 20 to 30 minutes. Sprinkle with parsley and cheese. Mix lightly and serve. Yield: 6 servings.

Pineapple Sherbet with Champagne

Sorbet à l' Ananas au Champagne

1 cup champagne
½ cup water
2 tablespoons quick-cooking tapioca
¼ teaspoon salt
1½ cups sugar
1 egg, beaten
1¾ cups pineapple juice
¼ cup Kirsch
1 teaspoon grated lemon rind
½ cup heavy cream, whipped

Put champagne, water, and tapioca into a saucepan. Bring to a boil, stirring constantly, until tapioca is clear and thick. Add salt and sugar, and stir until sugar is dissolved. Remove from heat; cool to lukewarm. Beat in egg; stir in pineapple juice, Kirsch, and lemon rind. Return to heat and bring to a boil. Cool thoroughly; fold in whipped cream. Turn into freezer trays. Freeze until almost firm. Beat in a chilled bowl until smooth, but not melted. Return to freezer trays and freeze until firm. Yield: Approximately 1½ quarts.

Green Bean Champagne Casserole

Haricots Verts au Champagne

2 tablespoons butter or margarine
2½ tablespoons flour
1 cup milk
½ teaspoon salt
1 tablespoon minced onion
¼ teaspoon celery seed
¼ cup champagne
2 cups cooked green beans

Melt butter in a saucepan; blend in flour. Stir in milk. Add salt, onion, and celery seed. Cook, stirring constantly until mixture thickens and comes to a boil. Stir in champagne. Add beans to sauce and turn into shallow baking dish. Sprinkle with topping.* Bake in 350°F oven about 20 minutes or until crumbs are browned and crisp. Yield: 6 servings.

*Topping

¼ cup butter or margarine
⅛ teaspoon powdered thyme
2 cup soft bread crumbs

Melt butter in a saucepan; stir in thyme. Add crumbs and toss until evenly coated.

Grapefruit Bouzy

Pamplemousse Bouzy

3 grapefruit
¼ cup white grapes
½ cup sliced pitted dates
½ cup pineapple tidbits
½ cup halved strawberries
¼ cup chopped green maraschino cherries
champagne

Halve grapefruit. Remove sections and drain. Remove dividing membrane. Cut the peel of the grapefruit shells halfway down into strips ⅓ inch wide. Curve the strips inward. Combine grapefruit sections with remaining fruit. Pile into the shells. Pour in enough champagne to moisten the fruit. Yield: 6 servings.

Crème Amande

1 envelope unflavored gelatin
¾ cup sugar
1 cup champagne, divided
4 egg yolks, beaten
½ cup finely chopped toasted almonds
¼ teaspoon almond extract
1 pint (2 cups) heavy cream, whipped

Mix together gelatin and sugar in top of double boiler. Stir in champagne and egg yolks. Place over boiling water and cook, stirring constantly, until gelatin dissolves and mixture thickens slightly, 7 to 8 minutes. Remove from heat; stir in almonds and almond extract. Chill, stirring occasionally, until mixture mounds slightly. Fold in whipped cream. Turn into a 6-cup mold; chill until firm. Unmold and serve with Sauce Grenache. Yield: 8 servings.

Sauce Grenache

1 tablespoon softened butter
1 cup sifted confectioners' sugar
½ cup light cream
¼ cup dry red wine
salt
nutmeg

Cream together butter and sugar; blend in cream. Place in a saucepan and cook, stirring constantly until mixture is heated through. Gradually add wine, stirring constantly. Remove from heat. Add a few grains of salt and nutmeg. Cool.

Champagne Cup Monique

Punch aux Liqueurs Monique

1 tablespoon maple syrup
1 large orange, thinly sliced
1 lemon, thinly sliced
1 teaspoon lemon rind
4 thin slices cucumber
2 teaspoons bitters
1 cup brandy
¼ cup Curaçao
½ cup Maraschino liqueur
3 whole cloves
2 bottles champagne

Combine all ingredients except champagne in a punch bowl. Add a large piece of ice and stir to chill. Remove ice; pour in champagne. Ladle into chilled champagne glasses. Yield: Approximately 20 half-cup servings.

Strawberry Champagne Punch

Punch aux Fraises et au Champagne

1 pint strawberries
2 cups rosé wine
½ cup sugar
1 can (6 ounces) frozen pineapple juice concentrate
½ teaspoon salt
½ teaspoon almond extract
1 lemon
1 bottle champagne, chilled

Wash and hull strawberries; crush coarsely. Combine with wine, sugar, undiluted pineapple juice concentrate, salt, and almond extract. Grate rind from lemon; squeeze juice; add to wine mixture along with empty lemon shell. Cover and refrigerate overnight. Strain liquid, discarding pulp. Pour over ice and add champagne just before serving. Yield: Approximately 16 half-cup servings.

Champagne Cup Ay

Punch au Champagne Ay

3 bottles champagne
1 bottle sauterne
3 lemons, thinly sliced
3 oranges, thinly sliced
18 sticks fresh or canned pineapple
3 sprigs mint
½ cup sugar
1 cup brandy
1 quart strawberries, washed and hulled

Put all ingredients except brandy and strawberries into a punch bowl; stir until sugar is dissolved. Add a large piece of ice and stir to chill. Remove ice; pour in brandy and add strawberries. Ladle into chilled champagne glasses. Yield: Approximately 44 half-cup servings.

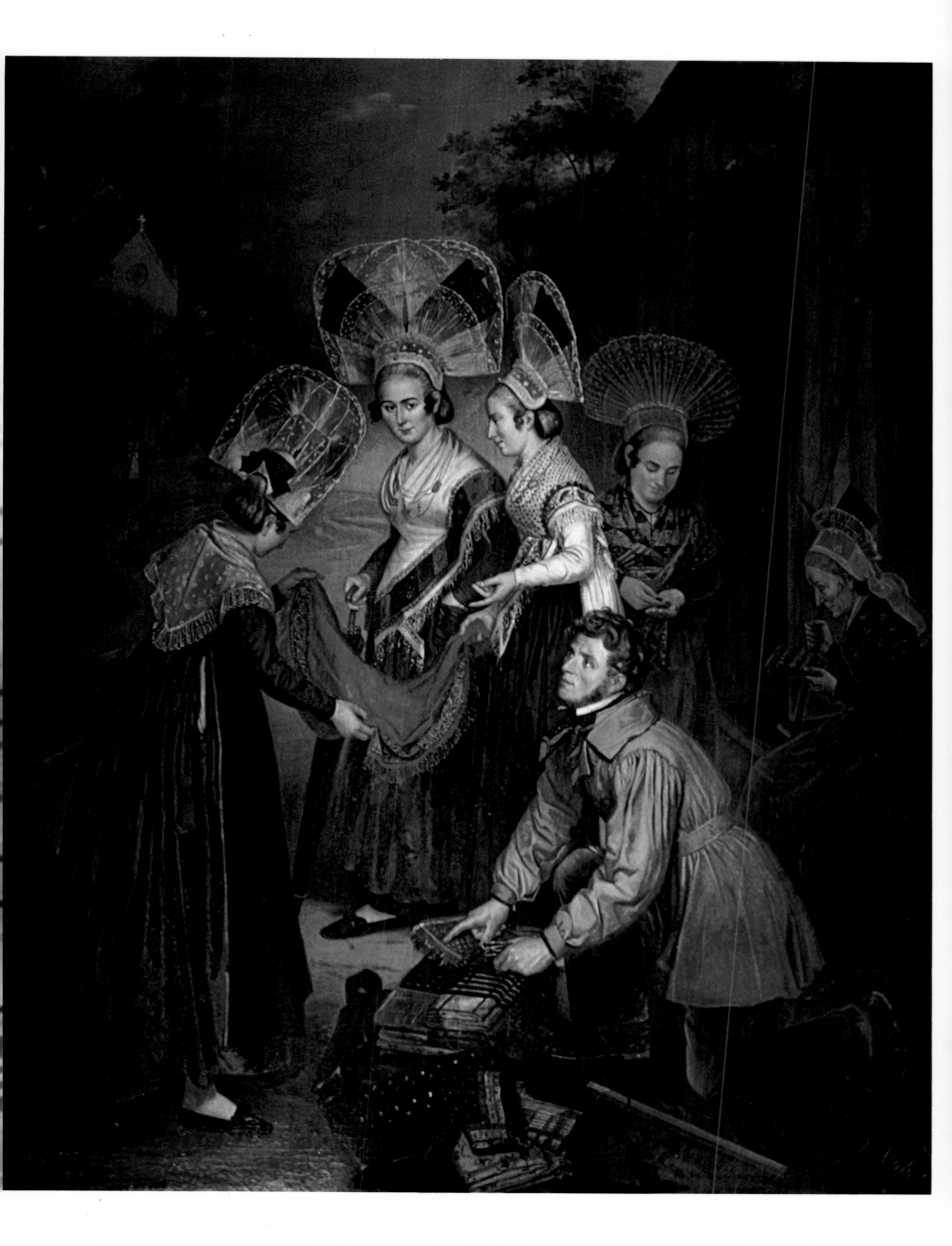

LIST OF ILLUSTRATIONS

INDEX

INDEX OF RECIPES

My Champagne

Oh! my Champagne,
Oh! my love,
I return to you forever.
Oh! my Champagne,
Oh! my love,
I return to you forever.

I ran away from a deceptive world,
And beneath your dreamy and overcast sky
I return to look for solitude and shelter
Where my heart is healed.

The recollection of twenty battles
Repeat the glory of your name.
In your valley bloodied by the victory,
Dreamily I wandered, Oh! my Champagne.

The vines of your slopes
Are the treasures that I prefer,
When tomorrow their light froth
Will flood us with its waves.

FARANDOLE

C. Gauthier